TO THE POINT

TO THE POINT

The No-Holds-Barred Autobiography

HERSCHELLE GIBBS

WITH STEVE SMITH

Published by Zebra Press
an imprint of Random House Struik (Pty) Ltd
Reg. No. 1966/003153/07
80 McKenzie Street, Cape Town, 8001
PO Box 1144, Cape Town, 8000 South Africa

www.zebrapress.co.za

First published 2010
Reprinted in 2010 (four times)

5 7 9 10 8 6

Publication © Zebra Press 2010
Text © Herschelle Gibbs and Steve Smith 2010

Cover photographs: Morne van Zyl

PUBLISHER: Marlene Fryer
MANAGING EDITOR: Robert Plummer
EDITOR: Ronel Richter-Herbert
PROOFREADER: Bronwen Leak
COVER DESIGN: MR Design
TEXT DESIGN: Monique Oberholzer
TYPESETTING: Monique van den Berg
INDEX: Sanet le Roux
PRODUCTION MANAGER: Valerie Kömmer

Set in 11.5 pt on 15 pt Adobe Garamond

Printed and bound by Interpak Books,
Pietermaritzburg

ISBN 978 1 77022 131 4

Over 50 000 unique African images available to purchase
from our image bank at www.imagesofafrica.co.za

Contents

Preface

I had not been playing for Western Province for long when a 16-year-old schoolboy called Herschelle Gibbs was selected to play against Northern Transvaal. I think he scored 37 runs on the day, but watching his style and flair for the game was enough to convince anyone that this youngster was going to be around for a long time.

And so, here I am, 20 years later, having been asked to write the preface to the autobiography of Herschelle Gibbs – an honour indeed! Naturally, I jumped at the opportunity, feeling that it is important that people know the views and opinions of the person who spent many hours and days just 22 yards from him on the cricket pitch, as we battled it out against the best opposition in the world.

It was here, in the middle and under pressure, that I got to see Herschelle Gibbs at his purest and best. There were times when I saw the fear in his eyes, when I saw him vulnerable and unsure who he was and whether he belonged in this arena. But, more often than not, I saw the determination and confidence of an entertainer who had a deep desire to display his talents and skills in their truest form and show the cricketing world what he was made of.

In the early days, when Herschelle's confidence was soaring (and the game had yet to dish out a few harsh lessons, as it does to us all), his stroke-making was audacious! His trademark back-foot drive, which regularly soared over the cover boundary, is such a difficult shot that I have yet to see the batsmen of the new era even consider it. Such was Hersch's skill that I would often watch him select an area to hit the ball with little regard of the delivery's line or length. With Herschelle at the crease, it was cricket entertainment at its purest, and he relished and flourished in the adulation that came with it.

But, as in any great pursuit, there are challenges and obstacles in cricket. Herschelle was not immune to this. As he started playing against better opposition, they worked out his shortcomings and would specifically target those aspects of his game – both mental and technical. He quickly realised he would have to adapt and work out new strategies that would give him the consistency to be a long-term fixture in the South African team. He did this and he did it well.

I'm not sure when it was or how it came about, but a decision was taken that Herschelle should open the batting in all forms of the game. This was the beginning of a long and enjoyable partnership, as he and I opened the batting for South Africa and Western Province. I look back on this period as one of the most memorable in my cricket career.

Herschelle and I complemented each other perfectly. He allowed me to play my natural game without the pressure of having to score runs freely. I encouraged him to play more of a percentage game when it was required. It was during these years as an opener that he tightened up his technique and became a difficult batsman to get out. Herschelle was able to combine his natural flair and skill with good control and organisation at the crease. Thus grew one of the best and most feared batsmen in the world.

Many people will be unfamiliar with Herschelle the person. The media have projected him as something of a maverick, prone to self-destruction and always living on the edge. On some levels, this is an accurate reflection, and Herschelle would be the first to tell you that. He has always done things to the extreme, so whether it is training in the gym, batting in the nets or going out for a party, he is going to give 100 per cent commitment to it!

What has not been as well documented is what a thoroughly genuine and generous human being he is. He would be more than happy to give the shirt off his back, if that meant making someone else's day. He has set a fantastic example to future sports stars in his willingness to give to others, and many people have benefited from his enormously generous heart. He has always been fully aware of the privileges that cricket has given him in his life and has never taken that for granted.

Herschelle has made many friends in the cricket fraternity. He is well liked because he has a tremendous ability to connect with people quickly. On many occasions I have seen him with a smile on his face, happily signing autographs and engaging with cricket fans and young aspiring players, while the rest of his team-mates are sitting in the comfort of the changing room. And let's not forget Herschelle's exceptional wit and humour. There was never a dull moment with Hersch around, and he always kept us well entertained when we were on the road.

I don't know when Herschelle will decide to retire, but I will make sure I'm at Newlands when he makes that decision to play one last innings at his favourite ground. I'm certain he will still be at backward point looking for the opportunity to take a great catch or hit the stumps. I'm also sure he will make every effort to entertain his loyal Cape Town fans with bat in hand and remind us of the stroke-making that turned him into one of the world's great batsmen.

Thanks, Hersch, for the great memories!

Gazza

GARY KIRSTEN
Dambulla, Sri Lanka, August 2010

Acknowledgements

So here we are, people … Twenty-odd years have come and gone. What a ride. I can honestly say it's been filled with every bit of emotion, from heartache and failure to celebration and triumph. I guess that's all part of life, and, for someone who is still fairly young, I can count myself lucky to have gone through so much already. These experiences will stand me in good stead, of that I'm pretty sure!

During the roller-coaster ride, I've met people all over the world, from all walks of life – from the man sweeping the streets to presidents and even the royal family. Not bad for someone who comes from an underprivileged background, hey?

I've only ever played team sports and, with this in mind, I want to say thank you to everyone who I've shared a team with, be it football, rugby or cricket. From the age of six till now! It's been a treat to play alongside each and every one of you lads, so thank you!

To all my coaches – especially Duncan Fletcher – who helped me through it all. Not sure how you men put up with me. Thank you. Fletch, you were the one who suggested that I open the batting, and we both know it worked out pretty well in the end. You are truly a legend.

To my manager, Donné Commins, who has stood by me through it all … If it wasn't for you, Don, I'm not sure where I'd be today. You're a gem of a woman. Thank you from the bottom of my heart!

To all my sponsors – sorry, just too many to name over the last two decades – thank you for allowing me the privilege of using and endorsing your products. They have all been of the highest quality! To have sponsors from the age of ten, I was truly blessed.

To my former opening partner Gary Kirsten ... Gazza, the touching words you wrote in the preface, bro, made me shed a tear or two, you shit! Thank you. What a complete man you are. It's been an honour indeed.

Where would I be without my friends? To all of you, shot for all the support and let's carry on with the good times, okay?

Now to my family – the people I've hardly seen because of my travels during these years. I know it hasn't always been easy, but without your encouragement and support I would never have made it through all the rough times I've experienced. I love you all. Daddy, Mommy, Cindy, Rashard, Clinton and family, we will make up for lost time once my cricketing days finally come to an end. For now, let's just enjoy the next couple of years together. Daddy, I think all your hard work and effort in my younger years eventually paid off to get me where I am today. I'm proud to say I'm your son. I love you immensely.

Rashard my boy, I've watched you grow and mature into a fine young man, and I can't believe you are turning fourteen in a couple of months' time. Exciting, exciting! Dad's extremely proud of all your achievements in the classroom and on the sports field. If you continue to enjoy your sport and maintain your dedication, hard work, and of course be a good boy, you're going to go very far indeed. You have the world at your feet, and I'll help you achieve whatever it is your heart desires, okay? Never forget how much I love you and what I always tell you: 'You're the man!'

Liesl, you've been a wonderful mother and you can be proud of raising such a beautiful and loveable boy. He really is a special young man. Thank you.

To all my fans and everyone who has enjoyed the style of cricket I've played over the years (and, yes, there is more to come), thank you for your support through it all, good and bad! For me personally, it's all about you guys and will always be that way. Big up to all of you.

So, with all this said and done, I hope you enjoy reading this book as much as Steve and I have enjoyed producing it! Steve, you're a champion; it's been a pleasure!

I've been asked by a few people: What made you want to do the book? My answer was simply, 'To celebrate life.'

Enjoy.

Hersch

HERSCHELLE GIBBS
September 2010

Author's note

Formalities seldom keep their shape when Mr Gibbs is around. I learnt that early on. Our first-ever interview was for a *Sports Illustrated* cover feature, and, as the magazine's editor, I was after a suitably meaty story. Armed with some tough questions, the plan was to uncover exactly what made this talented but controversial cricketer tick.

It started out as a formal interview all right – me trotting out the big guns on cue – but thanks to Herschelle's relaxed and open attitude, it soon changed … into a really good chat. That's his way. For a couple of hours he answered all my questions as honestly as good sense would allow. And that was the beginning of my understanding Herschelle Gibbs a little better.

After spending more time with him over the next six years – and especially during the week we hung out at the 2010 IPL in India – I've gained some insights into what makes this cricketer such a popular figure. And you really have to see how Indian fans respond to him to understand the depth of his popularity.

Which, when you think about it, is weird given how equally frustrating it has been to witness his career. This is the part that always puzzled me. How could a guy who has done time for match-fixing, been bust for sucking back some of Antigua's finest and been to rehab for alcohol addiction still be such a beloved sportsman?

And it's not like his on-field performances have always counter-balanced his off-field adventures either. There have been many innings in which Hersch appears to have chucked away his wicket. And when we're up against the Aussies and you need him to score runs, it really is flippin' annoying.

Why, then, has Herschelle Gibbs remained in the hearts of cricket fans around the world? Why, for example, aside from my sparkling way with words and the promise of some juice in the coming pages, are you reading this book?

Two reasons, I reckon. One: as frustrating as it's sometimes been to watch him play, Hersch has always delivered on that crucial contract between professional player and spectator. Your part is to pay the money; his part is to entertain you. With Hersch on the field, something is bound to happen. It could be a brilliant catch or a spectacular dive to cut off a certain four. It could be a couple of sixes in a brief but explosive innings. Or it could be 175 off 111 balls to pull off an impossible victory. From a value-for-money point of view, Herschelle Gibbs alone is worth the price of your ticket.

The second reason, though, is the more powerful one. It's the reason why there's an emotional bond between Hersch and his fans. It's the reason why messages of support pour in every time he finds himself in trouble. Thing is, Herschelle Gibbs, for all his flaws, has a massive heart. And throughout his life, Hersch has unashamedly worn it on his sleeve.

He's a genuinely friendly individual with the kind of demeanour that immediately puts anyone in his company at ease. I saw this first hand in India during the IPL. Hersch didn't just sign every autograph thrust at him or pose for every photo, but he did so in a way that made each of those fans feel like they had a real and personal interaction with him. Not many sports stars are able to do that.

What you see is what you get with Hersch. There's no hidden agenda, no sneaky manoeuvring for self gain. His ups and downs have been there for all to witness – from that beaming smile you see on the cover of this book to the scared and vulnerable man standing before the world during the King Commission. Whatever his faults may be, you can't help but like the guy.

And my thanks…

To end this author's note, I want to thank some important people. I can do this because I've recently read a bunch of other author's notes and I'm happy to report it's allowed. Obviously I've read a lot of books before, but no author's notes. Seriously, who the hell reads author's notes?

Firstly I have to thank my long-time friend, one-time colleague and fellow journalist Pieter Redelinghuys. The book was Piet's idea. He and I were having a few beers one night at The Shack, our local hangout, and Piet had just read the interview I'd done with Hersch for *GQ* magazine. In it, for the first time, Hersch talked openly about his time in rehab.

'*Kom nou, Smitty man, fok,*' said Piet in his usual forthright manner, '*dis nou tyd om a bladdy book te skryf. Vra vir Gibbs.*' Something like that … My Afrikaans is pretty bad, but he does call me Smitty and he loves saying 'fok'.

The very next day I emailed Marlene Fryer at Zebra Press.

And it's her I want to thank next. Marlene is this book's publisher and, while she knew a Herschelle Gibbs autobiography would make for interesting reading, she took a chance on me as the writer. This is my first book. Thanks for the faith, Marlene. Thanks too to your very efficient and professional team – Robert Plummer for helping me shape the book, Ronel Richter-Herbert for her editing (I take almost as many liberties with the English language as I do with Afrikaans), and Kim Taylor for making sure the world knows about it all.

To my family – Medina and Holly. If it wasn't for you, Dee, I would have been a lawyer. Ja. Words aren't enough. And Holly, thank you for remaining the cheerful little imp you are, especially through those months when the only sign of your dad was the clicking sound of my laptop's keyboard.

To Donné Commins, Herschelle's manager, thanks for all your help and insights. All professional athletes should find themselves someone like Donné. She looks out for her players like they are her own family. She's helluva nice. But fierce too. The perfect combination for the business she's in.

And finally to Herschelle. It can't be easy to sit down with someone you only sort of know and tell them the warts-and-all story of your life. That's pretty ballsy. So thanks, Hersch. Thanks for making the time in your hectic schedule and thanks for trusting me to tell it like you told it.

STEVE SMITH
September 2010

1

The early days

From school days to a tough start in the senior ranks ... and fun along the way

'Today,' he said, 'I am going to kill you.'

And there was no reason not to believe him.

He was tall and swarthy, with a mean look in his eye. I shat myself. What the hell was I doing here? I was only 16; I had my whole life ahead of me. Things were supposed to be sunny, bright and full of hope. Instead, as I squinted through the gap between the visor and metal guard of my helmet, I could see my killer thundering towards me. Tertius Bosch had a very long run-up, which, while it might have added a few extra seconds to my rapidly diminishing life span, also gave me what seemed like forever to contemplate my fate.

Fortunately I managed to survive the Northern Transvaal pace bowler's onslaught on 26 December 1990 at Newlands, but the moment was indicative of how out of depth I felt playing cricket at that level. I mean, the guy put the fear of God into me. From this baptism-by-fire debut, it took a good three years before I could honestly say that I was comfortable batting against bowlers of Tertius's calibre. Facing schoolboy fast bowlers was one thing; facing the likes of Tertius, Allan Donald and Brett Schultz in my first season of senior cricket was another ball game altogether.

Up until that stage, cricket had come easy to me. They bowled the ball to me; I made them go fetch it. That suited me. I reckon I was about 10 when I first began to get an idea that I was pretty good at the game. I attended St Joseph's College in Rondebosch, Cape Town, and every time a pupil took six wickets or made 100 runs, they used to have a little ceremony at assembly on a Monday morning and award you a wooden plaque with a ball mounted on top. The problem was that I was scoring so many runs that they eventually had to stop giving me the award. It was a little embarrassing for all concerned, I think. So ja, by then I was beginning to understand that maybe I was a bit better than other kids my age.

I was 11 when I first saw my name appear in the *Cape Argus*. Legendary Cape Town sportswriter AC Parker had written a report on the SA Perm Week – basically the national under-13 cricket tournament. The headline read: 'Herschelle's star on the rise'. My dad still has that clipping in his scrapbook. It was my first year at Perm Week – I was in Standard 4 (now Grade 6) then. I played for Western Province again the following year, in my final year at primary school.

It was in high school though that I really started making a name for myself, and not only in schoolboy sport, but at senior level as well. I was offered a scholarship by Bishops, an exclusive private school, after John Peake, the headmaster, had noticed my sporting abilities, and I started there in Standard 6.

I think I was on a full day-scholarship; I never asked my dad about the financial side of it, but I do know that he could never have afforded to send me there. My dad had struggled to afford St Joseph's, let alone Bishops.

But I didn't just excel at cricket; I was making a name for myself as a rugby player too. I think playing rugby had a lot to do with my scholarship, as school rugby was, and remains, a big deal at Bishops. But the big deal for *me* back then was neither cricket nor rugby. Football was my favourite sport and the one at which I reckoned I was most talented. I was already playing provincial football at that age.

So, in winter I'd play a rugby game for my school and then

rush off to play club football, aware of the fact that my team was deliberately delaying the start of the game so that I could make the kick-off.

I loved Bishops. I always felt completely at home there and, despite the fact that I was neither white nor wealthy (unlike the majority of my fellow learners), I never for a moment felt like I didn't belong. The sports field helped overcome any social barriers there might have been and I made a lot of friends quite quickly. The guys gravitated towards me once they saw how good I was at sport. I've always had an outgoing personality, and I think I'm easy to get along with, so that helped too. It is very rare that I don't feel comfortable in company and, irrespective of who the people are, I am always myself. I regard myself as very fortunate to have that gift, because there are a lot of people who struggle to chat and mix with strangers.

The teachers at Bishops took a shining to me too. They must have, or else I don't know how I managed to make it through high school. Ja, I was no great shakes academically. When it came to the actual studying side of things, I was way out of my depth. I reckon they just let me pass every year.

Except Standard 9. They kept me back then – perhaps they wanted me to play sport for them for another year. I reckon, though, that I never properly passed a year of high school. I have to mention, however, that I did once get 93 per cent for a business economics exam in Standard 8. No idea how that happened – it's not like I cheated or got hold of the paper beforehand. In fact, I've only ever 'cheated' once – or, more accurately, was involved in an underhand activity. And, as everyone knows, that got me into all kinds of trouble. But more about that later.

I remember that I actually enjoyed business economics as a subject, so perhaps that's why I did well in the exam. I also always passed English and Afrikaans, but I found it a monumental schlep to study history or geography. And biology ... man, I just couldn't understand why the hell we needed to take that subject. As it turns out, I would become very, very interested in biology later in life.

My dad pushed me a bit to try to improve my marks. When I was younger, he was a teacher and therefore fairly strict when it came to my studies. He taught physical education and a bit of history at a school called Bridgetown High in Athlone. Apparently he was very strict. I hear people used to genuinely kak themselves in his class. So my dad tried to encourage me to work harder and do better, even though he could see I obviously wasn't enjoying it. My head just wasn't focused on my books. My head was on the sports field and, increasingly, on girls.

We lived in Elfindale in Cape Town's southern suburbs, and I used to catch the train to school each day. Rondebosch Station was one of the stops. I used to check out all the hot girls there, then get off at the next station, catch the train back and check them out again. If there was someone I felt I needed to get to know a little better, I'd jump off and make a concerted effort to get her contact details. Obviously it meant I'd often be late for school, but I didn't give a damn – I'd blame it on the trains running late. What could they do? Certainly no one on the Bishops staff took the train, so they could only take my word for it.

I often bunked classes too, and enjoyed all the sorts of stuff that boys get up to when they are together in a group. In class we used to do stuff like put a drawing pin on a chair for someone to unsuspectingly sit down on, and we generally gave the teachers a hard time. I wasn't really naughty; it was just normal, exuberant, teenage-boy stuff.

But there was one time my exuberance did make the papers, though – clearly a precursor of what my life as a professional cricketer would be like in the years to come. It was the 1992 Nuffield Week – the prestigious interprovincial under-19 cricket tournament (now called Khaya Majola Week) – and I was 18 and in matric.

The tournament was being held in Stellenbosch that year, and we were staying in the dormitories of a local school. My fellow Western Province XI teammates and I decided to go out the night before one of the games, knowing full well that we had a midnight curfew. If you weren't back by then, they would lock the doors. There were, I think, five or six of us, and we just happened to walk past a wedding. It was a large affair with many 'coloured' families in attendance, and one of the guests at the wedding happened to notice me.

As part of the coloured community, and because I had been playing senior cricket for a couple of years by then and therefore had a public profile, one of the guests recognised me and invited me in for a few drinks.

Obviously I had my mates with me and I couldn't just drop them, so I dragged them in as well. Predictably, one thing led to another. A few beers were consumed and, the next thing you know, it's 12.30 a.m. I thought we might be able to sneak in quietly, but of course they had already locked the doors to the dormitories. One of my teammates was really pissed by now, and he started banging on the doors and causing all sorts of kak. So we got bust. Our coach, Keith Richardson – one of the masters at Wynberg Boys' High – was notified. We were in deep shit.

All of us were banned for one game, and the story made the papers ... but my name was the one that got dragged through the mud. A similar thing happened in 2001 when, in another moment of exuberance, some of my Proteas teammates and I decided to smoke a little weed in the West Indies. Everyone remembers that I was one of the *rokers*, while they probably couldn't name the other culprits. But more about that later.

So school ... ja ... The bottom line was that I was just not interested in spending any time in the classroom. As I said, my mind was on the sports field. For me, school was just about sport. That was it. During our 40-minute break I'd be playing sport; if we had 'civics' from 1.30 to 3.30 p.m. (cadets, or music ... all that nonsense), I'd get out of it and play football or touch rugby. Afterwards I'd return to class with my uniform soaked in sweat.

I couldn't sit in a classroom and apply my mind for 20 minutes, let alone for those double sessions of one hour. The only time I enjoyed a lesson was when they showed us a video, which meant that I could have a quiet doss in the back of the classroom. All I ever thought about were the weekend games that lay ahead. Basically, I was just like any other sports-mad South African schoolboy.

On the sports field, it was a different story. My cricket was going great guns and, at the age of 15, I was selected for the under-19 Western Province XI to play in the Nuffield Week. Although I was scoring plenty of runs, cricket wasn't a doddle all the time. I remember the first time I was pinned by a genuine quickie.

His name was Brett Chambers, and he attended Fish Hoek High School. I was 15 and never used to wear a helmet ... that was, until I faced Brett. The ball was flying past me – it was a real eye-opener. I'd never before faced pace of this calibre, and I didn't like it at all. I thought, shit, if this oke bounces me and hits me on the head, he'll clean my pipes ...

He did hit me. I was trying to get out of the way of one of Brett's lightning bolts when the ball hit me flush on the chest. It stopped me dead in my tracks. I was like, later for this, I'm out of here. I nicked off and walked back to the changing room. It was one of the few times I was happy to get out. Fortunately Brett came to Bishops shortly afterwards, so he became a teammate. He was a great guy, and easily the quickest bowler in school cricket in the country at that stage.

I'm not sure what happened to him. He played Nuffield for Province, but I don't think he made SA Schools. Funny, but now-adays I still think about those moments. When I prepare myself for an innings, I make use of pre-game visualisation, and those moments, when you've really been shaken up by a bowler, stick with you. It doesn't matter whether it's Shoaib Akhtar now, or Brett Chambers 20-odd years ago.

That was school cricket, but I was also making a name for myself in senior cricket by this time as well. By Standard 8, as a 16-year-old, I was playing senior men's cricket for Western Province. It all happened very quickly. Way *too* quickly, when I think back now.

I played my first-ever premier-league club game for Avondale against Tech-Mutual, and this was a time when club cricket in South Africa was at its strongest, with every club having at least one or two provincial players in their line-ups. I managed to score a 100 that day. This really made the headlines – 'schoolboy prodigy scores ton in first premier club game' – and the next thing I get called up into the Western Province B-team.

I played one game for them – against Transvaal B at Newlands over 10–12 December 1990, scoring 77 runs – and the next week I was invited to the A-team practice. I remember seeing the coach talking to some of the Province players and watching them just shake their heads before walking away. I knew then that they were going to pick me for the next game, but it also meant one of the established players would have to make way, which understandably pissed them off. And so I became the youngest guy in 130 years to play for Province. Clearly the coach, Hylton Ackerman, liked what he saw in me.

I wasn't so sure though.

I didn't share his confidence in my cricket. I knew there was a huge difference between facing schoolboy bowlers and facing the men in Currie Cup cricket. It was like chalk and cheese. South African cricket in the late 1980s and early 1990s consisted of a crop of 20 or so bowlers who could all have played inter-national cricket. Apart from the aforementioned Bosch, Donald and Schultz, you also had the likes of Rudi Bryson, Steve Elworthy, Chris van Noordwyk, Corrie van Zyl, Nico Pretorius, Brendon Fourie, Simon Base, Russell Adams, Adrian Holdstock and Dean

Payne, to name but a few. All these okes were genuinely quick. I kakked off against them, and my fear of getting badly hit was huge.

The only experience I'd had that even approached facing bowlers of this calibre was playing a warm-up game for the Western Province Nuffield XI against an invitational Mellville XI, made up of senior players. The match took place at the Cape Town Cricket Club. The Mellville XI had a quickie called Les Ryan, who came steaming in and hit me on the helmet, right on the badge. I remember him glaring at me and saying, 'Welcome to the big league, boet.'

But even that was nothing compared to A-section Currie Cup cricket for Western Province. My performance reflected my concerns. In that first year I hardly scored runs – 35 against the same Tertius Bosch and Northern Transvaal in the return game at Centurion Park was my highest score. It was a very frustrating time for me. I knew I was out of my league. I was just basically trying to survive. Walking out onto the field for that first game against Northern Transvaal at Newlands, I couldn't even feel my legs, I was so bladdy nervous.

I would be standing in the middle, at the end of an over, with senior players like Brian McMillan and Kenny Jackson, who'd try to give me advice, but their words would just go through me completely. I was far too nervous to comprehend anything they said. I was still way too young for this level of the game, and I found it really tough to make such a huge adjustment so quickly. I got nine in my first innings and 14 in my second in that first game for Province. I guess Daryll Cullinan is probably the only other cricketer who can relate to my experience, as he also began his first-class career at the age of 16 (for Border, in 1983).

It didn't help that I was also feeling the weight of expectation to perform. I was seen as a talented prodigy who, if he didn't score 50 or 100, had failed. I've had that my entire career. The fans can be demanding. It's almost like no matter what you get, it isn't good enough. I could come off three or four 100s in a row and the next innings I don't score and everyone's like, 'Well, what happened?' I'm also very conscious of the fact that people pay good money to watch me play. No one is more disappointed when I don't score runs than me. But that's cricket; no one in the world scores a 100 every time they go in to bat.

Knowing that some of the games were on TV was an additional burden. Being on telly was new to me – the knowledge that hundreds of thousands of people were watching me bat just added to my nervousness. It definitely took a while to get used to that!

The coaches obviously realised I had concerns and I was selected to play only three A-section games in that first season. I did, however, play in quite a few Benson & Hedges limited-over games. In the first game I played in that competition, they cocked up my name on the back of my shirt. It said 'Dibb' instead of Gibbs. Come to think of it, concealing my identity in that first, patchy season wasn't necessarily a bad thing.

But ja, I felt a lot more at home in the B-section, as I was more comfortable with that level of cricket. In those first years I knew that I couldn't yet hold my own in the top-flight provincial four-day game. The B-section was a lot more relaxed and, without any TV coverage, not so much in the public eye. I could go about learning my craft without bearing too much scrutiny. I had a decent record when it came to the B-section, averaging 50.69 in 26 matches with nine 50s and two 100s.

A major turning point for me was the day I got my first ton for Western Province A. In that innings I realised that I now had the skills to deal with top-level pace bowling and the *kop* to cope with it all. It was at Newlands against Boland in December 1994 and a new wicket had just been laid down. And, man, was it quick. Probably the quickest wicket I've ever played on in South Africa. Probably even quicker than the pitch at the WACA (Western Australian Cricket Association) in Perth, Australia, used to be.

Charl Willoughby and Henry Williams were firing in the balls and I remember my teammate Brian McMillan getting absolutely sconed by Henry. The ball hit Brian flush on his helmet and shot back over the wickets on the other side. You can imagine how fast the wicket must have been for a ball to do that. The ball hit Mackie really hard. Being the tough guy that he is, he just stood there, his face expressionless.

I managed to get on top of the bowling and I gutsily ploughed my way through to my inaugural A-section century, hitting 20 fours along the way. I may have got one or two 100s while playing in the B-section, but after four years of frustration and at 20 years of age, I had finally reached this significant milestone. Actually, I breathed a sigh of relief more than anything else. For four years the press and fans had been talking about this talented young cricketer, and their high expectations were getting to be a heavy burden to bear.

Once the monkey was off my back and I'd passed this big mental obstacle, I started to get 100s a lot more regularly. In those days, the Cape Town press dubbed us 'the four pups': me, HD Ackerman, Sven Koenig and, of course, Jacques Kallis. We were obviously talented players. Jacques probably had the strongest *kop* of all of us, operating out in the middle in his much-talked-about 'bubble of concentration'. I think Province management blooded him at the right time – he'd been out of school for two years already when he first played for Province. He'd played a lot of club cricket and had plenty of B-team experience before taking the step up.

Instead, I had played one club game and one game for the B-team before I was thrown straight in. And if I'm sounding a little miffed, I guess it's because I do have some regrets about that happening.

Batting at that level at such a young age became a struggle for survival rather than just trying to play a normal game. And I had to deal with the public's high expectations. Being thrown in at the deep end definitely set my progress back a few years.

But all that was on the field. Off the field, it was another story. As a 16-year-old, I had access to a world inhabited by South Africa's top sportsmen. And that world, let me tell you, was one helluva lot of fun …

It started with my little initiation ceremony into the A-team, of which teammate Kenny Jackson was the orchestrator. I would have to go through the infamous 'dip' initiation. My initiation took place before they remodelled Newlands, so the 'ceremony' took place in the old Pavilion, where the admin offices used to be.

'Get your boy out!' commanded Kenny, trying hard to sound authoritative, but not doing a very good job of it. So I had to drop my rods, get out my 'boy' and lay it out on a desk. Kenny had a piece of string – it could've been a bootlace – in his hand and he proceeded to lash my boy six times. Once or twice, it actually hurt. After the lashing – and this is where the little ritual gets its name from – the team pours you a glass of beer and you have to dip your boy in the beer. And then – you guessed it – you have to down the beer. It was a little bit cold putting the boy in the beer, but, you know, it was all smiles afterwards. It was a lovely little initiation.

The first few years I played for Province were wonderful, as my teammates were a bloody mischievous bunch of lads – both the A- and the B-team guys.

Of the B-team players, I would hang out with Alan Dawson and Lance Bleekers – two *very* naughty okes. Not that the rest of them were angels – not at all! The likes of Dean Payne, Tim Mitchell and Ian Solomon – and even our coach, Hylton Ackerman – certainly enjoyed a party or three.

I remember one evening in Pietermaritzburg when we went out for a team supper and had a few drinks. I was rooming with Vinnie Barnes at the time. Vinnie is currently the Proteas bowling coach, but he was then playing for Province. He and I went on to become close friends.

So, anyway, after supper, some of us – me, Bleekie, Dawsie,

Ian Solomon and Dean Payne – were in the lift on our way to our rooms when the decision was taken to hit the town. Out we went. The drinks flowed freely, as they tended to when we were socialising, and we stumbled back to the hotel at a late hour – I can't remember exactly what time it was, but no doubt it was way past any curfew the coach might've imposed.

It being summertime in Pietermaritzburg, a very hot and humid day awaited us the following morning. And, obviously, there was a game of provincial cricket to be played. What followed that morning was one of the funniest things I have ever seen on a cricket field. Dean was our opening bowler and he was way more hung-over than the rest of us. Now Dean was also a very hairy individual, and he used to wear these neoprene cycling-shorts under his cricket longs to prevent chaffing. And he'd have on long woollen cricket socks as well.

As it was, Dean used to sweat like a miner, and on this blazingly hot and humid KwaZulu-Natal day, the sweat was running off him in rivers. He could barely hold the ball, his hands were so sweaty. He had to abort his first ball, because halfway through the run-up it slipped out of his hand.

So in he comes again – all you can hear is the swish, swish, swish of his neoprene shorts – and he delivers the ball. Except no one can tell where it's gone. There's the blur of Dean's bowling action – he was a world-class quickie, remember – but then no sign of the ball. Next thing there's this crash as a cricket ball hits the sightscreen behind our wicketkeeper, Bleekie. The ball had obviously slipped out of Dean's hand, but this time it had sailed over the batsman, over Bleekie, and bounced once before hitting the sightscreen. Vinnie, fielding at fine leg, nearly kakked himself.

I remember standing there in the covers just laughing and laughing.

Our captain, Tim Mitchell, tried his hardest not to smile and to impose some sort of order on proceedings. He had word sent to the twelfth man that under no circumstances was Dean Payne allowed any water during play or at any of the drinks breaks. So we come off the field at lunch time, and poor old Dean is just lying there on the changing-room floor with ice blocks on his eyes, basically funnelling water down his throat.

Hylton Ackerman, or 'Dutchman' as everyone called him, made playing in the B-team a fantastic experience. He was a great coach and an astute reader of the game, but also a real character. I remember one game against Free State in Bloemfontein. We were in a bit of trouble early on, but I came in and Bleekie and I started to build a good partnership, as we often did in those days. I think we posted 100 in something like 90 minutes. It was a four-day match, but Bleekie and I were flying.

While all this was going on, Dutchman and fellow coach Mike Minnaar had disappeared off to the bladdy horse races. And, as luck would have it, they returned to the ground just in time to see me go out to the biggest slog ever. When I got back to the changing room, Dutchman laid into me: 'What the fuck do you think you're doing? This is four-day cricket – you can't just play these huge, big fucking hoicks like that!' I just laughed. I mean, the guy had gone off for a quick gamble, had missed the 160-odd runs Bleekie and I had put on, and had then given me a lecture on how *I* should be approaching the game!

But that was part and parcel of the team spirit in that squad back then. It was really fantastic. You couldn't help but be a little naughty. Even a guy like Gary Kirsten had his moments, let me tell you. There was this game we played in Queenstown – a one-dayer, I think. I was 16, and it was one of the first nights Gary and I ever went out together. I know Gary still remembers that evening very well, and I must add that this happened way, way before Gary met his wife Debbie!

So, anyway, we meet this gorgeous brunette and we're both very keen on her. I mean, *very* keen. Somehow we ended up back at her place – well, her folks' place, actually, but they weren't there – and we were all a little tipsy. The girl seemed up for a little fun, but Gary and I couldn't work out which one of us she liked more. It looked like we were both in the game. While she was off somewhere else in the house, Gary and I met up in the kitchen.

'What do you think we should do, man?' he asked. 'Do you want to go for her?' In a moment of consideration for my fellow teammate, I remember saying, 'No, you're older than me. You might as well go for it.' So Gary got the girl and I went back to the hotel for a cold shower. That evening was the start of what would not only become a successful opening partnership on the field, but also a valuable friendship off it.

Ja, those were really happy days. Everything was so new, fresh and exciting, I could barely sleep at night. Former Proteas bowler and later coach, Eric Simons, will testify to that. He was my first roommate at Province. I used to wake up at around 6 a.m. and open the curtains, switch on the TV – M-Net was still pretty new then – and generally make a racket. Poor Eric is 12 years older than me and needed a few more hours' sleep. Even today I don't need more than a six-hour kip.

I look back on those days with a lot of nostalgia. Those first few years were filled with laughter and naughtiness – hardly surprising, given the characters with whom I played. If they wanted to party on an evening during a game, then they would. And because I am a spontaneous sort of person, I was happy to go along with them. This set the tone for the rest of my career – something for which I am eternally grateful.

2

Me ... and my game

There's not a whole lot of difference between the two, actually. I'm impulsive, I like the limelight and I'm flashy. But I also have a big heart and I'm pretty generous. On the pitch I go for the big shots and I also often get out to rash shots. But I've also scored a lot of runs ...

Me ...

Look up the phrase 'what you see is what you get', and you'll find the name 'Herschelle Gibbs' written next to it.

And this is what you get ...

I'm always going to go for it. It's that simple. Whether it is on or off the pitch, it's been balls-to-the-wall in everything I've tried. 'Live life to the max' has pretty much been my mantra. With this default setting and an outgoing personality, I've had a lot of fun in my life. I'm also a pretty generous guy, both with my money and my time. And that's not a boast. Lord knows, it's got me into trouble often enough.

I find it impossible to refuse a drink bought for me by a cricket supporter or not to sign an autograph or talk cricket with my fans. And I don't refuse a drink simply because I *never* say no to a drink (as I know some of you wise guys might think), but because I feel a strong obligation to engage with cricket supporters. It's more than an obligation or a duty, actually; I really enjoy it. Similarly, and to my detriment, I've been way too generous with my money, often showering girls with gifts and all too regularly picking up the bill when I'm out with people.

Of course there are some downsides to my go-large-or-go-home attitude. Being a spontaneous person means that I've often not thought things through before making a decision. Frankly, my spontaneity has often landed me in deep shit. Once or twice up to chin level, and, let me tell you, it doesn't smell great. These are the kinds of things the tabloid media thrive on.

However, the flip side is that I've also had an unbelievable amount of fun, met some incredible people, had the pleasure of knowing many beautiful women, played some explosive innings and scored many runs. I won't give you the juice now, but keep reading and the following chapters get interesting, I promise.

I think my attitude to money is a pretty good reflection of my personality. It not only illustrates my general balls-to-the-wall approach to it all, but shows up the negative side of it too. Once I started earning money as a professional cricketer, I tended to spend it as fast as I made it. There wasn't too much in the way of forward financial planning, which was pretty indicative of my general attitude to life. In later years I learnt to curb my spending habits and, thanks to the valuable advice of people like my manager, Donné Commins, I've made some wise investments – particularly in property.

I'm still Herschelle, though, which means that there are still the occasional ill-advised little spending sprees. I do appreciate the finer things in life, and I have been very fortunate to have been able to afford some of them. So, thanks to my personality, I have definitely made some … let's call them 'rash' … decisions when it comes to money, but it's also allowed me to enjoy my life – one thing I have been equally determined to do.

When I first started playing cricket for Western Province over 20 years ago, I was still living with my parents. I was still a teenager and had no real money of my own. Almost all the cash I earned from my Province contract – about R3 000 a month, I think – went straight to my dad. He probably gave me about R500 or a little more for spending money.

He was like: 'You live under my roof and now you're earning

money. You've got to pay rent, you know.' I hardly had any bladdy money in those days. I remember saving up to buy a R120 striped shirt that I absolutely had to have. The problem was, I really liked the expensive stuff – clothes, cars, girls. Which is probably why, once I did get my hands on some real money, I would spend it like there was no tomorrow. Initially, anyway.

Money has given me a lot of pleasure, but it has also financed some excesses. I earned my first fairly decent income in 1996, when I signed a contract with the United Cricket Board of South Africa (UCB) to become a member of the national squad. It wasn't a huge amount – something like R12 000 or R13 000 a month, basic – but with match fees, win bonuses and a few sponsorships, I could afford some of the things I really wanted.

I remember saying to my first agent, Trevor Torrington, 'Listen, I've got a national contract now. Surely I can afford a Volkswagen Golf VR6?' My friend and teammate Paul Adams had just bought an Alfa, and I wanted a cool set of wheels too. I wasn't satisfied with average stuff any more. My tastes were expanding ... and so was my bank account. Unfortunately, though, my tastes often expanded way ahead of my bank account.

From 2000 onwards I started playing regularly for the Proteas, and that meant my bank account started to accumulate nicely. When you're in the starting XI, the match fee and a win bonus can add up to about R200 000 a month – though it does vary. That's just the Proteas money, though. Playing county cricket and, more recently, the Indian Premier League (IPL), increases your income significantly.

I've always been quite a big spender. I mean, we're not talking huge amounts of money, but when I started playing for South Africa, I started spending quite a lot of cash on clothing. I'd met these guys who worked at a very upmarket men's clothing shop at the V&A Waterfront in Cape Town, and I just kind of got convinced to buy all this expensive clothing – a lot of exclusive brands like Pal Zileri, an Italian label.

I was suckered, I guess. I've always liked suits, these guys figured it out, and I reckon they saw a good thing coming. I'd always wanted to wear whatever the latest fashion was, and those guys stocked it.

Ja, I used to spend quite a lot of money. I wouldn't think twice about paying R2 000 for a belt and double that for a pair of shoes. I'd go a couple of months without spending a cent and then blow 20K in one shot.

The most expensive item of clothing I ever bought was my Dolce&Gabbana suede jacket – more like a blazer, actually – but a stunning piece of clothing. It set me back about 16K. It's blue. But stunning, believe me. About a year later I was shopping in the UK and happened to come across a pair of D&G shoes in exactly the same colour as the jacket. Obviously, I bought them. Actually, I bought three pairs – in blue, red and black. The best pairs of shoes I've ever bought. I hardly wear them, though.

I still love my clothes – last year I was one of *GQ* magazine's Best Dressed Men in Sport – but I've cut down a *lot* on my spending. I don't see the point of it all any more. I've got everything I need ... and the clothes I bought five years ago are still in fashion.

The only problem is that they no longer bladdy fit me. I was on creatine back then and had more muscle mass. Now that I'm smaller, it means that I have a whole lot of shirts and suits that don't fit me properly. They fit my dad, though, and he's basically taken them all. The guy is looking pretty damn sharp these days, I can assure you. His girlfriend has just bought a Merc SLK, so my old man is cruising in designer gear with the top down.

Ja, I've also been into cars in a big way. Man, I've spent a lot of money on cars. I remember when the Audi TT first came out – I just had to have one. I must've been one of the first okes in South Africa to get one. I also had that old slab-shaped Audi Cabriolet. Ja – I don't know what I was thinking there. I looked like an old man in that convertible. It was nice-looking, though – a stunning car with a black interior, but not a car for a person my age. I've got a black BMW X5 at the moment – classy, but not too flashy, and practical. I think the car is a fair reflection of where my head is these days.

Booze has obviously also cost me a fair amount of money over the years. In the early days, Paul Adams and I used to hit a club called Sirens in Claremont. I can barely recall all the times I used to get *vrot* there, but it was a lot. During one winter in the off-season we went there every single night until 5 a.m. in the morning. 'The Month of Madness', we called it. As you can imagine, we were responsible for a large chunk of the club's income that month.

So, ja, I've always liked expensive things and I have sometimes bought more than my budget allowed for. On a couple of occasions, I'd try to draw money at an ATM, only to find a big fat minus in my account. With all my bond payments and after some enthusiastic shopping, I'd find my money ... you know ... blown.

But now I've organised my finances so that I've got two accounts. It's pretty standard stuff – all my debit orders come off my one account, and I use the other one for everyday stuff. I have this great banker at BOE – her name is Candice – and she transfers the money from one account into the other for me.

Unfortunately, at one stage I spent money faster than Candice could transfer it, though fortunately I've curbed my poor spending habits since then. Candice had to say to me, 'Listen, if you're going to carry on spending like this, you're going to blow all your flippin' money.' Maybe she didn't swear. She's a sweet lady. But ja, so I pulled up the handbrake quite a lot with my spending.

One thing I have been financially smart with is houses – I've made money on all the houses I've bought. I bought my first place in 1996, when I finally moved out of my parents' home. It was the year I started playing for South Africa. I bought a three-bedroom apartment in High Cape below Devil's Peak in Cape

Town. I think I paid about R340 000 for the flat, and I ended up living there for four years.

I eventually sold the apartment for double what I paid for it, so that worked out okay. Actually, most of the money I earned in those first few years of my national contract went into my mom's house and my parents' cars. When my parents got divorced in 2000, the bond still needed to be paid off, and my dad basically said, 'Well, it's your baby now. You've got to pay for it.'

So initially, for those first couple of years, I had to sort out my mom's house. And I bought her and my dad a car each too – my mom one of those little Toyota Rav4s, and my dad a Honda Ballade. Ja, I wasn't too fussy about the car I chose for my dad, but I was for my mom. She was very happy with the Rav – she still has it, in fact. And her house is paid off, and it's all good, you know.

As I've said, over the past few years I've made a bit of cash buying and selling houses. That's not to say I've got property everywhere. As far as my current house is concerned, playing in the IPL has been a blessing, that's for sure. Because of the IPL, I have been able to afford a great new place in Camps Bay, which I've just renovated. The property cost me a whack, but I'll be able to pay it off this year. My manager, Donné, was adamant about it: 'You buy this house, you pay it off this year.' I've learnt to listen to Donné when she uses that tone of voice.

As excessive a spender as I have been over the years, I've also been very generous when it comes to paying for people. If I'm out with friends for supper, I don't really think twice about paying for everybody, I really don't. Donné is always telling me, 'You can't be so generous all the time, Herschelle!' But I can't help it.

Look, some mates of mine have taken advantage of my generosity, but I've had a little word with them. Just one or two of them, but they know who they are. All in all, however, I've certainly cut down quite a lot on my spending.

Playing county cricket is not just a great experience in terms of learning your craft as a cricketer – it's also financially lucrative. At Glamorgan, where I am contracted, the guys are clocking in the region of £70 000 a season. That's good money right there, and it doesn't come back to South Africa; along with my IPL earnings, my county cricket money stays in the UK.

I've also had – and still have – a great relationship with my sponsors. Apart from being given great clothing and equipment, it has also been pretty lucrative cash-wise. I like to think that I give my sponsors' brands plenty of exposure too. I know this is going to sound like one big punt, but I've been lucky to work with a number of brands whose products and ethos I've really loved and with which I've identified.

Take Puma, for example; they are one of my main sponsors. I moved to Puma from Adidas before the 2003 World Cup, which took place here in South Africa. I'd been with Adidas for ages – from school, even – but our relationship was getting a little stale and they seemed to be focusing more on Jacques Kallis and Mark Boucher than me. That was their prerogative, I guess, but Puma were really interested in building a relationship with me and now we've got a really good thing going. I've always loved their stuff – I reckon Puma's technical and lifestyle ranges are the best you get, and I get to wear it every day of my life, which is cool by me.

Because I'm sample size, I am basically given free rein to take whatever I want from their sample stockroom – I've literally got cupboards full of Puma stuff. I've become a lot more selective these days, though. Obviously I'm a little bit older now, so I don't want to wear the same clothing as my younger Puma-sponsored Proteas teammates, JP Duminy and Albie Morkel. I love, for example, Puma's formal Black Label range – flipping classy stuff. Puma are also prepared to push the envelope a little with their design, which really appeals to me. I mean, they made me this wicked pair of black and silver boots specifically for the Deccan Chargers, which they also sponsor.

An International Cricket Council (ICC) rule states that your boots have to be predominantly white – which, frankly, I've always found a little strange. In limited-over games you wear coloured clothing, pads and gloves ... but still your shoes have to be white? Fortunately, the IPL doesn't subscribe to the ICC's rules and we're allowed to wear boots that match our outfit's colours.

I've also had a proud association with Oakley eyewear for 14 years – another brand I'd buy if they didn't give me stuff. The designs are cutting edge and comfortable, and they've got lenses for every type of light – I can choose from more than 20 different lenses. I like wearing Oakley's new Jawbone range at the moment, and, man, have they been generous. I recently went to Oakley with Boucher – he was with Adidas eyewear, but is now also with Oakley – and I left with an armful of new shades.

Bouch was like, 'Jeez, Hersch, you can't leave here with 10 pairs!' I just laughed. 'Of course I can! I've been with Oakley the longest, my boy.' I also often go on their website, and if I see stuff I like, they'll organise it for me, even if it hasn't arrived in South Africa yet. Great bunch of people there!

The sponsor I've had for the longest, though, has been Gunn & Moore – we go back to even before the start of my international career. I use their bats, pads and gloves, and they really have been fantastic to me. Just to give you an example, they gave me a set of Ping golf clubs when I made my first international 100 ... and quite a few sets since then too.

G&M tailor-make my bats specifically for me in the UK and then ship them out to wherever I am in the world. I'm using 212 (2 pounds 12 ounces) bats these days – I used to play with 208s and then 209s, but the way the game is going, you now need something heavier. I know Lance Klusener used to bat with a 213 or a 214, and rumours did the rounds that Graeme Pollock had batted with a three-pound bat. I don't know if that's true, as that is one bladdy heavy bat.

Bat making has evolved a great deal in recent years. Bats are still made of English willow, obviously, but the pick-up is now much better balanced. I can bat with a heavy bat with big, thick edges, but the pick-up – still the most important part of a bat's feel – makes it seem like it's a 208 or a 209.

However, the longevity of bats is becoming an issue these days. I was speaking to the guy who makes my bats at G&M and he was telling me how the cricket pros' bats just aren't lasting as long any more. With all the 20/20 and limited-over games these days, we aren't only playing more cricket, but also whacking the ball further and harder. Basically, the bats are getting knackered way more quickly.

Another factor: bowlers are all endlessly practising their limited-over death bowling, so you're facing yorker after yorker in the nets. The toe of the bat therefore takes a hammering – the bottom left of my bat always cracks and bombs out first.

But G&M really make phenomenal bats, and I'm not just saying that because they're one of my sponsors. They've just made me my 101st bat – every bat gets numbered – and they're so well made that I can hardly tell the difference between any of the six bats I usually have with me on tour.

... and my cricket

And that's a perfect lead-up to discussing my approach to cricket. As I said in the intro to this chapter, there's not a whole lot of difference between the way I've lived my life and the way I've played my cricket. On the field, the spontaneity of my personality has been bolstered by quick-firing synapses and above-average reflexes and coordination. It means I don't have to think myself into that 'zone' that sports psychologists are always talking about.

A lot of athletes are very analytical in their approach. They do a lot of planning, preparation and strategising before they compete, but I believe this can have a negative effect on their performance. Sports psychologists consequently make a lot of money coaching athletes to just let go and let their natural talent and ability take over. It's only then that goals are scored, passing shots are nailed and runs flow off the bat. It's easy for me, though. As I have never consciously thought about having to back my physical skills with a sound mental approach, I have never had to unhook the analytical part of my brain before I go out to play. I've always just done it. It's the only way I know.

In order for me to play to the best of my ability, I have to play my natural game. And my natural game is to go out and look for runs. For example, in my entire cricket career I've always played the pull shot against short-pitched bowling. It's an instinctive skill. Some batsmen simply have the ability to pick up length a lot quicker than other batters, and these are the guys who basically pull really well. If they see a bowler throw in a ball that's way too short, they just get underneath and hit it.

When I try to play defensively, by leaving the ball, for example, I inevitably end up in two minds about what to do next. And let me tell you, there's no time for second thoughts when the ball's coming at you at 150 km/h, boet. Steve Waugh, for instance, had worked out that trying to hook and pull would often cost him his wicket, and once he'd eliminated that shot from his repertoire, his average steadily increased. Waugh dropped what was a high-risk shot in his game. For me, the high risk would be if I *stopped* hooking.

Look at Matthew Hayden, Adam Gilchrist, Virender Sehwag – all of them attacking openers like me. You'll very seldom find that these guys play tentatively. Irrespective of whether it is a Test match or a one-day game, if they get 20 runs they are going to get them quickly, and if you are going to get them out, it will always be when they are trying to hit the ball.

That's always been my approach, too. Think about it … at its essence, cricket is a simple game of putting bat to ball. You can theorise all you want, but at the end of the day, you have to hit the bladdy ball if you want to win.

Obviously it's not all that simple. Occasions do arise when

I should give myself more time to study the bowling and get in properly before attacking. Of course there have also been occasions when I have taken a liking to a particular bowler right from the start and proceeded to clock him to all corners of the park from ball one. There's no point in me scratching around the crease trying to follow orders to 'bat responsibly', because I just don't score runs. 'Being responsible' has let me down so many times – I think about things too much rather than just going out and bladdy well hitting the ball.

I am a far more effective player when I take on the bowling and dominate. I've learnt that the hard way, believe me. I know a lot of people think that my attitude is limiting and more than a little selfish, but the fact is, asking me to play conservative cricket is like asking me to play with one hand tied behind my back. Of course there have been times when I have had to keep an innings together as my colleagues have fallen around me, but even then you'll see my run rate has been atypically high for that kind of situation.

Duncan Fletcher has been the one coach who's always understood me. From my early days, when he coached me at Western Province in the 1990s through to his advisory role for the Proteas in 2009, Fletchie has always told me to 'go out and just play. I don't care what the situation is; you just play.' It's great to have someone who backs your game, and when I have that kind of confidence, irrespective of who the bowler is, they tend to travel. I have often played my best innings when I've thought, 'Hersch, you've got nothing to lose. Just go out there and hit the ball.' My innings in the famous 438 game is a prime example of that attitude (more about that later).

Ja, Fletchie is always telling me to 'play it as you see it'. He never tells me to play myself in. Not ever. Graham Ford, who took over as Proteas coach from Bob Woolmer, wasn't too bad either, allowing me the freedom to go out and express myself. But the coaches who came after him – Ray Jennings, Eric Simons,

Mickey Arthur and now Corrie van Zyl – were all pretty conservative in their approach.

I don't know how many times I've been told that the first hour of a Test match always belongs to the bowler. Well, someone clearly forgot to tell Michael Slater. Or Sanath Jayasuriya. If the first ball asks to be hit over cover, they happily oblige.

Yes, the downside to being an attacking batsman – especially when you're opening and facing the new ball – is that you do often go out to rash shots. It's not as if I don't know this. Trust me.

There have been plenty of times I have been out on shots I know I should never have attempted, even as an attacking player. I wish I knew why I played those shots. I have never been able to figure that out about my game. It's just such an instinctive thing. I mean, I wouldn't purposefully want to play a bad shot. Fletchie always said I just play it like I see it … and unfortunately I haven't seen the ball so well at times. It's frustrating when you're back in the dressing room and you're watching a TV replay of your dismissal. But I've always taken solace in the fact that I got out trying to play a shot. In this case, obviously a kak shot.

But it's particularly hard for me to watch a replay of my dismissal when I know I've gone out playing tentatively. It pisses me off so much, I can't even watch it. If I've been defending against a good ball and I've nicked it or been bowled, then fair enough – all credit to the bowler. But I hate losing my wicket because I've been asked to play conservatively and, as a consequence, have tightened up.

The 2005/06 series against Australia in Australia was a prime example of how it messes up my game when I play too tentatively. We played three Tests against the Aussies in December and January, and then hosted them in South Africa during March/April. As you no doubt recall, we were humbled, losing the series 0-2 in Oz and then 0-3 in South Africa.

There's no doubt in my mind that I was way too hesitant, against Brett Lee in particular. I was too focused on trying to play myself in and to figure out what the ball and the bowler were doing. And with me, doing so always results in my feet getting heavy and my balance going for a ball of shit.

But if I had gone out there with a positive attitude, suddenly I would have been light on my feet and in perfect sync, ready to pull one of his short-pitched skull-splitters.

The best I managed was 94 in the first innings of the second Test in Melbourne, 67 later in Sydney, and then 53 at the Wanderers in the final Test of the series. I still look back on that series with a fair amount of regret. I should have just played the way *I* wanted to play. I've been thinking a lot about this particular issue, which is why my New Year's resolution for 2010 was that, for however long I'm still going to play – and it's likely that the majority of it will be 20/20 cricket – I am only going to bat the way I *want* to bat.

I know I frustrate a lot of people with my batting, and the press certainly love having a go at me, but that comes with the territory. It's a simple fact that I would have scored far fewer runs if I had been a more conservative batsman. It's the flipside of my personality. I've had a lot of great times, but I've also been in a lot of trouble. And, similarly, I've scored a lot of runs, but I've also often gone out too early.

Ironically, one of the best Test knocks I ever played was a hard-fought 85 at the Wanderers against England in 1999. It was the first Test of the series, and the opening day saw cloudy conditions and a damp, spongy pitch. England batted first, and within a couple of overs they were four wickets down for only two runs. Thanks to Allan Donald's superb two opening overs, it was England's worst-ever start to a Test match.

The ball was doing everything – bouncing, seaming, moving through the air. In fact, it was doing *too* much. It was so bad, the batsmen could barely get bat to ball. England managed to scrape together 122.

We were in trouble early on, with Gary Kirsten and Jacques

Kallis falling cheaply. As an opener, I defended for my bladdy life. I couldn't play an attacking shot even if I wanted to – the ball was just all over the show. Daryll Cullinan, who scored 108, and I rebuilt the South African innings in what was probably one of my top-three knocks in Test cricket. But fans will never remember that one.

While we're on the topic of irony: the fact that I ever became a cricket professional in the first place is somewhat ironic. Cricket was never my first choice, either as a sport or as a career. That's not to say that I hankered after a career in accounting – now *that* would've been interesting – but during my school days, rugby and football were the front-runners.

I played provincial schoolboy rugby, representing Western Province at Craven Week, and then later I played for the Villagers Second XV and Western Province's Under-21s. Former Springbok flyhalf and rugby legend Naas Botha even came up to me during my last Craven Week match and said, 'Ja, you'll be the next Springbok flyhalf.'

Things were looking really promising in that direction, and becoming a professional rugby player was tempting ... But that wasn't what I *really* wanted. Football was the game I loved the most and, to be honest, the sport in which I knew I had the most talent. I had people tell me – and these are guys who have gone on to play professional football in Europe – that when they played with me as youngsters, I was streets ahead of them.

I wouldn't say I was a football genius, but I really think I could have gone a long way in the sport. Unfortunately, any dreams I had of running out for my beloved Manchester United were ended by a knee injury sustained while playing rugby when I was 20. The doc I was seeing gave me some very good advice. He said, 'You can play cricket a lot longer than rugby or football. Just give up rugby and football, and concentrate on your cricket.'

It was wise counsel, and even though it was hard for me to hear it, as I'd already got so far in my rugby, the truth of the matter was that I just didn't really have the build to play another 10 years of rugby. Cricket, on the other hand, offered the chance of having a long-term career. Of course I loved the game, but up until then it was just the sport I played in summer. I hadn't ever thought of cricket as a potential career.

Studying further was obviously out of the question. As I mentioned, my academic record was less than stellar, and even my parents understood – and my dad was even a teacher, remember – that I best put those reflexes and coordination to work earning money, because it sure as hell wasn't going to happen if I went to college or varsity.

I knew there was a chance that I could go places with sport. I knew I had the talent to play professional football, rugby or cricket, but when the first two were no longer an option, it necessarily had to be cricket.

Fortunately, looking back now over a career that has so far spanned 20-odd years as a professional, the decision I made was the right one. I've made the most of my longevity. Whereas for a long time the rugby players made much more money than us cricketers (comparing their national team contracts with ours), with the advent of 20/20 cricket and the IPL, the wheel has turned.

At the IPL auction in 2008, I, for example, was bought for $575 000. That's $575 000 a year for three years – and that's around half of the $1.35 million my teammate Andrew Symonds went for. When you consider that you are paid this amount for only five weeks' work per year, it's pretty decent cash. Game for game, it's better money than the football players in the English Premier League earn.

So a professional cricketer is what I became, and while it might appear that I've had something of a laissez-faire attitude to my chosen sport, that's not entirely true. Yes, I'm only too aware of the natural talent I have for the game – it would be insincere of me to pretend otherwise – and I've never really possessed too much in the way of a game plan beyond hitting the ball towards the white rope (preferably without a bounce) when I've walked out to bat. But that doesn't mean I haven't prepared or put in the hard yards.

In order to prepare mentally for a game, I always use a variety of visualisation techniques I started when I was still a schoolboy. I would always see myself playing the particular school we were scheduled to play and could 'see' myself fielding and batting. I would basically play the entire game in my head. I don't know if it's a gift, but I can almost 'feel' the ball being bowled to me. In my mind I sense the speed at which it's coming and I can gauge the kinds of shots I'm going to need to play ... or the ones that I can't.

Because we know our fixtures months in advance, it gives me plenty of time to think about the upcoming games. Three days before a game, I'll start visualising who I'll be facing and what the wicket will be like. Having been around this long, there aren't many bowlers out there I haven't faced before, so that obviously helps too. There's no substitute for experience. I hated hearing that when I was a youngster, but being an old *ballie* now, I now know exactly what those older players were talking about.

For me, the visualisation technique has been even more valuable in preparing for a match than actually hitting balls. I find hitting balls these days a little boring, to be honest. A lot of the time we hit balls just for the sake of it, because we need to be seen to be putting in the hard work. Fielding is a different story altogether, because you can never get enough catching practice. So, ja, my innings is already played out in my mind when I walk out to the middle. Unfortunately, sometimes the script doesn't go quite according to plan ...

And then there's the physical training, which is one area where I reckon I've managed to work harder than most. I think a common perception exists that cricketers have it all laid out for them; that, like golfers, cricketers don't have to be in peak physical shape to perform well. Judging by the waistlines of some of my colleagues over the years, I can certainly see where that perception comes from. Sure, you don't have to be super-fit to be a cricketer, given that the game – especially as a batsman – is about hand-eye coordination, reflexes and a good *kop*.

But it does help. Bat out there for hours in the heat and humidity of the Indian subcontinent or the West Indies, and all that natural talent you have been relying on won't help you when you start to cramp up or see little black dots dance in front of your eyes when you're exhausted.

So ja, I have made a point of working hard to stay in shape. During time off between tournaments, I'm always at the gym. I do weights in the morning and then go back in the evening to do cardio on the treadmill. I never really run on the road, as I find it too jarring on my lower back and knees. You'll often see me at the Virgin Active in Green Point or the Sports Science Institute in Newlands at 8 p.m. or 9 p.m. at night, working the treadmill.

And that's after I've had supper too. There have been a lot of times after dinner when my mates have suggested that we go out, but I've turned them down because I had to go to the gym. I also value the peace and quiet at that time of the night. It allows me to go through some of my visualisation techniques.

I haven't changed my routine in 20 years. If there are no games during the week, I'll be at the gym four times a week. I'll do almost an hour of cardio – either run for half an hour and cycle for another half an hour, or I'll run for 40 minutes and cycle for 20 minutes. A lot of the guys train differently, but it is a routine I have settled into and stuck with. With all the drinking and partying I've done through the years, it's also really helped to keep me lean.

I'm always trying to instil this kind of work ethic into some of the younger guys in the Cape Cobras team. I always wanted to be fit; I always wanted to show my athleticism on the field. I never took those things for granted. I get a little frustrated with some of the guys who seem satisfied with the level at which they are playing now. They've had some domestic success and, in a couple of cases, have had a taste of international cricket, and that seems to be enough for them.

Stuff like the sponsored car, the fancy sunglasses and the latest kit – all the peripheries – seem more important to them than working hard to improve their game every season. I keep on telling them that nowadays there's just so much more opportunity to make real money, especially with 20/20 cricket.

For that to happen, though, these guys have to up their game on the international stage. And for that to happen, they have to make the final of our domestic Standard Bank Pro20 competition and then do well at the new T20 Champions League tournament against the world's other top franchises. Either that, or cement a permanent place in the national side, where one of the IPL or English county teams can notice you. Then you start making the cash. Unfortunately, we have a few lazy and overweight cricketers in South Africa.

Throughout my career it's been said that I am a naturally gifted cricketer, and that *is* true – I have been blessed. But I've also had to work hard at technical elements of my game. Sure, my natural abilities are a huge bonus, but these can't always carry me through. As I've said in Chapter 1, when I first started playing provincial cricket, I struggled a little when I started out – well, quite a lot, actually.

And for two or three years into my international career I also struggled with my batting form. My teammate, Brian McMillan, gave me some invaluable advice which I have stuck with to this day. 'Listen,' he said (you always listened when Mackie said 'listen'), 'when you line yourself up in your crease, make sure that your head is pointing over off-stump. And use that as a set-up and as a guideline, whether you're in a slump or playing well.'

It's all I've ever done since, and out there in the middle I probably focus more on following Mackie's advice than on the ball. Especially when I am up against express pace, I concentrate on keeping my head still instead of watching the ball. That might seem weird, but it works for me. Obviously I *do* watch the ball – that's instinct. You can pick up in the replays that my eyes are focused on the ball, otherwise I'd never make contact with it, but my basic guide is to keep my head still for as long as possible. If I don't, I often go out lbw when the ball nips back. My head has moved, I've planted my foot too early, and I'm off-balance and committed to playing the wrong line.

Sometimes the guys have odd bowling actions; so that if you watch the ball closely, your head tends to move with the action. Often a bowler will use the width of the crease, come wide over the wicket and angle the ball in. Part of the reason why they do this is to get you to follow them, so that you lose your balance a bit. And then they bowl a late swinging-away swinger that, now that you've moved across your stumps, either gets you plumb in front for an lbw, or gets you nicked behind.

A lot is made of getting your feet into the right position as a batter, but I haven't focused on that aspect too much. Again, for me, it's all about the position of my head and keeping my head still. In that bad trot I went through against the Aussies in 2005/06, mentioned earlier, I had a tough time dealing with Brett Lee because I was premeditating shots too often to try to deal with his pace. And he was probably at his quickest then – bowling at close to 160 km/h – and I played the short ball exceptionally badly in the Tests in Australia.

On some occasions Lee was bowling so fast that it felt as if he was coming in from 10 yards, not the actual 22-yard length of a cricket pitch. Because I was deciding on what shot I was going to hit before he had even bowled at me, my head would move as he released the ball, and consequently I'd be in trouble. What you don't want to do when facing a guy of Lee's pace is to get yourself on the wrong side of the ball. When you're off-balance instead of staying straight up, which allows you to either pull the ball or duck underneath it, you're unable to adjust. That's when you either get hit (which I did) or get out (again, which I did).

Bowlers have also discovered that when I'm playing tentatively, they have a better chance of getting me out. I have spoken to some of my Deccan Chargers teammates, whom I've previously played against in international cricket, and their general consensus is that when they get the ball to come back into me, chances are I'll be out either lbw or bowled. It isn't so much a technical flaw in my batting as it is playing tentatively early on, trying to predict what the bowler is going to bowl and not playing the ball on its merits.

Technically, my defence has always been pretty good – if you don't have a solid defence as an opening batsman in international cricket, you are never going to cut it. Any stuff written in the press about my defensive 'frailties' is, frankly, a crock of shit. As I mentioned, sometimes when my head moves – especially early on in an innings – I will plant my foot and get trapped lbw. That aside, my defence has been as solid as you can get. But I guess most of my opposition probably say, 'Stay patient with Hersch and he'll give you a chance or two. He likes to free his arms and hit through the covers. You've always got a chance with a straight ball.'

Another aspect of my game I'm proud of is my BMT … my big-match temperament. I love the big games, particularly World Cup games, and my averages there speak for themselves: 1 067 runs in 23 innings, averaging 56 runs and a strike rate of 87.38. A World Cup is the most pressurised form of the game you can play in any sport. You are playing for your country, and it's the one platform on which you really want to perform. I am prouder of my World Cup record than anything else, and I believe the record exists because of my ability to handle the pressure inherent in the situation.

From an early age I wanted to be the guy who scores the big

runs, the match-winning goal or the try in a final. I don't think there's one particular element in my make-up that makes me perform well in a big match, but, from my school days, if my team was in a final, they knew that I'd do anything to help them win the game, and that, in turn, boosted their confidence. And their belief in me motivated me even more.

I am definitely always determined not to let any situation get the better of me, and love performing for people on the big stage. From my school days, I've wanted to entertain crowds, and an element of showmanship has always been a part of my game. I won't lie; I love the glory too. I like taking centre stage and getting the attention – it motivates, focuses and brings out the best in me.

The famous 438 game at the Wanderers against Australia in 2006 is a perfect example. With the ODI series locked at 2-2, the fifth game was essentially a final. The Aussies posted a record score of 434, and with my innings of 175 off 111 balls, we managed to chase their total down. It was the ideal platform for me to do what I do best, and I did it. The greater the glory, the bigger the outcome, the more I'm up for it.

On the flip side, it's been fascinating to watch players who have scored more runs than I have, and who have better averages, fall apart completely in a final. Despite having all the experience in the world, when they are put in a do-or-die situation, the wheels come off. Take a look at the IPL finals over the past few years. Just about all the big names have had a mental meltdown, even when chasing very moderate totals. Ja, those big games do amazing things to people – they blow their minds completely.

Obviously I can't discuss my BMT without mentioning the elephant in the room. The Proteas don't exactly have a reputation as a team with big-match temperament, do they? We've fallen agonisingly short at the World Cups, due mainly to an alarming degree of brain fade at critical moments. And while my batting record at these tournaments has been great, I have to include myself among the faders with my 'dropped catch' in the Super Eight stage of the 1999 World Cup against Australia. But more about that later.

In the 2007 World Cup semi-final, once more against Australia, we were again a team in meltdown mode. Our game plan had been to attack, but it was unbelievable to witness what happened instead in our innings. 'Attack' became more like 'panic', and in no time at all we were four or five wickets down. There were some really strange and totally out-of-character shots being played out there. By the time I came in to bat, the game was virtually dead.

I had listened to some of our bowlers talk before the game, and they seemed genuinely intimidated by the prospect of bowling to Matthew Hayden and Adam Gilchrist. I could see that they were shitting themselves, and I was thinking, 'Come on, okes! Surely you are up for it?'

Perhaps I should've said something and tried to be more supportive, but generally I'm not really outspoken in team talks. I don't really say how I feel about things. Yes, I think I've gained enough experience to comment in team meetings, but, to be frank, I have never played a leadership role in a team. Even when I was at school, I left the big decisions to someone else. I still wouldn't want a leadership job in any team. Some guys, though, are happy to be the captain any time. I think Graeme Smith was born to lead. Perhaps the fact that my comments are not taken seriously is part of the reason why I don't speak up. Whenever I've made a suggestion on the field, it's been declined.

Sounds like I'm avoiding the topic here, doesn't it? So … do the Proteas have BMT or not? Well, put it this way – we have a lot of talented players – always have had – but there seems to be a missing factor. If we could pin-point what that was, we would have won at least one World Cup so far.

A similar pattern repeated itself when the Cape Cobras played in the inaugural 2009 Champions League semi-final against Trinidad and Tobago in Hyderabad. Before the game, during the team talk, I spoke up (something I'm doing more often now at the Cobras) and basically said, 'Listen, this is not the time for you to retreat into your shell. It's a one-off opportunity. You are going to be playing in front of crowds of 30 000 or 40 000 people – something that will never happen back home. And there are billions of people who will be watching you on TV. This is no time to freeze up. Don't withdraw into your shell.'

Being on TV is nothing – I mean, we are all pros; we've been on telly plenty of times. That shouldn't be an issue. And we're also used to crowds (although it's a different story in India, but still). But the pressure still got to some key players. Guys who had been playing for eight or ten years were suddenly dropping catches ... just because they were in a semi-final. We scored a respectable 175, with JP Duminy getting 61, and I anchored our innings with 42 up front. Unfortunately, those dropped catches cost us, and Daren Ganga and Dwayne Bravo won the game for Trinidad and Tobago.

It might be something I was born with, but I've never frozen in the big games. As I've said, perhaps it's because there's more glory in those games. Or perhaps it's because I have been playing the game in my mind in the days leading up to it, and when I actually get onto the pitch I've 'been there' already.

I really don't know ...

3

The good times

I could couch this chapter in a whole bunch of safe-sounding euphemisms, but given the book's title, I'll get straight to the point, shall I? Two words: 'women' and 'booze'.

Whatever else has happened in my life, I can say one thing for sure: I have had a huge amount of fun in my cricket career. Three things have undoubtedly contributed to this: 1) I'm a friendly and outgoing guy who's comfortable in anyone's company; 2) I have the gift of the gab, which I get from my dad, and clearly women love it. My open demeanour often comes across as flirting, but that's just the way I am. I guess you could say I am charming and, as I said, chicks dig it; 3) And this is the double-edged sword – I like to drink, and alcohol has only exacerbated points 1 and 2. It has lubricated some of the best evenings of my life, but it also nearly ended my international career in 2008.

We'll get to that in the next chapter, though. For now, let me tell you about some of the fun stuff. Parents … send your kids to bed.

The Aussie tour of 1997/98

As far as women are concerned, the Proteas' tour to Australia from December 1997 to January 1998 was like going shopping. To this day, the tour remains the most 'successful' one I've ever been on, by a long shot. The guys couldn't believe it – especially some of the single guys who were touring Oz for the first time.

From the day we set foot there, women were falling into our laps virtually every night. Australian women, I can tell you, are not afraid to speak their minds and make it crystal-clear what they're after. Especially, as we found out, if you're an international sportsman. There's none of this, 'Am I reading the signals correctly here?' crap. Nope, the message is hand-delivered to you in capital letters. Most of the time we didn't have to go and look for girls either. They came hunting, often in packs, and if they liked what they saw, you were in for the ride of your life. Fascinating social behaviour. They should study it … make a documentary on the Discovery channel. I'd watch it.

It started with the Perth Stripper, as she fondly became known. During one of the tour's warm-up games, a couple of the guys and I weren't playing and, as a result, we were sharing the twelfth-man drinks duties. We saw this pretty girl sitting right in front of the players' viewing area and, as we'd find out a little later, she happened to be a stripper. But, more than that, she was a stripper who enjoyed cricket. And there can't be too many of them around. No doubt she would've appreciated Gary Kirsten's great knock that day – he got around 200, if I remember correctly. An unbelievable knock, actually.

As any youngster in a team will tell you, being on twelfth-man duties can be a bit of a schlep. All you want to do is be on the pitch, playing; sitting on the sidelines gets really frustrating. One tends to turn one's attention to attractions in the stadium rather than the sparkling cricket being played out in the middle. And that's how our attention happened to fall upon this fine young Australian lass. The three of us started chatting to her, and eventually we invited her to join us for a drink at our hotel at 8 p.m. that evening. She was very punctual.

We all got together in one of the okes' rooms and we had a bottle of wine. More drinks followed, and things started to loosen up a little … And then the girl happened to mention that she was a stripper and that, if we wanted, she would strip for us.

Things loosened up a lot more after that. Various items of clothing were removed in an eyebrow-raising kind of way, and one thing invariably led to another. I led the warm-up session, but then left after about 40 minutes. The rest of them stayed behind.

And basically the tour just kicked on from there. It got the ball rolling in a big way. A few nights later, there was a matric dance at the hotel – huge party, girls galore. I spotted one particularly gorgeous girl, obviously dressed to the nines, walking around the hotel lobby. I thought, 'Well, hell, it's a matric dance. It's quite a big occasion. I might as well try to get to know her.'

So I did. After a drink and a few words, she came upstairs with me to my room and gave a little dance of another kind. She then left and went back to the dance proper.

In the lead-up to the last Test in Adelaide, one of my fellow single lads and I met these two really cool girls in a bar and had a great time with them. We sort of stuck with them for a while, and on the last night of the tour we had something special in mind. These girls were well connected and we said to them, 'Listen, you organise as many girlfriends as you can – we're going to have a huge party back at the hotel.' We must have had about 30 girls at the party that night – I told you those two were well connected. So: 30 beautiful girls, a few very enthusiastic South African cricketers (only the single ones, of course), an open bar at the Hilton, and the knowledge that we were only leaving the hotel at 5 p.m. the next afternoon. It was one fat party. From mid-evening to the next afternoon, I enjoyed the company of ... let's just say, more than one woman.

That was probably the most eventful night I have ever had. From a work-flow point of view, it wasn't as difficult as you might expect either. These girls were really up for it and, to be honest, I don't know if they knew what was going on or not, but no one seemed to mind. You picked a girl up, took her upstairs to your room, and afterwards both of you would go back downstairs and you'd go and chat to someone else. It was a phenomenal night.

And that was just during the Tests.

We also played a triangular ODI series against Australia and New Zealand. It was the first match of the best-of-three final against the Aussies at the Melbourne Cricket Ground. I was made twelfth man again for the finals. I wore number 13, which turned out to be an unlucky number for me on the pitch, but particularly fortuitous off it. We won the first game (lost the series 1-2, though), but any feelings of frustration I might have had because I wasn't playing quickly dissipated when this girl stopped me in the hotel lobby and asked me if I was 'Number 13'.

She had two friends with her and apparently they had been waiting for me. To this day I'm not entirely sure why, but, hey, you tend not to question people's motives when you are presented with such an opportunity. The girls basically invited themselves up to my room. The hotel had pretty big rooms, which was nice – more a suite vibe, with an open-plan design that included a lounge and two single beds. All in all, too much for one man. A quick phone call later and one of my single colleagues was knocking on my room door in what I can only describe as an enthusiastic manner.

Two beds, two cricketers and three women. One of them wasn't all that keen though; she just lay on the bed. Which was fine – there was enough for everyone. The other two girls, however, more than made a go of it. I got the ball rolling, but then I noticed that my mate was feeling a little left out. Now he's lying on the other bed, so, big-hearted chap that I am, I say, 'Well, you can't leave my mate all alone there.' And fortunately one of them was only too happy to transfer ship.

And that wasn't the only time my teammates and I were double-teamed by a couple of eager young Aussie lasses. During the third Test in Sydney on that 1998 tour, a teammate and I spotted two girls sitting next to the players' viewing area. Unbeknown to us, the two of them had a reputation: they were determined to make their way through the cricketing nations of the world, if you know what I mean.

My teammate invited them back to his room – we always seemed to end up in this guy's room, for some reason – though I wasn't there initially. As I was playing the next day, I was planning an early night. Next thing – it could not have been much after 10 p.m. – I get a call from my teammate: 'No, Hersch, we've got these two chicks here, but fuck, nothing wants to happen.'

So I said, 'Give me the phone. Let me speak to one of them.' So I spoke to this chick and said, 'Listen, now what's the bladdy story? Everybody is up for it, but no one wants to make the first move? Just hang on, I'm coming down.'

Anyway, so I put on my bathrobe, take the lift, go to the room, and there are the lads. And these two hotties. I seemed to be the missing ingredient in the cocktail, and with a few sweetly whispered words, it wasn't long before proceedings got under way. Without going into too much detail, let's just say that the evening came to a very enjoyable conclusion.

It certainly was one helluva trip. But that's Australian women for you. They were just always up for it. I remember a South African bowler coming back from the first World Cup this country ever played in 1992 and telling me the guys had had an absolute bladdy whale of a time with the Aussie women. During that World Cup, the Proteas had played good cricket to get to the semis before they were robbed by the idiotic system the ICC used back then to calculate revised totals for rain-interrupted play.

I had a mediocre time with the bat, though, in the 1998 series. It was my second year in the squad and, as a 24-year-old, I guess I was still a little green. As I said, I didn't play in the best-of-three ODI finals against the Aussies, but that's hardly surprising, given my lack of runs in the round-robin games against the Black Caps and the Aussies.

Aside from 54 against Australia A, the only other significant innings I had was scoring 131 in another warm-up game against a Bradman XI ahead of the third and final Test. I didn't crack the nod for the first Test, but played the remaining two. I'd love to say

I made a difference, but aside from a 54 in the second Test and a 37 in the final one, I didn't bother the scorers much. We lost the second Test and drew the other two to lose the series 0-1.

So, as all-conquering as we were off the field, we were equally frustrated on it. We also lost the ODI series after dominating matches for all but the final few games, and we should've won the last Test to level the series. About 10 dropped catches and the absence of our fast-bowling kingpin, Allan Donald, didn't help our cause.

Then there was the much talked about incident with Mark Waugh on the final day. He got hit on the arm by a short-pitched delivery from Shaun Pollock, and while walking away from the wicket clutching his arm, his bat knocked off a stump. We appealed. But Waugh was given not out, and rightly so, it must be said. He'd clearly completed his stroke, which meant that he couldn't be given out 'hit wicket'. Then Adam Bacher dropped him the next ball – we would drop Waugh four times in his match-saving innings of 115.

Hansie was seriously pissed off that day. At the end of the match, he speared a stump through the umpire's changing-room door. He was bladdy lucky to get away with a letter of apology.

So ja, not great memories of that trip *on* the field, but wonderful memories off it. We couldn't put a foot wrong when it came to women. In the six weeks we were in Australia, I got to know some gorgeous Australian women as well as they can be known. Yes, Christmas came early for young Herschelle Gibbs that year.

The 'French Evening'

During the Proteas' 1999 tour to New Zealand, I managed to befriend a certain young lady in Auckland during the second Test. Some of the guys and I were out for a bite to eat at a local restaurant and, as pretty girls often do, she caught my eye. I thought she was gorgeous – dark-haired, very good frame, though she did have a bit of a big nose. Mark Boucher called her *hakneus*

… but I reckon he was just jealous that I had made a move before he could.

For some reason, women loved our South African accents, no matter where we travelled. Whether it was in Australia, New Zealand, the UK or the West Indies, women took a liking to our accents, which certainly opened a few doors for us. That particular tour to New Zealand was no different. And I could tell this girl was keen right from the get-go. And so was I.

In those days I used to drink copious amounts of the energy drink Red Bull. Their South African sports manager, Tristan Werner, used to send me cases wherever I was in the world. Still does, actually. I've a huge amount of natural enthusiasm for life as it is – the Red Bull amped that up, so I was revved up and ready to fly.

I didn't take the girl home that same night, but managed to get her contact details and made arrangements to take her out the next evening. I decided to make plans for a special evening. You know … spoil her a bit.

I told her we were going to have a French-themed evening with a difference … French champagne and French fries, and the last French item would be a surprise. She smiled. I think she guessed where the evening was heading, but she was practically speaking in a French accent by then, so I knew my French-flavoured hat-trick was still on the cards.

It was a pretty romantic evening – I may have been horny as hell, but I'm also a big romantic at heart and enjoy all that mushy, soft stuff too. Part of the old charm, I guess. So ja, I did seal the deal that night, and for a few nights after that too. When I later told the guys of my exploits, the 'French Evening' – French champagne, French fries and, yes, a French letter – became a bit of a legend. They all found it very amusing.

It was a fun time for both of us – I really liked her and we hung out quite a lot on that tour. We kept in touch for a while afterwards too. The last time I saw her was about six or seven years ago in London. It was typical of 'what happens on tour stays on tour'.

The only problem is that – and no doubt I'll get flak from the Kiwis for saying this (it's clearly a touchy subject) – there just aren't too many lookers in New Zealand, which means you tend to spoil the ones you manage to lay eyes on. For a few days anyway. And this isn't just my opinion – a lot of the players will tell you that the quality there is not great, hey.

My most expensive 'date', ever

It was the 1999 tour to New Zealand, the final Test in Wellington, and my teammate Dale Benkenstein's birthday. This was a very successful tour for the Proteas. We did well out on the pitch too, winning the ODI series 3-2 and the Test series 1-0. As a team we scored over 1 500 runs in only four innings, and that fourth innings was only to get the 16 runs we needed to win the third Test.

In the first Test, in Auckland, Daryll Cullinan broke the record for the highest South African Test score with 275. (Gary Kirsten would, of course, famously equal that score 10 months later against England, before Graeme Smith would raise it to 277, also against the Poms, in 2003.) I was in good nick as well on that tour, scoring 211 in the second Test and 120 in the third.

Anyway, it was Benky's birthday on the Saturday night, the third day of the Test, and I was fresh off my century in our first innings, so I thought I'd let my hair down a little – so to speak – and enjoy his birthday with him. A few Proteas were also with us – I remember Nicky Bojé being one – but it was still obviously a Test night. The understanding with team management was that we could go out on a match night, as long as things didn't get out of hand. Right. So cool, out we went and, as is often the case, one thing led to another, and then took a further step that eventually left me R5 000 poorer.

I happened to see this particularly beautiful girl walk into the pub where we were having a few toots, and I think, like most of us do when we've had a few, I was feeling anything but shy. I decided to go straight in for the kill. I don't remember what I said to her – I was pretty juiced up – but whatever it was, it worked. It didn't take more than a minute and a half – dead serious – and the game was on. We left the bar to go to her place. To this day Nicky claims it is the quickest pick-up he's ever seen in his life.

When I combine my gift of the gab with a few drinks, things tend to happen very quickly. As I said, I can't for the life of me remember what I said, but she bought it right then and there. Unfortunately, memory loss is an issue when I drink heavily – especially if I drink a lot of shooters. They tend to give me blackouts, and a lot of the time I would be with a woman and not remember a thing the next morning. Every now and again I would wake up with somebody in my bed and have no idea how she got there. It's obviously a pleasant surprise to find a gorgeous woman in your bed, but it's a little embarrassing having a total blank about it. I mean, what do you say? 'Hi, what's your name, how did you get here, and what did we do? And can we do it again?' It's only happened to me a few times in my life, but I'm not proud of those moments.

No … I've seen enough movies to know that that line of questioning gets you a slap in the face. Deservedly, too. Anyway, so this girl and I left Benky and the rest of the party and went to her place to get to know each other better. Unfortunately, though, by the time we got there, I was too out of it to close the deal. I tried, but I simply didn't have enough energy to get a signal. I passed out. Not good, because we did have a team curfew. Nothing formal, but just an understanding among the guys that during a Test match we wouldn't a) tonk it and b) get to bed in the early hours.

However …

I did have an uncanny ability to wake up at sunrise, irrespective of how pissed I'd been the night before … which is why, I guess, most people had no idea how much I was drinking. There was still time to sneak back to the hotel and, hopefully, get in before anyone noticed. But before I left, I enthusiastically finished what I had started the night before – it would've been rude not to. Now it's Sunday morning, it's 6.30 a.m., and her place is a good 20 kilometres from the hotel. I needed a taxi, and quick.

By now I was really panicking, because by the time the taxi arrived it was getting light and people would be starting to have their breakfast back at the hotel. I'm thinking, 'Oh shit.' I have to find a way of getting into the hotel and into my room without anyone realising I hadn't slept there.

I was still wearing my T-shirt, jeans and trainers from the night before, so, if any of the guys did see me, I couldn't just say that I'd just got up. If I could just get to my room, I'd be okay – my roommate on that tour, Paul 'Gogga' Adams, would definitely cover for me.

I managed to make my way through the lobby without any-one noticing me, and even into the lifts. But the lifts in this particular hotel opened straight onto the rooms. Peter Pollock – Shaun's dad, a fine, upstanding gentleman and legend of the game – was the convener of selectors at that stage. He is also a very religious man. As I walked out of the lift, I looked up and saw Peter in his room – the door ajar – and he was reading a passage from the Good Book. When he heard the lift door open, he looked up. There was nowhere for me to hide. There I am in my jeans and T-shirt when, obviously, I should have been in team kit, ready for the day's play. What could I do but walk past his room and hope he didn't see me? No such luck.

He looked up at me over his reading glasses, the Good Book in one hand, and said, 'Morning, Herschelle.'

'Morning, Pete,' I mumbled. I was – and there's only one word for it – fucked. I got to my room and woke Gogi up to tell him the whole story. I made him swear that he wouldn't tell anyone about my little adventure. By now I had also thought of a plan that could get me off the hook ...

Our team physio, Craig Smith, could be my alibi. Craig was a great guy. He was a very good physio and also got on well with the guys. Craig was like one of the team and would cover for you just like your teammates would. I got hold of Craig and said, 'Listen, if anybody asks where I was, say I slept in your treatment room last night because my roommate had the shits and kept waking me up every half an hour. I decided the only way I could get some sleep was to kip down in your room.' When we sat down for breakfast, that was the story we told, but between Craig and me, it didn't quite add up. I could see none of the guys were really buying it.

I was feeling a little hung-over, though not *too* bad. We were fielding that day, and I was fine during the warm-up, taking all the catches that came my way. Unfortunately, once play got under way, I dropped two. Both were offered by Nathan Astle, and both were off Shaun Pollock's bowling. And it's not like they were screamers either. I was at cover, both balls came straight at me, and I put both down. Not good. Given that Peter had seen me sneak in that morning, I couldn't have chosen a worse bowler to drop catches off. And they were easy catches – on any other day I would have eaten them up.

Polly looked at captain Hansie Cronjé and said, 'Sheez. Was Herschy out last night?' At tea time Hansie came to me and said, 'Were you out last night?' I lied. 'No, man. Why?'

'Because PP said he saw you come in this morning past 7 a.m., still wearing your jeans and everything?' I was like, 'No, I just slept in Craig's room, you know, because I was …' But I couldn't lie any more. I told him the truth. So, at the end of the day's play, they called the team together in the team room back at the hotel and I had to apologise, saying that I had been very unprofessional and that it wouldn't happen again.

I was fined R5 000, which made my escapade the previous evening the most expensive shag I ever had. Easily.

The 'Two Nights Before Club'

During the 2000 season, Mark Boucher and Jacques Kallis went through a purple patch. On the pitch. We're talking about cricket now. And they both attributed their successes to the fact that two nights before any innings in which they scored big runs, they had been out for a few toots. As a result they believed that they had unwittingly discovered the secret to a flood of runs, and it would be criminal not to include the exercise in their meticulous preparations before each game.

This little ritual was still going by the time of the 2001 tour to Australia, and, by now, had gained some dedicated supporters. One of whom was me. True to form, two nights before the first Test in Adelaide, we were out at a nightclub called Heaven, diligently preparing for our forthcoming innings.

Being the team man that he is, both on and off the field, Bouchie got together those in the squad who were keen on a little socialising and requested they wear their drinking caps, and we proceeded to have a few beers in Heaven. So to speak. I got really hammered, though, even by my high standards, and got back to the hotel at about ... To be honest, I can't remember, but it was pretty damn late. Especially considering we had practice the next morning.

Anyway, the Adelaide Oval changing rooms were a little different from the way they are now. As you left the changing room and went down the steps along the passage and onto the field, the showers were on your left and the toilets on your right. I was sitting in the changing room waiting to play a little touch rugby as a warm-up before nets, and I was feeling really ill.

There were a couple of faces that were rather green around the gills that morning, but none of them compared to mine. I was *very* hung-over. I knew I was going to puke eventually, but I didn't want to use the toilets, knowing only too well that everyone would hear me, as the sound would've roared up and down that passage like one seriously annoyed tiger. I would have to park my cat in a somewhat more subtle fashion.

My plan was to casually saunter to the toilets, put my head deep into the bowl and pull the chain as I puked, thus cunningly disguising any sound effects. My plan worked, and one stealth-puke later, I casually sauntered back to the changing room and put my boots on. Only my stomach wasn't *quite* finished expelling the previous night's festivities. I could feel another movement on its way, and I couldn't execute the toilet action again – the guys would definitely smell a rat. I had no choice but to guts it out – so to speak – until it was time to go on to the field. I could then hang back and dive into the toilets.

As the last person walked out of the dressing room, I darted into the toilet and puked again. (I'm feeling queasy just remembering it.)

I eventually made my way on to the field feeling slightly less nauseous, but I was still bladdy buggered. We started the warm-up with a lengthy set of stretches. Lying there on my back on the soft Adelaide turf, the sun gently warming me, was exactly what my body craved ... and I promptly fell asleep.

One minute I was doing a stretch, and the next thing I knew our trainer, Paddy Upton, was tapping me on the shoulder to wake me up. The guys thought this was hilarious. During the game of touch afterwards I remember standing on the wing and somebody passing me the ball – the softest of passes – and me just missing it completely.

After that we had a net practice. South African legend Graeme Pollock was accompanying us for part of that tour to help the batters. The thing with the Adelaide practice area is that spectators can sit right behind the nets. They therefore have a clear view of how well – or, in my case that day, how poorly – batsmen are batting. I was shitting myself, thinking, 'You're in the kak here today, Hersch. You're about to face your own teammates *and* a bunch of unknown net bowlers who are no doubt dead keen on knocking you over, and you can't even see straight.'

I had a few throw-downs and then my net session proper

started. On the way in I had a word with Proteas fast bowler and all-round loose cannon Mornantau 'Nantie' Hayward.

'Nantie, fucking bounce me today in the nets and I'm going to fucking whack you with this bat.' He just laughed. And shrugged. Which Nantie does a lot. He knew I was hung-over, and of course he bounced me, but I managed to just duck under one of the three balls I could actually see.

That was Nantie, though – a bit of a nutter. And when you combine his ability to bowl a cricket ball seriously quickly with his personality, things tend to get interesting. Nantie loved to toss in the odd head-high beemer just to perk up the proceedings. Once, during a domestic game at Newlands, he bowled a beemer at me. It came straight for my helmet, but I managed to fend it off. It really pissed me off. I swore like a trooper and warned him not to try any more of that nonsense on me or I'd hit him. He apologised, saying the ball had slipped out of his hand. That was the funny thing about Nantie – for all his apparent aggro, he often backed down when confronted. I don't think it's because he's gutless – it's more to do with his unwillingness to unleash his true craziness. I think if Nantie actually had to genuinely lose his temper, there would be carnage. Breaking-news-on-CNN kind of carnage.

One thing's for sure about Nantie: he didn't like being on the receiving end of a fast bowler's wrath. On that tour, he and Makhaya Ntini were the two tail-enders, trying to dodge bullets from Aussie paceman Brett 'Binga' Lee. Binga was trying his best to hit Nantie, but Nantie was backing so far away to square leg that he was practically standing on the umpire's toes. Makhaya, on the other hand, was standing his ground and, even though he couldn't bat to save his life back then, he wouldn't budge. Binga hit him a few times too. Twice in a row. Unable to duck out of the way, Makhaya just dropped his chin and got klapped flush on the badge of his helmet.

It's funny how the quickest bowlers in the world don't mind

bowling – or even throwing – in a few short ones, but when it's their turn to bat, they don't want to stand in the firing line.

But back to me in the nets in Adelaide. Graeme Pollock was sitting on the bench next to the net and, after I had finished my 15-minute session, miraculously escaping both injury and embarrassment, I walked past him. All he said was, 'Looking good, Hersch. You're really hitting the ball well.' I could barely muster a 'Thanks, Graeme' before hotfooting it back to the dressing room for one last vomit.

So ja, that was the downside of being a member of the infamous 'Two Days Before Club'. That morning at the Adelaide Oval was easily the worst I've ever felt on a cricket pitch. Fortunately it was only a practice session.

I believe the club has long since closed its doors.

The night before the 438 game ...

The day before the famous 438 ODI game against Australia at the Wanderers in 2006, I got totally wasted. Which, given my performance the next day, scoring 175 off 111 balls to help the Proteas chase down Australia's record-breaking total of 434, probably comes as a surprise to most people.

We had a team practice the morning before the game and were given the afternoon off. I took the opportunity to fit in a signing session for my long-time bat, pads, and gloves sponsor Gunn & Moore. Two kids were among those standing in line – two brothers aged somewhere between 10 and 12 – both eager for my signature. Who really caught my eye, though, was their mom, one of those real Joburg yummy-mummies. We're talking proper quality here.

'Gee,' I said to the one boy, 'is that your mother? Ask her to come and say hi.' Obviously the kids were overawed and far too young to put two and two together. They introduced their mom to me in a flash. As it happened, she was going through a divorce at the time. I thought, 'Well, okay, cool, let me just see what happens here.' I invited the mommy to join me for a few drinks. She said yes, and we started drinking some white wine. This must've been around 2 p.m. We sat at the bar on the sixth floor of the Sandton Sun Hotel until about 6 p.m., when I had to attend a Proteas team meeting.

You're probably thinking, 'Four hours of drinking and then he goes to a team meeting? Surely they must've noticed that he was drunk? And that can't be a good thing, right?' Fortunately I can handle my drink pretty well – up to a point, obviously – and often I might be a little tipsy, but people won't know. Probably because of years of experience. Besides, we'd had something to eat that afternoon as well, so it wasn't just wine on its own *all* the time. I made it through the team meeting without getting any raised eyebrows.

So, afterwards, I met up with the woman again and we carried on drinking. We were getting on really well too, even making plans for her two boys to have playdates with my son Rashard. This carried on until 11 p.m., when the mommy and I went up to my room. I must've been pretty drunk by then, because from that moment on the evening is a bit of a blank. Apparently the Aussie team management was also at the bar and they could see the whole drama unfolding.

Someone must've phoned the Proteas bowling coach – and my good mate – Vinnie Barnes to let him know that, given there was a game the next day, I needed rescuing. This must've been about 1 a.m., and poor Vinnie, who'd been asleep, had to get out of bed. He knocked on my hotel-room door and found me with the mommy, still drinking wine and talking shit (just for the record, nothing happened between us that night). Vinnie was seriously pissed off. I tried to say that all was good, but Vinnie knew what was what. 'Look at you, Hersch, you can't even stand up *and* you're slurring. Tell this woman she must leave now!'

It was 2 a.m. before I got to sleep, and we had to get up early the next morning to be at the ground by 8 a.m. As I've mentioned,

99 per cent of the time I wake up at sunrise, but fortunately that morning I had set my alarm. There's no way I would've woken up otherwise. But wake up I did, my head spinning. I went down to breakfast, my head still hurting, and then left for the Wanderers in the team bus, feeling as green as the colour of our Proteas kit. Chapter 7 will tell you how I not only got through the match, but also managed to score 175 runs.

... and the night after the 438 game

Proteas 'fines meetings' ... man, they can be *hectic*. If you get nailed, you can go from sober to a dribbling drunk in minutes. Just ask Mickey Arthur.

If you haven't heard of them before, fines meetings are a common post-game festivity among sports teams: 'fines' in the form of a drink are handed out to various team members for any real, or trumped-up, 'transgressions' they may or may not have been guilty of during the game. After our brilliant victory against Australia, it would have been a serious understatement to say that the team was in 'high spirits', which meant the fines meeting was going to be epic. As usual Mark Boucher was our Fines Master, and he meted out the punishment admirably.

As Fines Master, Mark ran the show, making up any rules he saw fit – stuff like, if you wanted to say anything, or even ask to go to the toilet, you had to put up your hand and direct your request to him. If you didn't, you had to drink. The drink was a full can of beer. The Fines Master could also put you on 'death' if he decided you'd done something particularly stupid. Or it could just be that you were unlucky – Mark could decide that you just hadn't had enough to drink yet, and you'd be on 'death'. And you really didn't want to be on 'death', which involved drinking one full can of beer every two minutes until the Fines Master decided to take mercy on you. So ja, you can get pissed pretty quickly.

Everyone would get a chance to nominate an individual for a

fine. You'd have to outline the precise nature of the offence, but you had to be careful. If the Fines Master decided that your nomination wasn't good enough or it was just plain stupid, *you'd* have to drink.

There are other rules, such as 'spillage', which meant that you couldn't spill any beer down your chin when downing it. If you did, you'd have to drink another. I must tell you, though, that I'm proud to say that the guys can really handle it. They don't spill much. In fact, there are a couple of guys – did someone mention André Nel? – who would impress even Oktoberfest stalwarts with the speed and efficiency with which they can down a beer.

It was at this particular fines meeting that poor Mickey got nailed. Funny – American football teams pour a bucket of Gatorade over their coach when they win a big game … we get ours as drunk as a lord. The guys were gunning for Mickey at that fines meeting, and he had to down three ice-cold beers in quick succession. It's tough to recover when you jump the start like that. Those chilled beers just murder you. Mickey was sitting there, leaning against one of the dressing-room lockers, when he just unleashed … all over his chest. I can't say that I've seen a coach vomit like that too many times in my career. To Mickey's great credit, though, he simply fetched a towel, cleaned himself up and carried on.

It was just such a hell of a thing, the fines meeting that night. Even André Nel – he didn't play that game, but was part of the squad – was paralytic, and Nella is a guy who can handle his drink as much as anyone I've ever seen. I remember him standing up to say something … and no one could understand a bladdy word. He might have been speaking English, but he didn't make any sense. We were like, 'No, boet, I think it's time for you to sit down.'

I was really flying as well. We stayed at the Wanderers for a long time that evening. Some of the boys and I went to go and sit on the wicket itself. There we were, in the pitch-dark, after what had been a phenomenal day's cricket.

After we left the ground, we got together with the Australian team for a few drinks, as we usually do after a match. The venue, somewhat ironically, was the Sandton Sun bar. It was like I'd come full circle, ending the proceedings in the same place I had got so drunk in the night before. The staff kept the bar open very late, and I remember Brett Lee playing his guitar, although we didn't really talk to the Aussies much that night. We were on a different vibe to them – as fantastic as winning that game and the series was for us, it must've been correspondingly tough for them.

And that was basically the last I remember of that night. I've no idea how I got to my room. It's sad, I guess, that the day ended in a blank. It had obviously been a very special day, and when you have those days and they end with you so drunk you can't remember much, it's sad in a lot of ways. This has happened to me quite a lot over the years. Many times I look back on an event or an occasion and I can't remember how it ended, simply because I had just been so hammered.

The 2007 World Cup ... Karaoke in St Lawrence Gap

After we'd annihilated the Poms in the Super Eight stage of the 2007 World Cup, I was in the mood for a little celebration. We'd bowled them out for 154, with Andrew Hall leading the charge, taking five wickets for 18 runs; and then openers Graeme Smith and AB de Villiers made the majority of the runs in our innings. I didn't even bat. Still, a night out in Barbados was called for. This *was* Barbados, after all. Where the rum comes from.

The Proteas never hang out as a team much any more. I'll tell you more about that later, but the unfortunate trend had already been well established by then. On this occasion, the players did have a couple of beers in the changing room after the game, but I then decided to join a friend of mine, Brian Mahon, and his son Jonathan. Brian's a fairly wealthy chap who owns an apartment in the exclusive Sandy Lane Resort in St James, Barbados. Anyway, Brian looked a little knackered – an afternoon of beer and Barbadian sun can do that to a man – and he ended up having a little nap at the dinner table. I could only look at him and laugh, knowing that I'd done the same on a couple of occasions.

Brian had arranged a driver with a Bentley for the evening, so after dropping him off at home, Jonathan and I decided to hit the bars. Two good-looking guys and a chauffeur-driven droptop Bentley – it would've been criminal not to. There's this little area in Barbados called the St Lawrence Gap, which has lots of bars and clubs. After cruising up and down the main road in the Bent – obviously with the top down – staring at the beautiful women, we got the driver to drop us off and we went for a stroll.

We could hear music blasting out from one bar we walked past – they were having a karaoke evening, and it looked like a whole lot of fun. So Jonathan and I went in. Right then and there I decided it was time to fulfil a personal fantasy of mine, and that was to belt out Neil Diamond's 'Sweet Caroline' on stage. Needless to say, we were fairly intoxicated. I'm not right now, and in case you're wondering, I'm still not embarrassed by my love for Neil Diamond. My musical taste also includes the great Engelbert Humperdinck. Anyone who embarks on a musical career with a name and a pair of sideburns like his must have both an abundance of talent and a sizeable pair of balls.

At the bar, Jonathan and I see these five English cricket fans, also well juiced, and obviously drowning their sorrows, because England had just been given an absolute drilling by the Proteas. They recognised me and we had a few toots together, and it was then that we all decided, no, bugger this, all six of us are hitting the stage for a rousing sing-a-long. They asked me what I wanted to sing, and I said, 'Sweet Caroline'.

'Great fookin' choice!' was the unanimous response. We gave it the full kitchen sink. I've never sung so loudly in all my life as I sang with those guys. And I didn't even know them from Adam.

There I was, with a mate's son, in Barbados, singing with a bunch of Poms I'd met minutes before, and I was having an absolute blast. It was one of the best nights I've had, and with total strangers too. That's me, I guess. I can happily chat to anyone, be it the tea lady at Province, the CEO of a big corporate or a complete stranger, and genuinely enjoy the company. I've always been like that, and it is something of which I'm quite proud. Irrespective of the success I've had, and despite all my experiences, I've always remained true to myself.

As I recall, Jonathan and I even managed to pick up two women that night, and we went back to his dad's apartment to bring the whole evening ... and indeed this chapter ... to a fitting climax.

4

Alcohol ... and rehab

Getting an ultimatum from the Proteas, going through a month of rehab ... and emerging on the other side the same, yet different.

Having read this far – and if you knew anything about me before – it's pretty obvious that alcohol played a big part in my life. There has been a drinking culture in cricket for so long, the game's roots are practically pickled in alcohol. Perhaps this is something that may change over time as the sport becomes increasingly business-orientated, with the sums of money involved growing ever larger and the players' schedules filling up with T20, ODI and Test matches.

My drinking undoubtedly contributed a lot to the fun-filled memories I have, but there were times – particularly between 2006 and 2008 – when it had a very negative effect on me, my career and, most importantly, the people I loved.

I'm not using cricket's drinking culture as an excuse, but that, coupled with my outgoing and fun-loving personality, made refusing a drink practically impossible. And there were many times when I'd be drunk the night before a game, yet the next day be able to deliver an outstanding performance. I've already talked about the evening before the 438 game, and I'll tell you about another occasion as well.

Shaun Pollock's last-ever ODI game at the Wanderers, on 3 February 2008, was also the final match in a five-game series against the West Indies. While we may already have been 4-0 up, I hadn't scored too many runs in those games. Thirty-nine off

52 balls at Kingsmead was as good as it had got for me. You would've thought getting drunk the night before my last chance to score some runs in the series would've been the worst thing I could've done. As it turned out, it wasn't.

The night before the game, we had a team dinner at Vilamoura restaurant at the Sandton Sun Hotel in Joburg, where we were staying. I had a big piece of steak for dinner and drank some wine. Quite a lot of wine. I wasn't too concerned about getting a little tipsy in front of my teammates and the team management. As I've said, people can seldom tell when I'm drunk, unless – obviously – I'm properly slaughtered. Or maybe I should say: I don't think people notice when I'm drunk, but I can't really tell when I'm the one who's pissed, can I? I guess people I know – for example, my teammates – can see I'm acting differently, but I never notice it. So that evening, I kept on drinking. And I had another steak.

The team all went to bed, but I stayed at the restaurant. Although an actual curfew did not exist, you were, of course, expected to get some decent sleep the night before a game. Anyway, a mate of mine came round and I carried on drinking – I probably only got to bed at about 1 a.m. By rights I should've been in shocking nick the next day, but I ended up scoring 102 off 84, during which I klapped 13 fours and three sixes.

Just as he did after the 438 game, coach Mickey Arthur came up to me and said, 'Hersch, I do not fucking know how you fucking do it.' He was half annoyed, half pleased: never a comfortable mix. 'I was about to give you the lecture you deserve, but how can I when you get 100 off 80-odd balls?'

It became a running joke after that game. The guys would egg me on to drink lots of wine and to eat two steaks before every game so that I would get a big score.

Perhaps the alcohol had relaxed me, allowing me to just go out and play my natural game. Or perhaps I just operate better on very little sleep.

When we were touring Zimbabwe in September 2001, I had

a raging argument with a girl I was seeing at the time, and I probably didn't get more than a couple of hours of sleep that night. I was rooming with Claude Henderson on that tour, and I don't think he got too much sleep either. Anyway, I scored 147 the next day. It was the first Test and Gary and I put on an opening stand of 256, with Gary eventually out on 220. Jacques Kallis added to the Zim misery by also scoring 157 not out. I have an inborn energy that allows me to not only function on little sleep, but function really well.

I'm telling you this so that you know why, up until 6 November 2008, I didn't see any reason to stop drinking. I mean, why should I? I was having a lot of fun, and getting slaughtered only seemed to improve my batting. But obviously that was not a healthy attitude. Things had to change ...

My road to rehab began when Mickey Arthur and acting team manager Doc Moosajee sat me down on that November day. Mickey wasted no time in getting to the point: 'Hersch, I think you need to get some help.' I protested that I was fine, that everything was under control, and that I wasn't drinking any more than the other guys. Mickey wasn't buying it, though – he'd obviously seen enough by then. 'Hersch,' he said, 'this is your ultimatum: You either get help, or you don't play for South Africa again. We need you to sort this out.'

I'll never forget that conversation; it was the day before the first ODI against Bangladesh during their tour to South Africa in October/November. The three of us were sitting in the changing room at the Wanderers gym and I was being given an ultimatum, because what had transpired two nights earlier had been the last straw.

On the Tuesday, we had had an early team meeting at about one or two in the afternoon, which meant that for the rest of the day we had nothing scheduled – no team dinner or any reason to get up early the next morning. The T20 game against Bangladesh was scheduled for the next day, starting at 6 p.m. I had time on my hands and I was in a hotel. Not always a good combination when you happen to be me.

I called up a girl, a friend I hadn't seen for a while, and had a couple of glasses of wine with her in the hotel bar. She left at about 3 p.m., so I phoned another young lady and told her to come around. And all the time I kept drinking. Unfortunately, I hadn't had anything to eat, and the wine was beginning to hit me. Later a few mates joined me as well, and some shooters were ordered ... and that's when things start to get very hazy. By now it was around 7 p.m. and I had been drinking for about five hours, on an empty stomach.

I'm embarrassed to admit that I also got aggressive that night – I was later told that I had verbally abused my teammate Monde Zondeki, who was there with mates from Joburg, as well as some other people in the bar. Apparently, I had been completely out of line. Normally I'm not at all aggressive or obnoxious when I get drunk, but rather subdued and quiet. But that evening – perhaps because I was mixing my drinks – I insulted people in the bar, including Monde's buddies.

Eventually the bar manager phoned the Proteas bowling coach and my good friend Vinnie Barnes to come and get me. I know there were some reports that Graeme Smith and some of the players had come to fetch me, but it was Vinnie who hauled me up to my room.

So ... by 8 p.m. I was in bed and gone for all the money you know. The next morning I couldn't remember a thing. I played the T20 game that evening, scoring a quick-fire 18 runs off 10 balls before being bowled, stupidly getting an inside edge off a somewhat wide ball.

The next day I faced the music with Mickey and Doc. I was dropped from the squad with immediate effect and either had to pack my bags and check into rehab, or my international career was over. Not much choice then, really.

I remember feeling very frustrated, because, despite what

Mickey and Doc were saying to me, I didn't think that I had a problem. I believed my drinking was no different from that of the other guys in the team. You know, when the guys party, it's not like they have one or two beers – if they are going to drink, they are going to go the full hog. If they want to drink 20 beers, they'll drink 20 beers. Mickey was adamant, though, assuring me that no one else was behaving the way I was. Obviously I had to take what he said on board ...

I phoned my manager, Donné – man, I've put her through some tough shit – to tell her about the whole deal, and she was in tears. Donné had obviously suspected that my drinking had got out of hand, and she was quite emotional about it. She's a very considerate person and has always had nothing but my best interests at heart. In fact, Donné has always been far more than just my agent or business manager.

On this occasion, she asked me straight: 'Do *you* think you have a problem?' I said to her, 'No, I don't think so. Just because when I drink, I drink a lot more than the other guys doesn't mean I have a problem.'

But she wasn't buying it either. She was brutally honest. Donné said: 'Listen, Hersch, this is *it*. You're not going to play for South Africa again. You've got to give this some very serious thought. I think you need to get help, because you are throwing your life and your career away.'

At this point it's appropriate to tell you a little more about my agent, manager and guardian angel ... Donné Commins. Donné has been like a big sister to me. No doubt she'll be embarrassed that I'm saying this – but that's Donné for you. She'll do anything in the world to help you, but she gets all *skaam* when praises are heaped on her. Donné is exceptionally hard-working, and she makes sure that I'm up to date with my finances.

She's also fiercely protective of my welfare, always saying, 'Herschelle, I don't want people to take advantage of you just because they think you have money.' And she's right – I do tend to get a little overly generous when I'm out with my mates. In the past, some folk also tried to make some extra cash off me – I know of a couple of estate agents whose little ruses have been shot out of the sky by Donné. Ja. She's a lawyer too.

Besides that, though, Donné has always been there for me on a personal level as well. I trust her 100 per cent. Let me put it this way: the first person I would call when I'm in trouble is Donné. I know this for a fact, because whenever I got into trouble over the years, Donné was always the first person I called. On the odd occasion when I was in the dwang and didn't call her, she kakked me out properly.

It doesn't matter what I do, I reckon not telling Donné first is always the scarier option! I have the greatest respect for her. She's a great human being, and a world-class manager and agent. I mean, the woman has three small kids of her own, *and* she has the big kids she represents … me, Bouchie, JP Duminy and the two Morkels, Albie and Morné.

Basically Donné allows me to concentrate on my cricket and enjoy life, while she does all the hard work. And ja, for me the world would have been a very different place if I hadn't had her in my life for the past 10 years. She's just a great individual, end of story. I could never, ever thank her enough.

Right, so back to the little decision I had to make. I thought about it for quite a while – about three weeks or so. A large part of me still wanted to deny everything, but there was a nagging voice inside my head insisting that I do the right thing. Donné and my lawyer, Peter Whelan, helped me a lot in that tough time. Eventually I phoned Donné and said, 'Okay, fine, if they want me to check into rehab, I'll check in.' I heard an audible sigh of relief over the phone. And that was it. I flew back home to Cape Town.

If you think this sounds like I was going into rehab only to satisfy other people's wishes, then you'd be spot-on. I didn't believe I was an alcoholic, and I still don't believe it. Sure I was drinking too much and sure it was affecting my life, and I certainly needed some help to control that, but I've never seen myself as an alcoholic.

I know it is pretty standard behaviour for an addict to declare that he or she doesn't have a problem. The good folk at Harmony Addictions Clinic, where I went to rehab, certainly drove that point home. In their opinion, if you finish their programme and, say, have two huge drinking sessions a year – two and no more – they still consider you to be an alcoholic. I find that bizarre, to be honest. So if you only drink two out of 365 days, but those two days you go at it hammer and tongs, you have a problem with alcohol? I mean, it's pretty damn harsh to call somebody an alcoholic in that case. That would make just about everyone I've ever played cricket with an alcoholic.

I never spoke to my parents about going into rehab – we've never been a family who discusses anything deep. When my dad found out – he's a sports journalist, so he would've got wind of it early on – he was quite blasé about the whole thing. His take was that it was unrealistic to think Herschelle would never drink again. And besides, he thought it could only have a negative effect on my bubbly personality. Some might call his stance irresponsible, but I think his is a pretty accurate assessment.

Anyway ... ja, I thought about it and then I made up my mind to give rehab a try. I checked into Harmony Addictions Clinic in Hout Bay on 4 December 2008. Donné took me in. I chose to have my own room – it was more like a suite, actually, and quite nice too. So in I go, and, as all new 'guests' do, I get the full search. They check every item of clothing in your possession, even your shoes, and also go through your suitcase thoroughly. And then they strip you completely naked to check that you're not hiding anything where the sun don't shine. While it's not the full-on latex rubber-glove number, you *are* basically standing there completely starkers, and a member of the male staff (unfortunately) checks if you have any crack – or whatever your drug of choice may be – up your crack.

Obviously I was like, 'Whoa, mate. No need for that. I don't do drugs. I'm just here for alcohol.' So that was quite embarrassing. Afterwards I went to my room and tried to make myself at home. I had a TV, which was great. Unfortunately I had had to hand in my phone as well – in the first week, you're not allowed any contact with people outside. After that, you're allowed one 10-minute phone call a day. Funny enough, as much as I always relied on my phone – and still do today – at the time I didn't even miss it.

That one phone call a day became a big deal. As soon as the last session of the day was over, I would race to the phone to make my call before supper, which they served at 7 p.m. There was always a queue of people wanting to use the phone. Despite the fact that the phone was at reception and you had no privacy, as someone was always watching you, on some nights there were so many people wanting to use the phone that you never got a chance.

As a – you know – 'public figure', I never felt embarrassed about being in rehab. Many of the other 'inmates' recognised me, and some of them couldn't believe that I was actually taking part in a session with them. The counsellors initially had to stop these guys from discussing cricket with me. I was happy to talk cricket, though, and during breaks we'd chat away. The Test series against Australia was taking place while I was in rehab, and there was one particular guy – an elderly chap, I'll call him George – who kept on asking me for the score. The room he was in didn't have a TV.

George was a huge cricket supporter and a fan of mine, and every morning I'd hear the tapping of his walking stick as he came towards my room, wanting to find out how the Test was progressing. The counsellors eventually got pretty pissed off with him. They said, 'Herschelle is here to deal with his alcohol problem. You can't keep on talking sport all the time.' I didn't mind George at all. I actually grew quite fond of the bloke. But eventually the counsellors threatened us with a 'warning' if they heard us talking about sport again. Apparently, if you accumulated three warnings they could kick you out the programme.

But George was a funny old oke – sneaky as hell. The minute the counsellors turned their backs, he would come and natter with me through my window. 'What's the score? What's the score, man?' He had a great sense of humour.

The actual rehab part of rehab would start at 7 a.m. with a group meeting. The first half an hour would be a quick recap – stuff like how were we feeling, were we missing anybody outside, was there something we wanted to get off our chests? People would talk about what it felt like to go cold turkey, and what they were craving or missing – booze, sex, friends, family. I never said much. I'd say something like, 'Well, I had a good night's sleep.' And I'd give them the latest cricket score.

Each night you had to write your thoughts and feelings in your notebook. You would go over it with your counsellor the next day. We'd finish the early session with a reading of the 'Serenity Prayer'. It took me a while, but I actually learnt the prayer off by heart ...

God grant me the serenity
To accept the things I cannot change;
The courage to change the things I can;
And the wisdom to know the difference.
Living one day at a time;
Enjoying one moment at a time;
Accepting hardships as the pathway to peace;
Taking, as He did, this sinful world
As it is, not as I would have it;
Trusting that He will make all things right
If I surrender to His Will;
That I may be reasonably happy in this life
And supremely happy with Him
Forever in the next.
Amen.

Then it was breakfast at 7.30 a.m. The food at the clinic wasn't too bad. I ate a lot of toast, though, but actually got pretty thin, which happens if I don't go to gym – I lose a lot of muscle mass. There were some treadmills in a small gym at the clinic, but there weren't too many free weights. Ja, and a tennis court too. I played a little tennis as well.

Anyway, after breakfast, the day's sessions would start at 8.45. We worked from manuals and had to do a lot of written work, too. The sessions comprised various aspects of your addiction – its consequences, the people in your life whom it has affected, the causes behind your behaviour …

The classes were also the only time we had any contact with the female 'guests'. And even then we had to sit in separate rows of chairs. After the sessions, they would file out and go to their own section of the clinic. Naturally I found this highly amusing. Not to mention challenging. I missed not chatting to a girl way more than I missed alcohol.

I mean, you weren't even allowed to wink at the women or you were given a warning. And after three warnings they packed your bags and escorted you to the front door. But no, I was never given any warnings. Believe it or not, I was actually very disciplined and observant of the rules when I was at Harmony.

There was even a girl I knew at the clinic – a pretty Italian girl I'd met a couple of times at Caprice, a bar in Camps Bay. Lovely girl … and I couldn't even talk to her. Until the last day of my stay, that is. The day I was due to leave, I said, 'You guys can warn me all you want. This is my last day. I'm going to flipping talk to her.'

The rest of a routine morning was taken up by lectures and written work, as well as some group meetings. After lunch, we sometimes attended meetings outside the clinic … Alcoholics Anonymous, for example. For me, this was probably the hardest thing to do. Once, sometimes twice a week, I'd have to stand up and utter that well-known line: 'Hi, my name is Herschelle and I'm an alcoholic …'

Not only was it embarrassing – this wasn't within the protective and safe confines of the clinic – but I didn't even believe what I was saying. I knew I had to say the words in order to sort out my issues, but I didn't, and still don't, believe that I am an alcoholic. I simply don't buy into the notion that getting fall-down drunk a couple of times a year means that you're an alcoholic. Still, there I was, standing up and saying those words every week.

At these meetings, once everyone had introduced themselves and the 'chairman' had said a few words, the floor was opened to everyone. You're not allowed to speak if it is your first meeting, but even at subsequent meetings I didn't say much. I preferred to listen. Some of the stories you'd hear ... jeez man, they were mind-blowing. I didn't think it was humanly possible to drink as much as some of those people did.

One guy basically drank away the entire value of his house in the space of six months. Mind-boggling stuff. And that did hit me quite hard. I was given a glimpse of how my life could turn out if I didn't slow down.

Another guy told us how he'd shot and killed his brother when he was high. He still doesn't know why he did it. Just shot him. I mean, I could relate to these stories, as I was going down that same road. I would drink so much that I'd have blackouts, and the next day I wouldn't have a bladdy clue what I had done the night before. As I talk about this, it's been nearly two years since rehab ... and memories of those meetings are still very fresh in my mind.

It was amazing to see that there were some people coming to these meetings who hadn't had a drop to drink in 10, 15 or even 20 years. Obviously these meetings had helped them stay off the booze. On the other hand, the meetings can also serve as a crutch for these guys, as if you can't actually quit without attending them. To quit cold turkey has got to be tough, though.

I can't imagine living the rest of my life without having the occasional drink. I know that Aussie paceman Brett Lee never touched a drop of alcohol in the year leading up to the 2003 World

Cup. That's one helluva effort. You've got to take your hat off to people who can do that.

Back at the clinic, we'd also have our own group meetings, and we would have to take turns to be the group leader, who would voice the concerns of the group. I sort of took over the role a little bit too much and they actually banned me from talking for a few days. I made some valuable contributions, though, during my short tenure in the spotlight. I instilled the importance of little things, like punctuality – I actually asked the counsellors why they were always late. I mean, we arrived on time, at 8.45 a.m., but they'd stroll in only five or ten minutes later. Not on as far as I was concerned. I questioned the kind of example the counsellors were setting.

My comments raised a few eyebrows among the counsellors, but I wasn't trying to be disrespectful. My viewpoint was that we were all in the same boat, trying hard to improve as people. A small issue like punctuality goes a long way in my eyes.

But the counsellors took it well, to be fair to them, and we agreed that anyone who arrived late would be on dishes duty. All the dishes – and there were a lot of them – were washed by hand. It was a kak job. No one was late after that first week. I did dishes *once*, and I wasn't late again. We all had our normal chores to do, which often involved cleaning up or drying, but dishes duty would be in addition to your normal chores. The boys weren't keen for it, hey.

The other issues I raised were the flies and the pool. It was summertime, so it was pretty warm and, unfortunately, the clinic is near a horse farm – which meant there were flies everywhere. Look, the place was very clean, but there just always seemed to be a plague of flies in our dining room, and it's off-putting, you know. I had a word with one of the counsellors and said, 'Listen, you can't allow this, boet. We are bladdy human beings. You can't let us eat in a room with so many flies around. It's flipping un-healthy, man.'

Then the pool – it was a nice little pool, but it wasn't clean. And, as I said, it was really hot. I put my foot down, saying not only could I not eat with flies all over my food, but the clinic couldn't even bother to sort out the pool! I politely reminded them that we were people, not animals in a zoo. I was a little melodramatic, but my complaints had some effect, as within days the pool was sparkly clean and I barely saw a fly again for the rest of my stay.

The other patients were both impressed and annoyed. They said, 'Shit, we ask for things to be done and they just ignore us. But *you* complain and they jump to it straight away.'

I became quite friendly with one of my fellow 'guests'. He was the only guy there other than me who had his own room, so we were in the same part of the clinic. This guy was a sex addict, and for obvious reasons I won't call him by his real name. I won't call him Dick either. I like the guy. 'Dave' is a far better alias.

Dave's addiction was so bad that every time he just thought about having sex, he shot his load. I remember one night we were watching a video and suddenly Dave bolted out of the room. I realised his hasty departure was the result of a scene in which a couple were kissing. Just *kissing*. Hectic.

He was married too. And his wife had said, 'Listen, we can't carry on like this. You need to sort this out.' So that's why Dave was in rehab. In rehab, when people are open and honest with themselves, you see them change in a matter of weeks. And when you're going through rehab with other people, you tend to grow quite close to them. When the time then comes for a person to leave the clinic, one of the patients is asked to give a farewell speech. I gave one for Dave.

The only problem was, I got too emotional. You have to make the speech in front of everybody at the clinic, including the counsellors and both the male and female patients. I tried to tell them how much Dave had impressed me: he loved his wife, and rehab had been the only chance he'd had of saving his marriage. Dave's situation had obviously made me think of my own life. He was doing his damndest to try to hold on to his marriage, whereas after just a year of married life, I had thrown in the towel. So, ja, I tried to give Dave a farewell speech, but I had to cut it short … I just broke down in tears.

My ex-wife Tenielle was actually one of only two people who came to visit me at Harmony Clinic. My manager Donné was the other one. I had to apologise to Tenielle for all the heartache and shit I had caused her. Tenielle said to me that had we still been married, she would gladly have gone through the whole thing with me.

By then Tenielle and I had been divorced for about six months, and I'd only seen her a couple of times since, when we'd bumped into each other by chance. She was still angry with me, which is understandable, but she still came to see me. It was part of the clinic's programme to have those you have hurt come and visit so that you could apologise to them.

Still, Tenielle didn't *have* to come. It was an emotional experience for both of us. I wasn't just saying sorry to her, I was really speaking from my heart. And that – for me at least – was a very traumatic experience. I still love her, and every time I see her it hits me in the chest, because I was besotted with her at one stage. I couldn't even think straight or hit a cricket ball.

I was just as emotional with Donné. Donné couldn't even speak to me – she was too emotional. So she wrote me a letter and burst out crying before she could even finish reading it. There were more than a few tears in my eyes too. I also asked Donné to clear all the alcohol out of my house and to pass the message on to all the cricket teams I played for that all alcohol was to be removed from the mini-bar of any hotel room I was staying in. But yes, those were two very stressful sessions.

My folks never visited me. I have no idea why … I haven't asked them. I guess it's sad in a way, but we've never had the deep connection other families may have. I suppose part of the reason is that I've never spent much time with them as an adult. I started playing professional cricket at 16 and I've been on the road for 21-odd years now. That's more than half my life. We see each other when I get a bit of time off, but my parents are also divorced and have lived separate lives for the past 10 years.

My mom's always been very affectionate and still speaks to me like I'm her 10-year-old boy, but I think most mothers are similar. It's not as if I don't show emotion when I see my parents. Wine always brings out emotion. Whenever we sit down and share a few glasses of wine, and talk about things dear to my heart, it always brings out all these emotions in me and I invariably start crying.

I have a warm relationship with my dad. I might not speak to him every day, but we do chat and he's always willing to help me out. He will pick me up at the airport and he comes by my house twice a week to open up for my domestic worker. If I have to get something done, he'll organise it for me. But we don't really speak too deeply about what's on my mind or in my heart. We keep our relationship on a very even keel.

My dad's always allowed me to do things my way. He let me learn how to manage my own life. And so I've never really spoken to him much about the mistakes that I've made. It might sound a little strange to some people, but I think it stems from the days when I had my first real girlfriend. My dad was against the relationship from the start, and from then on I wouldn't speak to my parents about my personal feelings at all. So, ja, my dad and I chat a lot about sport and life in general, but we don't discuss anything personal.

I have a lot to thank my dad for: he provided me with the opportunity to become a professional cricketer. The guy had obviously busted his ass off to get my sister and me into private schools – my sister Lucinda went to Springfield. The Bishops bursary was my ticket to professional sport. I might have made it had I remained at St Joseph's College, but as good as St Joseph's was, it simply wasn't in the same league as Bishops. At Bishops I played sport against all the top youngsters in the country, and my successes got me recognised very quickly.

I see my sister Lucinda every now and then. She has her own busy life as a tennis coach, but again, we never talk too much about our private lives and I don't really know what she's up to. I have a half-brother too – Clinton Crayenstein – from my mom's first marriage, and he and I are pretty close.

I'd say we're a warm, loving family, but it's not your typical family. Both my sister and I have been on the road for so long with our sport that we were never able to develop a close bond. And because my parents are now divorced, we never get together as one big family. My parents still speak, but I can never get them together socially. My mom's completely against my dad's girlfriend, so if I had to invite my dad for a braai, he would have to come on his own, without his girlfriend. So, ja, it's a little different.

At Harmony, you are required to write your life story. The counsellors give you guidelines on how to approach the task, and when you've finished writing it, you have to read your story to your group. If the guys feel that you've left anything of importance out – say, for example, that you haven't been truthful – they will tell you so and then you've got to write more.

That's exactly what happened to me. They reckoned that I wasn't being completely honest and that I might have left a few important issues out … They also suggested that I explore other issues in more detail. Up until then my life story had been around 20 pages long, but my critics weren't happy until I added six more.

All in all, writing my life story turned out to be a very valuable exercise for me. It's funny … It was only when I got to the bit where I wrote about myself that I broke down. It had suddenly dawned on me that I was causing a huge amount of kak both for myself and for the people I loved. I had never considered what I was putting my family through. I mean, every time I was in the paper because of some or other controversy, my family's name was in there too. Everything I did also had an impact on my parents and my sister.

It was a huge realisation for me – how selfish I'd been all those years. I'd always thought that it was only me going through all the drama, but in reality my family was going through my shit too. The newspaper headlines impacted on their lives too. I wasn't only bringing myself down, but the family name too. When that penny dropped, ja, it was a real wake-up call.

Writing my life story had made this hit home, and it hit home hard. As I said, rehab helps you to be completely honest with yourself, which is probably the best part of it. If you're not open-minded and honest with yourself there, you're just wasting your time.

As the last couple of days of my stay at Harmony approached, I was really starting to itch to get out. I was counting down the days. A week before the end of my stay, I had already started to visualise playing cricket for South Africa again. As it happened, my stay was cut short because I'd heard from Donné that I'd been picked for the ODI squad to tour Australia. I had kind of expected to be selected, anyway. I was a senior player in the squad and had plenty of experience playing the Aussies on their own turf, which had to be a valuable asset to the Proteas. Besides, a month in rehab wouldn't have adversely affected my cricketing skills – in fact, probably just the opposite.

Looking back on the whole rehab experience, it had certainly been a *very* tough month; a very emotional and draining time for me. But it taught me a helluva lot too, mostly about myself. The counsellors kept telling me, 'Hersch, we know that you are wearing a mask. You put on this happy, jovial face, when we know that you're not always happy and jovial. Just be yourself.' As I've said, Harmony taught me to be honest with myself, as day in and day out you have to tell your innermost thoughts to people you don't really know. I'd never before spoken that deeply about what was in my heart and on my mind.

While I learnt some very valuable life lessons at the clinic, I wouldn't for a moment say that rehab changed the kind of person I am. I still have all this energy – I can't help it – and I'm still the last one to leave a party. But I now control my alcohol intake. Look, the people at the clinic obviously want you to stop drinking completely, but the thought of not drinking for the rest of my life is quite daunting. Society makes it tough on you. It's a cultural thing. But I'm a lot more hesitant now before I order my first drink. It's amazing; it's such a beautiful space to be in. Before, I didn't give having a drink a second thought, so going from a balls-to-the-wall attitude to thinking about what I'm about to do is a huge step for me.

Since rehab there have been a couple of occasions where I threw in the kitchen sink and got completely hammered, but I don't like it much any more. I wake up the next day and I want to kick myself. I ask myself: 'Why did you do that? You don't need it. You've been down that road so many times, *and* you're just fucking up your body! I mean, you train so hard ... what's the point of it when you're going to drink excessively and smoke the odd cigarette?' So I definitely now think long and hard about my actions. I've also noticed that the longer I go without alcohol, the better I feel.

Rehab could not have come at a better time in my life, which had been in a downward spiral over the preceding two years. I had got divorced and experienced various off-the-field incidents. Spending a month in rehab at Harmony Clinic was the most beneficial thing I'd done in 15 years, and it allowed me to pull up the handbrake. Its knock-on effect is that I'm thinking about life a lot more ... in fact, I've never done so much thinking as I have in the past 20 months.

But, as I've said, I haven't stopped drinking completely, though ...

At my first post-rehab Proteas fines meeting, during the ODI series in Australia in January 2009, I downed Energade. Now downing warm Energade isn't great, I can tell you. Neil McKenzie

My second birthday, I think. I hope so, anyway – hopefully my mom, Barbara, didn't make me wear that hat on a daily basis

Me, aged seven, at a Springbok Radio Christmas party. Ja. Even then I enjoyed the spotlight

My mom, my sister, Lucinda, and me (jeez … I hope those are pyjamas) at our flat in Elfindale, Heathfield

With my mom and my sister for Christmas lunch at my paternal gran's house in Bonteheuwel

Receiving my under-13 Western Province colours for football. I was 11 then

The 1991 Bishops 1st XI. I am sitting in the bottom row, in the middle. I was in Standard 9 then. Funny, I played senior cricket for Western Province from '89, but made the SA Schools side only in '91 and '92

Punting one upfield during the annual Bishops/Rondebosch derby in 1991. I remember scoring a try in that rugby game, running from inside our own 10-metre line. We never lost to Rondebosch Boys

Meeting the legendary South African rugby player and administrator Doc Craven at the same game

© TC Malhotra/PictureNET Africa

© Gallo Images

Portrait from my first ever South Africa tour to Kenya in 1989

Jonty Rhodes and me celebrating our win over the West Indies after the third Test at Kingsmead, Durban, in 1998. It was a genuine privilege to play alongside the greatest fielder ever to play the game

© Gallo Images

Makhaya Ntini, Paul Adams, me and Mark Boucher – all youngsters then and part of an under-strength South African team that famously beat a full-on Aussie squad to win gold at the 1998 Commonwealth Games. I remember the guys being helluva relaxed during the Games … up for a pint or three every night. And we won the bladdy thing. Incredible

© Gallo Images

Hansie guiding me to my first ODI 100 against the West Indies at St George's Park,
Port Elizabeth, in 1999

© Gallo Images

Despite all the match-fixing drama, Hansie remains the greatest captain I've played for.
The young pups – me, Jacques Kallis (left) and Mark Boucher (right) – worshipped the guy

The man who started it all congratulates me on my 211 not out against New Zealand at Christchurch in 1999. It was also my first Test century. If we hadn't lost 90 overs to rain I reckon I could've got close to 300

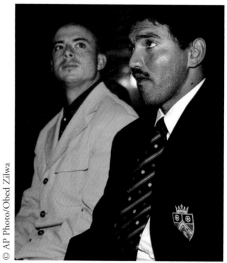

Me and Henry Williams facing the heat at the King Commission enquiry in to match fixing in June 2000. Poor Henry was kakking himself; he could barely remember his name. Ja. Pretty much the same for me

Arriving at the Delhi Police headquarters in 2006 to face the Indian authorities. That's my wingman and lawyer, Peter Whelan, on my left shoulder. The shades were more for my hangover than for the bright sunlight

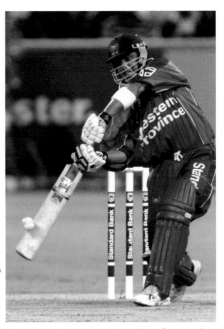

Right at the start of my career for Western Province during the 1989/90 season's Benson & Hedges series

It's been an honour to play a lot of my cricket at Newlands, and I'm proud to have represented this great province for 21 years. That's got to be some kind of record, surely?

Celebrating our win in the 2003 Standard Bank Cup final against Griquas at Newlands

© Gallo Images

With Gary Kirsten, doing what we did best … scoring a lot of runs. This is us helping to whip the Bangladeshis by 10 wickets at the 2003 World Cup. Gary got 52, I got 49

© Gallo Images

This photo says it all. Gary and I knew each other's games so well it felt like we were always in sync. Gary's a great cricketer, coach and all-round human being. Thanks for the memories, bud

was the Fines Master, and a couple of fines came my way. It didn't feel right to be drinking beer with them, given that I had just come out of rehab, but, honestly, the thought of drinking a warm energy drink for the rest of my career would've done my bladdy head in.

It didn't take too long before it was 'later for that' to the Energade and I was back, doing proper justice to a fines meeting. Later, before the Cape Cobras Pro20 final against the Diamond Eagles at Newlands, I promised myself that even if we won the game in front of our home crowd, I would refrain from joining my Cobras teammates in the traditional beer-soaked celebrations.

I couldn't do it, though. I couldn't keep my promise. We ended up winning and, predictably, the beers were flying in the changing room. I reasoned with myself: 'Well, okay, we did win after all. I might as well tonk a few beers too.'

It was a great evening. We had a fines meeting and drank and drank. Professor André Odendaal, the Western Province Cricket CEO, came into the room at one point and I said, 'Doc ...' (I always called him Doc.) 'Doc, I think we're going to need some more beer here.' And the beers just kept coming. We went out afterwards and had a big night.

The next morning I hated myself for going overboard. This was six or seven weeks after I had left the clinic, and sitting in my car the next morning, I was thinking, 'Why the hell did you do it? Like, why did you do this?' For many, if not most people, once they've come out of rehab, they manage to stay away from alcohol for the rest of their lives. I take my hat off to them, but that's not me, I'm afraid. Even though I was upset with myself for getting drunk, I also knew that I would probably never be able to give up drinking entirely. Not even in rehab did I say that I was never going to touch a drop of alcohol again.

But rehab allowed me to see what I was like when alcohol ruled my life, and it showed me how it affected those close to me. I won't let that happen again. But I'm still going to drink like the average person. I see no reason why I have to stop completely.

So I give it the proper horns on the odd occasion, but I also have nights when I go down to Caprice, where I've had many serious piss-ups, and drink no more than a couple of strong cappuccinos. And I still find it a highly enjoyable experience. I might go down to the bar to watch a Champion's League football game – I'm a lifelong Manchester United fan – and have a cool time just drinking coffee. The simple fact is that I've cut down on my alcohol consumption by a huge amount.

I'm happy and calm, but I've still got a lot of energy, you know, and that combines into a person I'm still getting to know. My dad always worried that if I gave up alcohol altogether, I'd become boring and lose my sense of humour. But that has not been the case. For one, my personality isn't based on my alcohol consumption; and, two, although I still have that energy, I also have a different mindset now. I'm a little more reflective and I'm quieter.

I do a lot of thinking in hotel rooms when I'm on tour (not so much at the ground, because there's just no time to think about anything else but the game, really) or at home between games.

Whereas before I'd always want to go out on the town, I actually enjoy this time now. In these quiet hours I find myself contemplating all the things that I've done in my life and what direction I want my life to take now.

I'm in a good space.

5

Fatherhood,
marriage ... and divorce

As a 22-year-old on the cusp of an international cricketing
career, fatherhood was the last thing I wanted. My relationship
with my son, however, has gone from strength to strength.
Unfortunately, my marriage a decade later was the exact
opposite ...

Fatherhood

Not everyone knows this, but I have a son called Rashard. It's not
a secret; it's just that I became a father at a very young age and my
relationship with my son's mom soured after I found out she was
pregnant. This part of my life hasn't been given too much attention
in the press, for which everyone concerned is grateful. However,
I've got to a point in my life where I'd like to tell people about my
relationship with my son, a youngster I love very much. Our relationship didn't start off too well, but I'm now happy and grateful
to have a healthy bond with a son of whom I'm very proud.

I met Liesl Fuller in my last year at school in 1992. It was
Nuffield Week – the provincial schools cricket tournament –
which was being held in Stellenbosch that year. Liesl was still at
school as well. She was five years younger than me, and on holiday
with her parents from Joburg. Nothing happened in those early
years – she was obviously pretty young – but we kept in touch.
After I left school and started playing cricket full time, I'd see her
whenever I was in Joburg. Gradually things got more serious and
by 1996 we were sleeping together.

Then one night, later that year, she phoned me at my parents' house, where I was still living. By now I was 22 and Liesl 17. 'Listen,' she said, 'I'm three months pregnant. I've been sick … I thought I had the flu or something.'

I shat myself. I had no idea what to do and responded very angrily. 'Don't talk kak to me,' I said, and put the phone down. I remember thinking, 'The fucking witch.' I had just made the South African team and all I could think to do was to keep it nice and quiet. I didn't even tell my parents.

I wasn't sure whether or not Liesl had got pregnant on purpose. I mean, she lived in Joburg and my international career was just taking off. It's not like I was ever going to make any adjustment to my life to go and look after her. Man, I was pissed off. I had no idea what to do about the situation and I didn't breathe a word about it to anyone.

My mom found out first. Via the post. Not ideal. This very formal-looking letter arrives in the postbox addressed to 'Mr H Gibbs'. My dad's name is Herman, so my mom opened the letter, thinking it was for him. But it was the maintenance contract Liesl's family lawyer had drawn up. They were asking for R3 000 a month, starting straight away – the kid wasn't even born yet. That was a lot of money back then, especially for me. It was ridiculous. They must have thought I was loaded.

My mom was like, 'And this? What the hell is this, Herschelle?'

Man, I was frightened, but I had to come clean. All I could say was, 'Well, listen, this is the story and this is how much I have to pay. What else can I do?' I had no choice but to pay the money. Fortunately Liesl became less demanding later on. Maybe she realised that you can't expect to get that sort of money from anybody.

But I was so angry with her that it took me a year after my son was born before I could actually bring myself to see him. I was in Joburg to see Liesl's dad about the maintenance and she asked me to come and see Rashard. 'Look,' she said, 'you don't have to stay with him long. Just come and hold him.' Her dad was in the car, she was driving, and I was holding Rashard, who was crying. I tried to sort of shut him up, and I remember feeling very cold towards him. It was just this complete anger, you know, for what I figured Liesl had done to me. I couldn't stop wondering, 'Did she do it on purpose?' In hindsight, it was obviously unfair to suspect her of that.

As a result, I didn't see much of Rashard as he grew up, especially in his early years. Now the situation is improving, though – in the past few years I've seen him much more regularly, and I phone and talk to him a lot too. We see each other whenever I'm playing in Joburg, and I've also gone to watch him play cricket a few times. I can't tell yet whether he's going to make his career in sport. I guess now that he's turning 14, you can start to see how good he is at a sport. I think once a kid gets to that age, you can form a good picture of how good he'll be. You still can't make a definite call on whether or not he'll make the big time, but you get a feel for what he can accomplish and what sort of levels he can reach.

I haven't seen enough of Rashard's abilities yet, but I know he enjoys his cricket and football. He's going to be tall as well – he already takes a bigger size shoe than me! And he's a good boy ... he's got brains, this one.

In personality, I see a lot of similarities between the two of us. I went to his birthday party last year and, like me, he loves to be the life and soul of the party. He definitely likes the attention; it was funny to see. And, just like me, he gets shy and nervous at times too. I can see when he is not entirely confident in a situation. Like me, when I have to make a speech. I don't like standing up and speaking in public at all. I find it completely bladdy nerve-wracking.

My relationship with Liesl is all right these days. Although we don't really talk much, I think she can see that I've made a real effort to stay in touch with Rashard. I don't think it's been easy for him to have me for a father: a public figure *and* one who doesn't see him that often. Kids at his primary school used to hassle him for being my son, which I think bothered him, because he got into a bit of kak every now and again. These days he's at St John's and he's made some good friends there. He's doing okay now.

I still help him financially, but the amount varies from month to month. I contribute to his school fees, for example, and sometimes Liesl and I split the costs. I make a point of not spoiling Rashard, because I wasn't really ever spoilt as a child, and I don't believe kids should get stuff just because they want it. But now I can't give him my old Puma shoes any more, as his feet have grown too big!

I am grateful to Liesl for having raised him the way she did. He has been well looked after and he's happy and healthy.

So that's fatherhood and me. It started off shaky, but the future looks bright. Of course, I can say the exact opposite about my marriage …

Marriage
I first met Tenielle Povey at the legendary Billy the Bums bar in Durban during the 2003 World Cup, where I was hanging out with my teammates Robin Peterson and Monde Zondeki. And, if memory serves, we met a couple of days before the fateful game against Sri Lanka when, thanks to Messrs Duckworth and Lewis, we exited stage left from a home World Cup we were heavy favourites to win. Anyway, in walked Tenielle with a friend of hers. I looked at her, she looked at me, and she walked past me to sit outside. A little later she came over and said, 'Can I buy you a drink?' Naturally, I said yes.

I don't think she knew who I was – obviously I was trading only on my good looks! So she bought me the drink, but she didn't join us – I think she and her friends were on their way to a club. As it happens, the guys and I were planning to go to the same club, so I arranged to meet Tenielle there and return the compliment by buying her a drink. I didn't get her number – which is not like me. And when we got to the club, I looked everywhere for her, which wasn't like me either – normally the girls are the ones doing the looking. But this girl had made an impression on me. Problem was, I couldn't find her anywhere. And I looked *everywhere*. High and low.

Eventually she found me, but by that time – as luck would have it – there were about six or seven girls around. I stayed. And I drank. The rest of the night was a complete blank for me. Tenielle, I'm happy to say, didn't give up. She found out where the team was staying and left her cellphone number at the hotel for me. Clearly she was keen. And that's how it started. The attraction between us was immediate and it was physical from the word go. Although I do remember this one time where, despite all my intentions, I couldn't quite ... 'follow through'.

We were at a club near the Cullinan Hotel in Cape Town – also during the World Cup – and I got horribly drunk. Tenielle pretty much had to look after me that night. Anyway, I got the munchies on the way home and insisted we stop at a KFC. I remember ... actually, I don't ... Tenielle remembers me demanding, 'I want six pieces of chicken.' I got my six pieces of chicken. But when we got home, I fell asleep with a drumstick in my mouth. So, ja, being so out of it meant that nothing happened that night. Tenielle teased me about it for a long time.

At first, our relationship was pretty casual. Tenielle had a boyfriend, but she made an effort to stay in touch with me. I loved seeing her when I went to Durban. Then, the West Indies tour came up in 2005. I'd obviously been to the islands before and knew what a nice place it was. I wasn't planning to take anybody along, but I thought, 'What the hell,' and asked Tenielle to join me on the tour. And she said yes.

When partners want to come along on tour, it's automatic if you're married – your wife comes with you. If you're not married, we refer to a sort of points system: if you've played long enough and have earned enough points, Cricket SA will fly your girlfriend over and pay for her accommodation. Fortunately I had accumulated more than enough points by that stage.

So Tenielle came over to Barbados, which obviously meant it was the end of her relationship with her boyfriend. I know the break-up was pretty messy for her … in a lot of ways. But man, I just couldn't wait to see her. And we had a really great time. We went swimming in the ocean every morning – it was a real honeymoon situation. I was bladdy besotted. It was in the West Indies that I realised how much Tenielle meant to me, and I was like, 'Hersch, you're in your early thirties now. Maybe it's time to make a proper go of it. This is a nice time of your life to get married. You're so crazy about this woman, she must be The One.'

So I asked Tenielle to relocate to Cape Town so that she could move in with me. We lived in my house in Higgovale for a while, and then we got a place in Green Point. We did up the house together and lived there for about two years. Things were great most of the time, but even then I often felt a little tied down. Every time I used to come back from a tour, I knew that the days were gone when I could just go off and play golf with my friends or have a boys' night out. I actually felt guilty every time I asked Tenielle if I could go out without her, and, understandably, she wasn't happy about me wanting to have boys' nights. She wanted to know why I didn't want to spend all my time with her.

And she was right … Why did I not want to spend all my time with her? After all, hadn't I been so in love with her in the West Indies?

Looking back now, I can see I just wasn't ready for commitment. And I'm still not, which is why I'm not in a relationship now. I'd rather just spend time with my mates. Or if I want to do sweet bugger all, I can do that too. When I was with Tenielle, it was like I'd get itchy feet. I loved going out for supper and a movie with her, for example, but then, after a few hours, I'd be like, 'Where's the party? Where's the party?' I just couldn't relax; I always wanted to be on the go. After a few nights at home I'd want to be out with my mates. And it wasn't the promise of hooking up with some other woman that was driving me either; it was the buzz of getting pissed with my mates. You know, just having a fat old party.

Look, there were times when Tenielle and I entertained at home and we had unbelievable fun. That, for me, was one of the real positives of being in a relationship. We'd have some other couples over, Tenielle would cook great food and we'd have an absolutely awesome evening.

Tenielle knew me, though, and she tried to keep track of what I got up to when I was away playing cricket. Obviously I was experiencing a bit of freedom when I was on tour, and I'd duck and dive a little and not always take her calls. On one or two occasions when I was out and about, she worked it out for herself that I'd lied to her about being in the hotel, or that the phone in the room wasn't working properly. I also sometimes said – and this was often true – that the hotel reception hadn't put any calls through to my room. The hotels generally don't put calls through to the players' rooms, irrespective of who the callers say they are. Obviously when I got home I'd be questioned left, right and centre – something Tenielle had every right to do.

Eventually the penny did drop that I was hurting her with this kind of behaviour. I did not want to do that any more, and so I thought it was time I married her. I really was head over heels in love with Tenielle when I proposed to her in 2006, shortly after the famous 438 ODI game against the Aussies. I remember that evening very well ...

I had come home from gym and decided, 'No, shit, I better just do it.' I already had the ring. Earlier in the year, when we were touring Australia, Tenielle was with me for about three weeks. We were in Brisbane and she was out shopping one day. She came back and announced that she'd 'found the ring I think I should have'. So I bought it. Obviously I didn't tell her I was going to buy it, but once she returned to South Africa – all the players' partners go home early – I flew back to Brisbane to go and buy the ring. And I proposed a few months later.

So, anyway, I got home, we had a quiet little braai, and over a glass of wine I proposed. She said yes. And then we proceeded to phone everyone to tell them the news.

My mother wasn't very happy. She'd never really seen eye to eye with Tenielle – she always had an issue about how much Tenielle smoked. My mom would say, 'Ag, she's a very pretty girl, great personality … but jeez, she smokes a lot, hey?' Actually, to be honest, my mom's never got on with any of my girlfriends. I don't know why, but it's been going on for years. She always wants to find fault with the woman I'm seeing. Perhaps she thinks they're after my money.

I've told her, 'Mom, but I don't *have* money. What makes you think I've got all this money?' But she's never bought it. I'm financially well off, but I don't have millions in the bank, like the very wealthy. If I did, I wouldn't be playing the UK lottery as often as I do! I always spend a little money on the lottery when I'm there. I mean, why not? Fork out £6 a week for a few lottery tickets and, who knows, it could turn into a win of £6 million. It would be fantastic! Six million pounds is quite a lot of money. Tax free. Nice.

So ja, my mom wasn't exactly over the moon about the news of my engagement, but my dad, on the other hand, was completely overwhelmed. So that was all good.

Tenielle and I were engaged for over a year and I think she definitely wanted kids, so I felt a bit of pressure from her. I guess I was just going through what every man goes through, contemplating whether or not he's ready to take the big step. I thought to myself, 'If you don't know by now, you'll never know.' But I genuinely wanted to get married. And to be truthful, out of all the women I'd dated, I really thought Tenielle was the one.

We had a very strong physical bond between us – it's there even now when I see her, and I don't think it will ever go away. I am a very affectionate person and we were very affectionate with each other. I'd look at how some of the other guys in the team treated their wives or girlfriends and it appeared odd to me, as they never seemed to show their partners much affection. Perhaps they were embarrassed or shy, but for me, it didn't matter. Even in public I was always helluva affectionate.

But whether or not I was going to be faithful to Tenielle was another story, and it was an issue that preyed on my mind. As a professional sportsman, a lot of temptations come your way and, obviously, you know, it fuels the fire when you're drinking a lot as well. Alcohol definitely lowers your moral barometer.

Despite my misgivings, Tenielle and I decided to get married on the island of St Kitts and Nevis in the West Indies. After playing the 2007 World Cup on the island and hitting six sixes in a row off an unfortunate Dutchman, the Minister of Sport for St Kitts and Nevis – a gentleman by the name of Ricky Skerritt – had awarded me a free 10-day holiday on the island, which included accommodation. Tenielle was obviously cool with that.

The wedding was a small ceremony attended by only a couple of mates whom I had met on the island during the World Cup and took place at a resort called the Rawlins Plantation Inn, which was basically an old sugar plantation that had been converted into a hotel. The hotel kindly organised the whole event for us, including the priest. It was great. Very romantic.

I don't have one photograph of the wedding, though. But that's typical of me. I never keep any snapshots. I've got some of my son Rashard, but otherwise I never keep photos.

Tenielle looked gorgeous. Man oh man, absolutely divine. But as I was standing there, taking my vows, I was asking myself whether I was doing the right thing. Right there, as I was speaking the words, a thought just suddenly dawned on me. I remember thinking, 'I hope you realise what you're getting into.'

The marriage lasted for about a year.

Divorce

The actual year itself wasn't too bad. I was away for the majority of the time – six months in all – so I basically only saw Tenielle for half the year we were married. Apart from one occasion during our engagement, I wasn't unfaithful during the marriage. Well, not technically, anyway.

Tenielle and I had a lot of great times, make no mistake, and I loved – and still love – her. But there were also some very bad times. Most of which were my fault.

One such time was at my cousin's wedding. I got really pissed, and on the way home Tenielle and I had a massive fight. She kept shouting at me that I was driving too fast, and I was getting really annoyed, as you do when you're drunk. She kept on at me, though, on and on: 'You're driving too fast … you're driving too fast.'

We were physically fighting while I was driving. I was trying to prevent her from grabbing the steering wheel and hitting me … and in the process I managed to pull some of her hair out. She was just trying to get me to stop the car, but I was having none of it. It's one of the effects alcohol has on me: I'm a bladdy stubborn drunk. Only when I'm on spirits, though. If I drink wine, I'm the most peaceful drunk around.

Eventually Tenielle says, 'No, I'm not going home. Take me to my parents' place in Camps Bay.' By then I'd realised that I had pushed things too far and was in a fair amount of kak, so I took her to her folks. Her dad comes out of the house and I give him this whole speech about how I know he's obviously going to stick up for his daughter, but all I was trying to do was drive home and she was shouting so loudly that I couldn't take it any more and she was then trying to push the steering wheel and I was sort of preventing her. Basically all that sort of crap. I was angry and said they should just take my car and that I would walk home.

It's a long way from Camps Bay to Green Point.

Fortunately her dad was like, 'No, no, don't be silly. Let's all just go home. Everything will be okay in the morning.' They're great people, Tenielle's folks. Very loving and understanding people.

Another big fight occurred at our house one night. We were giving a braai for some friends, and, again, I had plenty to drink. Tenielle and I would fight a lot about stupid little things, but never when I was sober. This particular evening we ended up having a huge argument in the bedroom. It got very physical. No hitting – I never hit her, or any other woman, for that matter. We were sort of pushing each other. One of my mates had to come in to see whether things weren't getting out of hand.

There was also an 'incident' with celebrity model Minki van der Westhuizen, which happened at former Miss Universe Michelle McLean's engagement party. The next day Tenielle said to me, 'You know, last night ... do you remember what happened? You tried to kiss Minki right in front of me.'

I'm like, 'What? Really?'

I didn't remember a thing. Funny things happen to me when I get pissed.

The whole drunk-driving incident in March 2008 was a perfect example ...

Tenielle and I went to Pigalle in Green Point for supper, because she had been saying to me that I never wanted to go out with her, just with the boys, and that we never went out and enjoyed ourselves together. So I said, cool. I remember it was a Thursday night, and Thursdays at Pigalle are generally good.

I had a few bottles of wine over supper and decided, no, we were now going to go to a bar in Camps Bay called Ignite. Where I proceeded to get slaughtered. Apparently, a bunch of students kept on buying me shooters. I only know this because Tenielle told me afterwards. My problem is that I can never say no to people who buy me drinks. I always feel rude and disrespectful.

At that time we were renting a place on Kloof Nek Road in the city – a development called the Summit. To get there from Camps Bay is just a short drive up and over the Nek, but I decided to take the long way round via Green Point in order to stop by Steers, a burger joint.

So we drive through Camps Bay to Green Point Main Road, both of us happy as hell. The music is blaring in the car, and at the traffic lights outside the old News Café, we get pulled over by the police. Apparently I had been driving pretty fast. I was in a confident frame of mind. 'Don't worry,' I said to Tenielle. 'I'll handle this.'

I was sure they would know who I was and that things would turn out all right. As it happened, these two didn't know me from Adam. 'Sir,' the one officer asks, 'have you been drinking?'

'Ja,' I said, confidently. What else could I say? So he said, 'Okay, will you come to the station with us, please?' They put me in the back of the van and took me to Sea Point Police Station. Tenielle had to drive our car back to the police station, and she sat there for a while before eventually going home.

For some reason the cops didn't have breathalyser equipment at the station, so they carted me all the way to a roadblock set up on the N2. As a result of my drunken state, I can vaguely remember sitting in the back of the van and abusing the cop, because he was driving at what felt like 160 km/h. 'What the fuck? You pull me over for a little speeding down the main road and here you are, driving 160 kays an hour. What's with you?'

Quite quickly we arrived at the mobile police station on the N2, and there's a queue of seven or eight people, all lining up to get breathalysed. Now I'm starting to get irritable – really irritable – and I am not being my usual jovial self. So I abuse the good officers a little more and suggest they phone President Thabo Mbeki and tell him who and where I am, and he would order them to let me go. Of course the officers declined to call the president.

Instead they made me blow into the breathalyser, which was apparently a new type of device. After doing this I saw a woman officer and demanded to make a phone call. I went on about knowing my rights, etcetera. So she gave me her phone but told me to keep it short, as she didn't have much airtime left.

This annoyed me even more, and I had a go at her, saying, 'In that case, you keep your bladdy phone.' Obviously that didn't make her too happy. I believe 'ungrateful little shit' was among the colourful phrases she used. Ja ... I didn't make any friends there.

Anyway, they then put me back into the van and took me back to the Sea Point station, where I was chucked into a cell. Another guy was already in the cell, also for drunk driving. I must have been locked up for a couple of hours, but I don't remember too much beyond loudly singing the Engelbert Humperdinck classic 'Please Release Me, Let Me Go' at the top of my voice and then passing out. I dossed like a champion.

Out of the fog I heard someone calling my name: 'Mr Gibbs ... Mr Gibbs ... Mr Gibbs ...' It was about seven in the morning when I was allowed to go, and by then there were some reporters outside the police station. Obviously someone from the police had tipped them off ... That's how they managed to get a photo of me, which appeared in the paper the next morning.

As it turned out, the charges against me were dropped a year later. Not too long after that incident I decided, however, to drop my marriage. 'Well, this is it,' I said to myself. 'Just stop all the shit and stop putting Tenielle through this.' She was too nice a woman, and I couldn't keep doing bad things to her. I needed to break the cycle. I think she was also starting to lose patience with my drinking.

I decided I just couldn't be in the relationship any more. By now I was thinking, 'No more marriage,' but not, interestingly enough, 'No more drinking.' I knew it was pointless for me to continue with the marriage. Despite my good intentions, I knew I just wasn't equipped or ready for it.

I still loved Tenielle – I probably always will – but the more I thought about it, the more I realised that it just wasn't the right time for me to be married. As a professional sportsman who played international cricket, I wasn't at home long enough to actually work on the relationship. If one partner in a marriage is home for only a few months of the year, it follows that the relationship is going to struggle. You simply don't spend enough time with your partner to actually build a strong bond.

When we first got married, I started feeling very claustrophobic after only a couple of weeks, despite the fact that I'd also been away for a month. I think that that's the result of being on the road for years and growing a little selfish. I felt guilty when I wanted to play golf with my mates, whom I hadn't seen for a couple of months. I felt like I had to get Tenielle's permission. Then I'd really feel bad because I wasn't spending enough time with her. You know, here I am at home at last and the first thing I want to do is play golf with my mates or go on a boys' night out?

In a normal, healthy relationship you're supposed to want to be with your wife all the time. But we didn't have a normal relationship, and the problem lay with me ... which I acknowledge. When we'd first moved in together, Tenielle didn't yet have a full-time job in Cape Town, so she obviously hung around the house quite a lot. When I had time off from cricket, I'd do my gym in the morning and then, if I wanted to see my mates in the afternoon, or play golf – and that takes, like, five or six hours – I'd have to cut things short because I needed to be home. Not that my mates gave me a hard time – I mean, quite a lot of them understood because they're married as well.

But I was also really excited about being with Tenielle. I wanted the house, the white picket fence, everything. And the funny thing is, I had the right woman. I always knew I had the right woman, and I really thought that I was ready to settle down. I grew comfortable with living in the same space as Tenielle during the years we shared a house. But then again, I wasn't home a helluva lot.

Of course it didn't help that I wasn't the most faithful boyfriend and husband. I didn't have sex with anyone else while I was married, but at that stage I was going balls to the wall with my drinking. And when you get drunk, your sense of responsibility diminishes. So, ja, I'd kiss the odd girl – nothing more than that – but then again, I'd get so hammered that I genuinely wouldn't know what I'd done.

Sometimes my mates would tell me what I had got up to the night before, and how can I put it? I'd be very surprised. So, ja, I kissed one or five girls during my marriage, but I don't remember most of what happened because I was *that* tanked. I'm not proud to admit it; it's just the way it was. I wasn't being totally unfaithful, but, still, my actions reflected where my head was.

Being in a steady relationship meant that I could never leave my phone on when Tenielle and I went to sleep. I always had to put it on silent, always, as I might have got the kind of text message that one's girlfriend definitely did not want to see. Even once I'd got engaged, I didn't tell any of my lady friends that I was now unavailable and that they shouldn't contact me any more. I always used to lie awake at night and think, 'Shit, who's going to SMS me now, or phone me?' I never, ever had peace of mind. Even when I was driving in my car with Tenielle, I'd worry about some chick ringing me up.

As I said, I'm not proud to admit to my behaviour, but it proves that I wasn't ready for marriage. Even though I had *really* thought that I was. Now, I don't know if I'm ever going to be ready. Travelling is a big issue for me. How one builds a relationship with another person when you're home for a couple of weeks and then gone for a couple of months at a time is beyond me.

Obviously other guys manage it. Take Shaun Pollock, for example. But Polly is a different kind of guy from me – he doesn't drink, just for starters. At team dinners he might have one or two drinks with the guys, but he never hit the bars and clubs with us. That just isn't Polly. Polly was probably the most together person I've played with. I mean, I played with him for 14 years. Guys like Makhaya Ntini and Ashwell Prince are also cut from the same cloth.

Having said that, some cricketers also appear to be a lot more together than they actually are. There's a lot of stuff that just gets pushed under the carpet; it doesn't come out in the media. I won't mention any names, as that will get me into even more trouble than I already am, but I can tell you that there are some guys in the squad who are not quite as straight up and down as their public image suggests.

I mean … just look at the former Proteas player Jonty Rhodes. His divorce must've come as something of a surprise to the public. And Daryll Cullinan's marriage has also broken up. I didn't even know about his divorce until relatively recently.

And so I ended my marriage. I discussed my feelings with Tenielle before I left for India to play in the inaugural Indian Premier League tournament in 2008. And while I was there I thought long and hard about the whole sad situation. It was there that I finally made up my mind … and I SMSed Tenielle from India saying, 'I think I've put you through enough trouble and heartache and I don't think that this is going to work. I can see it's not going to go anywhere. I don't think I could possibly change and it's best we just go our separate ways.'

Perhaps not the classiest way to end a relationship, I guess, but I had to let her know where my head was as soon as possible, rather than wait to tell her when I got back to South Africa.

My phone rang as soon as Tenielle got the SMS. And again I said, 'Listen, this is it. I've been thinking about it, and when I come back, I want a divorce.' I remember her saying okay, perhaps she should move out and we should separate for a while. We hardly spoke again during the IPL, and then after the tournament I was only in South Africa for a week before I had to travel to England to play county cricket for Glamorgan.

During that week, though, Tenielle and I met and had a pretty traumatic discussion. Ja, it wasn't nice. She cried a lot, not believing that I wanted to split up or even understanding why I wanted to end our relationship. She kept on asking, 'Why?' and said that she'd gladly work with me through all my issues and concerns. I hated seeing her cry – I hate seeing anybody cry, for that matter – but I was determined. I just said, 'No, I've put you through enough.' I told her that it wasn't appropriate to carry on and that she should try to find somebody who could make her completely happy. Tenielle didn't take it very well. It might be a little bit selfish of me to say this, but I still think I made the right decision to get out.

So I set off for Glamorgan, Tenielle moved out, and Donné and Peter Whelan sorted things out. Ironically, the day I landed in London to play county cricket was 8 July, our one-year wedding anniversary ...

The divorce went through on the grounds of 'irreconcilable differences'.

If you read the papers in that time, you will know that the saga didn't quite end there, though. Tenielle took me to court, demanding some very sizeable amounts of money – in the region of R100 000 a month. Clearly she was either smoking her socks or she and her lawyer were using that amount as a bargaining tool. It was money that she would never be able to get. I wasn't even worth half of what they made out.

Unfortunately, the press depicted Tenielle as a bit of a gold digger, which was basically a load of rubbish. She wasn't at fault. She did nothing wrong in our marriage and did not deserve what I had put her through. Although I wasn't in the country when the story went down, I heard about it, and I can tell you that Tenielle isn't the person the media made her out to be. The divorce was entirely my fault. I know how hard it had been for Tenielle and how bad she was feeling. For her, marriage was supposed to be a lifelong commitment, and she was exceptionally hurt by the divorce. Obviously she wanted to hurt me back, and the way to do that was to smack me in the wallet.

Fortunately I have good lawyers and they handled the case on my behalf. All I had to do was sign a few papers. I ended up paying off Tenielle's new car and giving her about R550 000 in cash. She took some pieces of furniture from the house, but the house itself remained in my name. Basically she didn't get anywhere close to what she thought she would.

The divorce did knock me a little financially – 550K is 550K – but thanks to tournaments like the IPL, I would survive.

Tenielle was one of the two people who came to see me when I was in rehab, but today I know we're finished. I can't really say I'll never get married again – I think, ultimately, I'd like to tie the knot one day. Perhaps after I've been on the road for 20-odd years, which will be in another five years, then I'll think about it. If this means that I stay single until then, so be it. I'm sure my life will take on a whole new direction once I've finished playing cricket. I've just bought a new house in Camps Bay that I'm renovating, so maybe that is the beginning of the process.

It is something I look forward to.

6

The controversies

Over the years, a lot has been written about the various controversial situations I have found myself in. Once and for all, let me set the record straight.

As explosive as my batting can be, it hasn't quite matched the pyrotechnics of my life off the field. Unfortunately some of my escapades have filled as many newspaper column inches as my cricketing performances. As you now know, I've managed to land myself in the kak with alarming regularity right from the start of my cricket career. A stint in rehab for alcohol abuse and a messy divorce would be more than enough controversy for most professional athletes, but with me, that wasn't the half of it. Here's a run-through of my own personal highlights. And why not start with the biggie?

The match-fixing scandal

It was 6.30 a.m., and knocking on my door was the Proteas team captain, Hansie Cronjé. We were touring India in 2000, and in Nagpur about to play our final ODI match against India. My roommate, fast bowler Henry Williams, was in the shower when Hansie sat down on the bed. He got straight to the point. 'I've got a mate here in India,' he said, 'and you can make some good money if you do what he's asking. He's offering US$15 000 if you go out for less than 20 in today's game.'

I'd like to tell you that this was one of those moments when someone says something so unexpected to you that you first frown like you can't quite believe what you're hearing and then your jaw drops as the words sink in. But that wouldn't be entirely true.

This had happened before.

During a tour to India in 1996, we were due to play a benefit game for one of the Indian players – it would be the last game of the tour. The night before the game, Hansie got the whole team together and dropped a real bombshell. 'I know a guy,' he said, 'who is going to give us US$250 000 if we lose this game.'

The offer was tempting, because we were probably going to lose the game anyway. We were well below strength, with six of our guys off sick – we were going to be on the back foot. I remember that I was fielding at point, which meant Jonty Rhodes wasn't play-ing, and Gary Kirsten was wicketkeeper. That's how bad it was.

Of course the team decided against taking the bribe, but, even so, it hadn't been an immediate and strong reaction to an activity totally abhorrent to the notion of sport. Instead, we talked the offer over. Pat Symcox – always an oke willing to look at all sides of the equation – thought it was definitely worth *some* consideration. He wasn't the only one. We decided that this was either some-thing the whole team bought into or it was a no-go. Some of the guys, though, were dead against it, Andrew Hudson in particular. So that was that. We declined the offer. Sachin Tendulkar ended up getting a 100 in that game and, predictably, we lost.

Again, when Hansie came out with this second offer to chuck a game, I'd like to tell you that my first response was one of shock and horror, but again I'd be lying. The first thought that popped into my head was, 'Well, my mom's house needs to be paid off. I might as well try to make some money.' The consequences of what Hansie was suggesting didn't even enter my head. So I said, 'Okay, cool.'

And just like that I made a decision that would get me into a world of trouble and that I would bitterly regret. It's not like I agonised over the offer for days or had huge dollar signs in my eyes. Typically of me, I make spur-of-the-moment decisions, and sometimes these backfire. I genuinely didn't give it too much thought, as it simply didn't seem like that big a deal. I mean, we were down 1-3 in the five-match series, so it's not like the game meant much either.

And besides, *Hansie* was doing the asking. And Hansie was one of the most together people I'd ever known. If he said throwing the match was cool, it was cool. Hansie then spoke to Henry, who said, 'If Herschy says yes, I'll go along with it too.' The deal was that I would score fewer than 20 runs, and Henry had to bowl so poorly that he would be hit for more than 50 runs in his allotted 10 overs.

Fortunately, I came to my senses …

Before the game started, I began to have second thoughts about the whole affair. It just seemed too risky, even though I didn't really believe that chucking my wicket for less than 20 would have much impact on the game. But I realised that if I was caught, I'd be out of the game for a very long time. Possibly for life … It was just not worth it. I told Hansie how I felt, and he said, 'Don't worry about it, Hersch. Let's just forget about the whole thing.'

With Hansie, you could never tell whether or not he was being serious about something. He was really tough to read. And he was playing this story as if it were a bit of a joke, like it wasn't that big a deal. Like … if we went for it, it was cool; if we didn't go for it, it was also cool.

I ended up scoring 74 off 53 balls in the match, playing a cracker of an innings, with 13 fours and a six. And it wasn't like I was just slogging, either. I played a range of proper cricket shots – drives over cover, controlled pulls and hooks – I basically had a fat jol out there. I remember Indian cricketer Ajay Jadeja (himself later bust for match fixing and banned for five years, though this would be overturned) chirping from slip, 'Hersch, you got a train to catch or what's the story?'

Hansie played a blazing innings as well, really teeing off. He smashed a quick-fire 38 off 28 balls and only got out to an amazing catch by Rahul Dravid at slip. Henry Williams, who had obviously also decided to bin the whole match-throwing idea, injured himself after one over and didn't bowl again in that game, so he was also in the clear.

We ended up scoring 320 and then bowling India out for 310 in an entertaining game. And that, I thought, was that. I reckoned I'd had a small brush with a nasty part of cricket, but that it was probably small potatoes. Thankfully I'd passed on the offer, and I subsequently never gave it another thought.

That is, until 7 April 2000, when news broke that Delhi's Chief of Police, KK Paul, was charging Hansie, Nicky Bojé, Henry Williams, Pieter Strydom and Herschelle Gibbs with match fixing. Indian police were allegedly in possession of 14 taped phone conversations between Hansie and Delhi-based Indian bookie Sanjeev Chawla, discussing match fixing. And my name apparently came up several times in these conversations.

Hansie called me the next day and told me to deny everything. He was such a great captain and leader, everyone was in awe of him, and it was very difficult to say no when he asked you to do something – which was how I got myself into this bladdy mess to start with. I agreed with Hansie's request and kept my mouth shut.

I received similar advice from the head of the United Cricket Board of South Africa, the much respected Dr Ali Bacher. Of course he knew nothing about what had gone down in India, but he also told me to save my statements for an official inquiry, should one be opened. Under Hansie's instructions, I also denied any knowledge of match fixing to Dr Bacher.

As it began to emerge that the taped telephone conversations actually existed and pointed to match fixing in international cricket, the King Commission was set up in Cape Town to investigate the allegations against Hansie. Along with Hansie, Nicky, Henry, Pieter and I would be called before the commission to answer its questions. I was to appear before Justice Edwin King and Chief Prosecutor Shamila Batohi on 8 June.

To put it plainly, I was shitting myself. Hansie kept in touch during this time, wanting to know if I had spoken to anybody about the matter. And obviously every Tom, Dick and Harry was asking me questions. I kept my mouth firmly shut, though. I even denied everything to my much-trusted manager, Donné Commins, and my lawyer, Peter Whelan.

But in those months leading up to the King Commission, denying the truth took its toll on me. During a round of golf at the King David Golf Club in Cape Town I got a really bad migraine for the first time in my life. It was so bad I vomited on the course, and at one hole I chucked my club into a tree. I was so frustrated, I snapped my four-iron. Threw my toys completely. Obviously my actions and symptoms were all stress-related. In fact, the whole match-fixing episode was the most stressful time I have ever experienced. Knowing that I was consistently lying, week in and week out, wasn't nice at all. Ja, I had months of sleepless nights worrying about this thing.

Although Hansie and I had decided that we would deny everything, eventually I couldn't do so any longer. As I said, the stress was really getting to me. I remember sitting down with teammate Mark Boucher at the Long Street Café in Cape Town about a week before the King Commission was due to start and, over a bottle of Jack Daniel's, we had a long chat about what I should do.

When the whole drama had initially broken, Bouch phoned me to say that Hansie had also approached him and Jacques Kallis to take bribes to underperform, so he knew what was going on. Bouch didn't hold back. 'Hersch,' he implored, 'if you lie, you could go to jail.' And that's when I decided to come clean.

Right then I phoned Donné and Peter and told them to come to the Long Street Café … And I told them everything. I'm pretty sure that Donné knew all along that I was hiding something – I don't think there's anyone who knows me as well as she does. She took the news quite well, as she always does when I have to tell her about my latest indiscretion. She was just relieved that I was finally telling the truth. I'd had about two or three meetings with Peter before this as well and, following Hansie's instructions to keep denying everything, I had basically just lied in response to all his questions. I think Peter also knew that I wasn't being honest, and I felt pretty shit about it. I knew I had to be truthful, but I was being as plainly dishonest as one could get. Of course, in the back of my mind was also the knowledge that if I lied in front of the King Commission and was found out, I would probably be banned from cricket for life.

After my meeting with Donné and Peter, I phoned Hansie to let him know I would be telling the King Commission the full story. I would tell the commission how he had put the offer to me and Henry, and that we had initially accepted it, but that we had then changed our minds. I said I would also talk about the offer he had made to the whole team in 1996.

To his credit, Hansie wasn't angry or bitter. He simply said, 'Okay, fine. I understand.' I think that by this time Hansie had resigned himself to the fact that the only thing for him to do would be to tell the truth. Despite what he had done, I knew Hansie to be a very principled man. The guilt must have been eating away at him. In his testimony before the King Commission, Hansie admitted that he had received US$140 000 from Indian bookies, including the infamous MK Gupta, between 1996 and 2000. He denied, though, that he had conspired to fix any matches.

Once I had admitted the truth, Peter and I sat down to prepare for the commission. I felt a great sense of relief as I gave Pete all the details of what had happened. It was like a burden was being lifted off my shoulders. We must have got together three or four times before I was due to appear before the commission, and with Pete's help I felt confident that I could answer any questions Prosecutor Batohi would have for me.

What I didn't really expect was the hype around the hearing on the day that I was scheduled to appear. I had woken up feeling really nervous that morning, and seeing the number of reporters and photographers waiting outside the building just amped me up even more. I had managed to make it to Peter's offices relatively unseen, but walking from his office to the court, man, that was another story. The number of reporters and cameras outside the courthouse was just scary. And then I walked into the courtroom and it was packed to the rafters. It was full, full, full – 10 rows deep. I was so nervous I couldn't even take the oath properly. When they said, 'Please raise your right hand,' I put up my left hand.

Shamila Batohi had a pretty hard-core reputation, and she now also had a very public platform on which to make her name. Surprisingly, though, she didn't come at me quite as hard as we expected. Peter had also prepared me well, though. There was one key question that Peter and I knew would be coming and it was crucial that I get the answer right. It wasn't a matter of lying, but just of making sure that I used the correct words.

Peter, though, was really worried that I might get the words wrong, as I was so nervous. As it turned out, I absolutely nailed the answer. I was very happy with how I conducted myself in the end. The way in which I gave my answers was both honest and professional. The toughest thing by far was apologising to everyone on worldwide TV – I would never like to be in a similar position again. I couldn't stop the tears …

As you can well imagine, it was a huge relief to get the interrogation behind me and escape to Advocate Mike Fitzgerald's chambers. Straight away, I had a shot of whisky and a cigarette. Hansie was there too. He was wearing this really awful tie with ducks on it. I said, 'Jeez, bru, the amount of money you've got and you still bought a tie with fucking ducks on?' Hansie packed up laughing. He then apologised again for getting me into this mess, but I told him not to worry; we were both to blame.

After hearing testimony from other players and Hansie himself, proceedings wrapped up. On 28 August, the UCB announced that Henry Williams and I would be banned from playing international cricket for six months. Henry was fined R10 000 and I was fined R60 000. But that was nothing compared to Hansie's punishment. On 11 October, the UCB announced that Hansie was banned from playing and coaching cricket for life. Naturally I wasn't happy with my sentence – not only did I not take any money or try to influence a game, I couldn't quite work out why I had been fined substantially more than Henry.

Sixty thousand rand was a lot of money, but nothing compared with what I would lose by not playing for six months. Under the circumstances, I guess I can understand the UCB's desire to make an example of us.

As Donné pointed out to me in no uncertain terms, I could've been banned for life, and then I would've been well and truly – sorry, again there's only one word for it – fucked. 'Just accept the sentence and say thank you,' said Donné. 'And apologise, obviously.'

While I was expecting a monetary fine, getting banned for six months meant I *really* lost out on a lot of money. So, ja – it was a little harsher than I'd anticipated, but I could handle it. Which is what a well-thought-out punishment should be, I suppose.

Those next six months were both good and bad; bad because it was quite embarrassing to go out in public. The match-fixing saga had turned into something way bigger than I could have possibly conceived, and it's not easy knowing that you have let your teammates, your family and your friends down. The upside was that I got to play a lot of golf, which helped keep my mind occupied. I reckon during those first three weeks I probably played golf for 19 days. It really helped to get me hooked on the sport.

Fortunately I was banned only from playing international cricket, so I could still play for my domestic team, Western Province – or the Cape Cobras, as we're now known. It would help make the transition back into the international arena a lot easier than if I hadn't played any cricket at all. Graham Ford was the Proteas coach then, and he remains one of my favourites. He's a very low-key, chilled coach, and I never got the feeling during my ban, from either him or the UCB, that they would shun me once the ban was over. As soon as the six months were up, I was invited back into the fold and the guys were genuinely happy to see me again.

Still, it took a couple of months for me to settle in at that level of cricket again. Fortunately my first Test back, in January 2001, was at Newlands against Sri Lanka. I was very happy to play in front of my home crowd that day, but the first morning was still nerve-wracking. We would bat first, and I wondered what kind of reception I could expect. Thankfully the crowd was great – I got the odd chirp, but it wouldn't be Newlands without it, now would it?

However, I didn't score any runs, as I was just too anxious. It reminded me of the day I'd made my debut for Province at 16 – I couldn't feel my legs walking onto the field, I was so nervous. This time, I lasted three balls before getting bowled by Chaminda Vaas for a duck. Not great, but at least I was back playing international cricket. My teammates all scored big runs, and we declared on 504/7. It was enough to thrash the Sri Lankans by an innings and 229 runs.

For me, the match-fixing saga didn't end with the King Commission and my re-admission to international cricket, though. The Chief of Police in Delhi, KK Paul, had publicly stated that if I ever visited India again, I would be brought in for questioning, and he could not guarantee that I would not be arrested. With the Proteas scheduled to tour India in 2004, this obviously posed something of a problem. On Peter's advice I took the safe route and asked the selectors to leave me out of the squad. Fortunately, they were very understanding about it all.

But after I had to decline playing in the 2005 ODI series in India as well, the UCB wanted to know whether the time had not come for me to consider finding another solution. I knew

I couldn't go on refusing to tour India. Prior to the 2006 ICC Champions Trophy – the ICC's biggest ODI tournament after the World Cup – which was to be held in India, Peter and I discussed the matter and decided that enough was enough. We'd travel to India and meet the relevant authorities. We initially suggested that we meet on neutral territory outside India, but they didn't bite. To India I would have to go. And, thankfully, Peter would be with me.

Before the meeting, Peter had been in correspondence with KK Paul, and, while he'd told him privately I wouldn't be arrested, the Indians would not put this in writing.

The plan was for Peter and me to fly to Mumbai, where we'd join the Proteas team, and then fly to Delhi the next morning for the meeting. Our flight to India was via Dubai, and Peter spent about eight of those flying hours coaching me on the upcoming grilling I was sure to get. Remember that the King Commission had been five years earlier and we knew the Indians would be looking for any discrepancies between my testimony back then and what I would say to them now. I've got to hand it to my lawyer, by the time we got to Mumbai I was once again 100 per cent up to speed.

Still, I was very nervous about the upcoming questioning. This was India. It's a long way away – and a very different place – from South Africa. That became apparent as soon as we landed in Mumbai. It was around dawn and the arrivals area was pretty deserted. We got our bags, walked over to the guy at the customs area, who promptly snapped to attention, saluted, and very enthusiastically said, 'Welcome to India, Mr Gibbs!' And that was just the start of the kind of attention my visit to India attracted.

Peter and I walked outside … and straight into around 1 000 members of the press – photographers, TV crews and journos. This was 6 a.m. in the morning. It really threw me, and even though we were met by our team manager, Goolam Rajah, and one of the team's security guards, Faizal (fantastic oke), I was pretty spooked. With Faizal on point guard, we basically had to shoulder charge our way to the car. It all really drove home the fact that it didn't matter how well I knew my shit, I was still going to be facing what appeared to be some very fired-up Indian fellows.

Now, given that I would be flying to Delhi the next morning, you'd have thought I probably had an early night to leave myself fresh and ready for battle, right? Ja. No.

I proceeded to get absolutely smashed at a bar around the corner from the Taj Hotel, where we were staying.

In the bar, I apparently became closely acquainted with a very friendly German girl, and she and I indulged in a little tonsil hockey right there in front of the other patrons. I say 'apparently', because I don't remember any of it. Faizal had witnessed the scene. 'That was one serious show you put on for us in the bar last night,' Faizal said on the aeroplane the morning after. I was like, 'What are you talking about?' This, by the way, was after Faizal had to just about break down my hotel-room door to wake me up. I managed to have a quick shower and get on the plane in time.

Faizal told me that apparently I had also arranged to meet the girl back at the Taj Hotel's nightclub, but when she pitched up – who knows why – I had ignored her. The girl broke down in tears. (If this book ever gets translated into German and she reads it, I hereby apologise for my rude behaviour.)

Pete had taken one look at me that morning – no doubt he was smelling me too … it gets hot in India – and said, 'Hersch, have some bladdy breakfast, and catch an hour's sleep. That's going to help you way more than us going over this stuff again.'

The South African High Commissioner in Delhi, Francis Moloi, met us at the airport – I think the Indians were pretty taken aback when I turned up with both my lawyer *and* the High Commissioner! – and we pulled up outside the Delhi police head-quarters to a throng of media that made our little reception party at Mumbai airport look like a genteel Hare Krishna celebration. Peter reckons there must've easily been more than 3 000 press people there. I was hustled inside to see KK Paul, who had been my Indian nemesis for the past six years. 'Hello, Mr Gibbs,' he said. 'I'm a big fan of yours.' Not exactly the reception I had been expecting from him!

He offered me some tea, and the two of us spent the next 10 minutes talking about cricket and the interrogation that would take place later. Not that he attended that either. Here was the guy who'd basically made his career out of me – the case was high profile and often reported on in the media, which had made KK Paul something of a big deal and had resulted in several promotions for him – yet he wasn't even going to question me!

After our tea and chat, I was taken to an adjacent building – an officer's mess, I believe – where a four-man panel, headed by the joint commissioner of the Delhi Police Crime Branch, Ranjit Narayan, bombarded me with questions for about three hours. I was in a chair, with Peter behind me, and four individuals sat behind a desk facing me. It was a hostile situation, make no mistake, and it wasn't helped by the fact that I'd publicly said Commissioner Narayan was 'hard-arsed'. The commissioner wasn't happy about that at all, and he even brought it up during questioning. I had to apologise. His arse was not hard after all.

The Indian authorities had already banned quite a few of their country's players, so they were obviously taking the whole match-fixing affair seriously. It was clear from the start that they wanted to have a go at me, and they did. During the game in which I was supposed to go out for less than 20, I'd almost gone out on 18, which they were alleging was proof that I was trying to fulfil the conditions of the bribe. Ja, they were interrogating me thoroughly, to the extent that one of the guys – a tough-looking old Sikh gentleman who headed up Delhi's Murder and Robbery team – said, 'Sir, you had better come clean. We still have the death penalty here.'

Nice.

Needless to say, Peter jumped in with both feet and threatened to end the meeting right there if they tried this kind of intimidatory tactic.

While I couldn't be 100 per cent confident that the interview would turn out okay – I was in a foreign country and not sure of their agenda – I reckoned I had all my bases covered. I went into the interview knowing that I would be completely honest and that I would say exactly what I had said at the King Commission. My interviewers obviously had the transcript of my testimony to the King Commission with them, and they were clearly hoping that I'd say something contradictory to what I'd said before. They also seemed to be fishing for the names of other Indian players or bookies whom I might accidentally implicate.

Fortunately I was on top of my game and, according to Pete, answered their questions even better than I did the King Commission's. What, by the way, Pete 'neglected' to tell me (notice how I'm giving him the benefit of the doubt here) is that he had a full legal team on standby if the Indian police did arrest me. He'd got the top legal firm in Delhi on full alert just in case. And that's exactly why Pete is my lawyer.

Some of the questions were completely irrelevant. I mean, completely off the topic – probably a tactic to throw me and make me lose focus. But I just answered as honestly as I could and repeated exactly what I had told the King Commission. Interestingly, when Pete asked any questions about the mysterious audio tapes of Hansie that had started this whole investigation, Narayan would duck and dive. Needless to say, no tapes were produced at this meeting. At the end of it all, Pete shook Commissioner Narayan's hand and said, 'If you still need to question us after this, you can do so any time.' We haven't heard a word from them since.

The press were waiting for me outside, but Faizal was great and made sure I got into the car without being hassled. Straight afterwards, Peter and I went for lunch with the High Commissioner. Of course we had some butter chicken – my staple diet in

India – and a bottle of wine. Ja, something of a staple diet as well, I guess. I was relieved that the whole drama with India was now over, but it would still take a while before I could put the whole episode truly behind me.

Of course, it didn't help that Narayan then held a press conference after our meeting, where he hinted that I had implicated more Proteas players in the whole drama. We first got wind of this at the above-mentioned lunch when Peter got a call from Hansie's lawyer, Leslie Sackstein, who wanted to know what the hell I had said. It was pure political opportunism on Narayan's part – clearly the guy was looking for as much media mileage as he could get. Certainly the meeting he was talking about was a very different one from the meeting Peter and I had just attended.

The next day, once we were back in Mumbai, Pete got the Proteas together to tell them what had really gone down in front of that police panel. His reassurance worked and my teammates and I could finally get on with what we do best: play cricket. Even that, though, was tougher than I anticipated. The whole affair preyed on my mind a little during the ICC Champions Trophy over the next couple of weeks.

To this day I'm not sure whether the King Commission managed to uncover everything. As I've mentioned, when the story first broke, Mark Boucher revealed that Hansie had also once approached some of the other players, Bouchie included. And that came as news to me. This was happening right under my nose and I wasn't even aware of it.

Is it still going on in cricket today? Unfortunately, looking at the fun and games that have gone on with the Pakistan team in England recently, it seems that it's still around. It doesn't totally surprise me, to be honest. I've watched a couple of games on the subcontinent and I've had my suspicions. But I obviously can't be sure. Match fixing has certainly not come up in any team I have been a part of since Hansiegate.

One thing I do know for sure, and that is that it is impossible to fix a game without having 90 per cent of the team in on the deal.

You could get a player to underperform in order to influence a particular spread bet, as allegedly happened with Messrs Asif, Amir and Butt, but as for fixing an entire game, no way. When we were asked to chuck that game in 1996, Hansie had an actual plan on how we would go about it – targets would be set, right down to what the score had to be and how many wickets had to be down by a certain over. That's the level of strategising required, and that's why the majority of the team's buy-in is necessary.

But there's not a chance of that happening now.

Apart from the fact that players are just not prepared to risk their careers – and remember, these days, with tournaments like the Indian Premier League, we make a *lot* more money than we did a decade ago – the ICC's anti-corruption laws make it practically impossible for players to fix a game. Players are not allowed to use their cellphones at stadiums any more, they no longer share rooms with their teammates, and the ICC has special security personnel present at all games to ensure that everything stays above board.

One could say, if one looked at it from a different angle, that if it weren't for Hansie and me, those security guys wouldn't have jobs, nor would the players have the luxury of their own rooms! At least some good things emerged from the whole sorry mess.

Weed in the Windies

The Proteas were to tour the West Indies for the first time in 2001. Although the Proteas had played a few ODIs and one Test in the West Indies in 1992, this was the first full-blown South African cricket tour to the islands. You could say that it was a fairly big deal.

Shaun Pollock was the Proteas captain, and when we got to Antigua for the fourth Test, we were leading the series 1-0, with two to play. By the fourth day of the Test, it was already clear that we were going to win the match and, therefore, the series. We just needed a few wickets on the last day, and that would be it – we would have beaten the West Indies in their own backyard.

So, sitting in the changing room at the end of that fourth day, enjoying a few beers with the guys, I suggested that perhaps it might be fun – not to mention highly appropriate – for us to celebrate the sheer momentousness of the occasion by partaking of the local herb. Neil McKenzie was like, 'Great idea! Great idea! Let's do it.' Obviously we had had a few toots by then, and pretty much all the guys were keen to smoke some of Antigua's finest, A-grade marijuana.

As it happened, our liaison officer – the local man who looked after us – was nicknamed 'Smokey'. Seriously. We never knew him by any other name. Great guy too. Anyway, so Roger Telemachus, the Proteas bowler and a good mate of mine, was really keen on the idea. I remember him saying, 'I'm going to smoke the fattest spliff if we win tomorrow.'

So anyway, we had a few more drinks and the idea took root and grew some lovely green leaves. Later, on the bus on the way back to the hotel, I had a quiet word with old Smokey: 'Smokey, what are the chances of organising us some weed? We're probably going to win tomorrow and the boys want to partake.' All he said was, 'Cool.'

Smokey was very cool.

The next day, as we walked into the changing room for the final day's play and the formalities of victory, true to his promise, I saw Smokey standing there with a big plastic bag ... and it was just bulging with weed. A whole bunch of loose heads and five already-rolled, fat joints. I had the biggest grin on my face, but I also didn't want the coach or any of the support staff – or Polly – to see it, so I quickly put it in my bag.

So now I'm sitting through the whole of the last day with The Shit in my bag. We end up winning the Test and now have a 2-0 lead with only one more Test to play. In other words, we have the series (and The Shit) in the bag. (We ended up losing the final Test, but I'm pretty sure our little game of Pass the Reefer did not influence the outcome of the match.) Anyway, so there was one very happy vibe in the changing room after our win. It was basically carnage, actually. The selectors were celebrating, our good friends Jack Daniel and Charles Glass were present … ja, the guys were getting properly hammered.

I was so keen to get goofed that I wanted to light up right there and then, but Roger said, 'Whoa! No man, are you nuts, bru? We can't smoke it in the changing room in front of the selectors! We'll take it back to the hotel.'

Everyone was still in tremendous spirits on the bus back to the hotel, and now we wanted to have a bit of a smoke. A few of the guys who had been really keen the day before – like McKenzie and a couple of others – decided that they weren't going to go through with it after all. Fair enough. The rest of us were committed, though. There was me, Roger, Paul Adams, André Nel, Justin Kemp and our physio, Craig Smith.

I've got The Shit, we're all very keen on a toke or three, and all we need now is a venue. Craig Smith always had his own private room, where he could treat the players. Perfect. Besides, we were all firm believers in alternative medicine. By now it was probably around six or seven in the evening, and by the time we eventually got to the treatment room, I was already flying, thanks to some bourbon.

Time to lock the doors and light up. I decided to have one of the joints all on my own, but some of the ous were too scared to inhale the stuff properly. Roger and I, however, decided to give it a proper crack. Pretty soon, we were *finished*. I mean, it was the first – and would be the only – time I ever smoked the stuff. So ja, I was blitzed. I just made it back to my hotel room, where my girlfriend at the time was waiting.

The team was supposed to meet back at the bar, but I was too high … I never made it out of my room. I remember knocking and knocking on our hotel room door and just laughing myself stupid. She looked at me weirdly and innocently asked, 'Why are you laughing so much? What? Have you been smoking something?' She always did have a great sense of humour.

It had been great fun nonetheless, and, even though we got bust, I wouldn't have swapped the thrill of celebrating a win over the Windies in Antigua by smoking a joint for anything. But, ja, we did get bust. And this is how it happened ...

The whole story came out a few days later when, during a two-day game in Montego Bay, Daryll Cullinan and Roger Telemachus had this huge altercation. The two of them had never really seen eye to eye, and neither of them ever backed down for anybody ... especially Roger. That guy did not take a step back, ever.

I was doing twelfth-man duties during the Montego Bay game – never a favourite way to spend my time.

So we're all sitting in the changing room during one of the breaks – I don't recall whether it was the lunch or tea break – and Roger breaks wind. At which Daryll completely loses his marbles. I mean, Roger just *farted*. Sure, it might have been loud and lengthy, and not at all pleasant on the nose, but all of us were laughing. Except Daryll. Who knows why? Daryll is Daryll. I've never understood or liked the guy. I'm a pretty easy-going individual and I got along with most of my former Proteas teammates, but Daryll wasn't one of them.

Daryll had been my very first roommate on my maiden tour with the Proteas in 1996 for the Kenyan Cricket Association's Centenary tournament in Nairobi, which would be my very first games for the team. So I'm sharing a room with Daryll, and his wife Virginia – they're now divorced – phones him and he isn't in the room. So I say, 'Virginia, I'll give Daryll the message. I'm sure he'll get back to you soon.'

Anyway, Daryll comes back to the room and I give him the message. After an hour or so, I asked him if he's remembered to phone his wife. All he said was, 'Fuck off. It's got nothing to do with you.'

It just blew me right out of the water – I mean, I was basically just covering his back, you know? And since that day I've never liked him. He has my respect as a cricketer, but that's where it ends. It's obviously tricky when you are teammates. You just stay out of each other's way and never really engage too much. The shit thing, though, is when you have to bat with the guy! I mean, you're out there in the middle and the oke hits a bladdy four and you don't really like him … now you have to say 'good shot', and you know – and he knows – that you don't really mean it.

Personality clashes are bound to happen, I suppose. Everybody can't always get on with everyone else.

Anyway, back to the fart in Montego Bay. Daryll and Roger were having a proper go at each other – we're talking a nose-to-nose altercation here. (Ironic, now that I think about it, given that Roger was the source of the smell to which Daryll was taking such great exception.) Roger ended up shoving Daryll, and the floor was covered in really slippery tiles, so Daryll went flying into some chairs. Not good. By now he was apoplectic with rage and stormed out of the changing room, shouting, 'That's it! Fuck this! I'm not going back on the field.' And he went straight to Goolam.

Goolam Rajah was, and still is, the Proteas' much-respected team manager. So Daryll stormed back to the hotel, which meant I had to go and field. 'Cool,' I thought. 'This is better than being twelfth man.'

What wasn't cool, though, was what Daryll apparently did next. We subsequently heard that he had told Goolam that he wanted to pack his bags, as he was tired of this team … and, by the way, they were smoking marijuana in the physio's room a few nights ago.

Ja …

So, we got back to the hotel after the day's play, and The Shit had hit the fan. The team was asked to assemble in the team room, where we were told that management had been notified of a certain incident that had taken place in the physio's room, and would the guilty parties please stand up. Daryll had sold us out. Most of the guys knew we'd had a couple of spliffs – I don't know if Polly knew, as he was the captain, but the rest all knew.

But Daryll was the one who had squealed because he had had an altercation with Roger. He might only have wanted to get even with Roger, but the rest of us got nailed too. I was still on a suspended sentence from the match-fixing drama at the time, so I got fined R10 000. The other guys were fined five grand or thereabouts. All in all, one of the more expensive farts Roger had ever let rip.

Still, I look back on the whole pungent episode rather fondly. You know, 'when in Rome' … It was the only time I ever smoked weed; I've never needed to do it again. I had just thought, well, it's a one-off thing. We've won the series, so we might as well celebrate in true Caribbean style.

I don't have any regrets. But we were obviously all pissed off with Daryll, because if it hadn't been for him, nothing would have come of it. But, ja, it was quite funny. The locals certainly found it bladdy amusing, as everyone smokes the stuff there, even though it's illegal.

While we're on the subject, and in case you're wondering, you should know that while alcohol is available all over the show, recreational drugs are not part of the cricket scene at all – especially now. Back then there weren't so many drug tests, but these days you probably pee into a test tube more often than you do into the toilet bowl. The rules are also a lot stricter on what we can and cannot use.

The guys tend to get the doctor's clearance first before they take or use anything. It's just not worth it to take any chances. Obviously many of us love a few drinks, and quite a few of us smoke the odd cigarette, but I certainly don't know of anyone who does drugs. If you test positive for illegal drug use, you are banned for life. No one is stupid enough to take that risk.

The Pakistan racial slur

I may have said and done some things I regret in my life, but calling those particular Pakistani cricket fans a bunch of animals and inviting them to make their way back home was not one of them. The incident occurred during the Proteas' first Test against Pakistan at Centurion Park in 2007.

For some or other reason, the fans – a combination of South Africans and native Pakistanis – were going ape-shit. I've never seen fans misbehave to such an extent at a cricket match. For the first two days they went really crazy, as if they were bladdy possessed. They made a huge noise and even kicked Rashard, my son, and his mom, Liesl, out of their seats when they took over the area next to the pitch entrance that leads up to the changing room, where they wanted to shake hands with, or throw idiotic insults at, the players as they left the field.

All of us Proteas were getting pretty irritated, and unfortunately the stump microphones picked up our displeasure. I was standing at gully, Graeme Smith was at slip and we were both looking at these morons. We agreed that a little verbal retaliation was in order. 'Stop acting like a bunch of fucking animals!' I said. I can't remember what Graeme said.

Then, after the close of play, the team was notified that a complaint of racism had been laid against one of the Proteas. Me. Typical. I mean, we all had had something to say about those supporters on the day, but after listening to the recording, it was decided that mine was the one voice that they could identify. I listened to the recording later, at the hearing, and you could hear Graeme's voice loud and clear. He still laughs about how he got away without being charged to this day. I guess I had to take one for the team.

After the game, match referee Chris Broad called a disciplinary hearing, where I had to appear with Goolam Rajah, our team manager. The Pakistan manager and their captain, Inzamam-ul-Haq, were also in attendance. 'I've had a complaint,' said Chris, opening the proceedings, 'from the Pakistan manager that you've broken one of the clauses in the ICC rules, relating to racist remarks.'

Fortunately, the Proteas management were behind me on this one. You could call me many, many things, but a racist was a bit of a stretch, to say the least. Especially concerning Muslims. I'm coloured, for goodness' sake. I've got four Muslim aunts and about 10 Muslim cousins. How could I be a racist? My damn family is Muslim. Goolam Rajah had echoed my surprise when he first heard what the charge was. 'You've got Muslim family; how can they call *you* a racist?' he asked, aghast. He's good at looking aghast.

Anyway, that was the charge. I couldn't deny that that was my voice on the tape, so I admitted that I'd said those words. I was found guilty, but I did make a point of apologising to the Pakistan captain, Inzy, asking him to convey my apology to the rest of his team. I told him that I had a Muslim family, so they shouldn't believe I was racist. 'Okay, cool,' said Inzy. That's all. He doesn't talk much, does Inzy.

Their manager looked really pissed off, though. He wanted me banned for longer than the sentence eventually handed down. The judgment was a two-match Test ban, which we appealed. The ICC's code of conduct commissioner, Richie Benaud, then changed the ban to one Test, one 20/20 game and one ODI match – all against Pakistan. To be honest, I think it was a tactic aimed at getting me out of the team rather than them being mortally offended by the 'racial' slur. It was a gambit to disrupt the Proteas more than anything else.

Mavericks

A few months after my divorce from Tenielle, and after I had returned to South Africa from playing county cricket in the UK, I attended the launch of a Hugo Boss store at the V&A Waterfront in Cape Town. I knew the Hugo Boss guys pretty well, and a few mates of mine from another Waterfront clothing shop also came to the launch. After a few drinks, a few of us decided – as sometimes happens with a bunch of single guys – that it would make for an entertaining evening if we patronised one of the city's strip clubs.

We first went to the House of Rasputin, but couldn't find anyone there who really whet our appetites. So we decided to try Mavericks. Already well on our way, we got ourselves a little booth and carried on drinking in the company of some very pretty ladies. Many of them had Eastern European accents, as I recall. One of the guys in our group was a chap by the name of Brett Canterbury.

'Brett,' I said, 'come, you and I are going to double up. We are going to go in for a little lap dance.' Both of us were flying by then – it must've been almost 2 a.m., and we were all well past our sell-by-date. My wallet was on the couch next to me. Brett and I were soon on the receiving end of a great exhibition of the art of lap dancing. The girl took off my tie and my waistcoat and just left my shirt on. She undid my pants too.

For the record, I still had my jocks on. Funnily enough, my tie disappeared. When I eventually came out of the cubicle, I was sans tie. I never did figure out what had happened to it. I really liked that tie.

Anyway, so the next day I met another mate of mine for lunch at Col'Cacchio Pizzeria in Camps Bay. I took out my wallet and noticed the credit-card slip of the previous evening … R6 000. This was a helluva lot, but the guys and I had had a great time and, as I often do, I had picked up the tab. 'Phew,' I said to my mate. 'I was out with a couple of buddies at Mavericks last night. Top evening, but it was a little pricey. I really need to stop picking up the bill all the time.'

Then I noticed *another* credit-card slip from Mavericks for … wait for it … R15 000. Fifteen grand, I kid you not. I got the fright of my life. There was no way I would've knowingly dropped that kind of cash.

As I've mentioned, there's only one person I call when I've landed in the shit, and that's my long-suffering manager, Donné. Something definitely smelt off here. Besides the fact that I would not have spent so much, I would also not have spent so much in such a short space of time. On the R6 000 tab, the time read 02h30. But on the R15 000 tab, the time was 03h15. I mean, how do you spend 15K at a strip club in 45 minutes? All we'd had were drinks and a lap dance.

Donné and I decided that the only thing to do was to get hold of the two credit-card slips and check out the signatures on both. We spoke to Mavericks' accountant on the phone, and she faxed us both slips. It was clear that the 02h30 tab's signature was mine. My handwriting is very distinct and I can be drunk out of my head, but I'll still sign it that way. The slip signed at 03h15 was another matter entirely, though. They said that I was so hammered that I could barely write, which was why the signature looked so odd.

'Ma'am,' I said – I was very polite – 'I've got a very unique signature. Have a look at it – that can't have been signed by my hand.'

I could only come up with one explanation: one of the dancers had taken my card during the lap dance, while my wallet was lying next to me, and she had swiped and signed it. They found out who the girl was, but they still insisted that I had signed the tab. There was no way they were going to pay me back the money.

We got my bank to send someone around to Mavericks to investigate the alleged fraud and the next step for us would have been to sue. However, Donné's advice was to let it go – she didn't think the money was worth the energy or the negative publicity. Wise counsel once again. We therefore decided to drop the matter. But the incident left a very bitter taste in my mouth.

It also wasn't over yet.

True to form – as you will have read, earlier actions of mine have a nasty habit of returning to bite me on the arse – a year and a half later I opened a daily newspaper to see a grainy picture of me enjoying that very lap dance. It turned out that Mavericks had fired one of its bouncers, and before the guy left, he'd helped himself to a whole lot of their CCTV footage. He then gave extracts of the footage to the newspapers as a way of getting back at his former employers. As I was a well-known public figure, he'd selected images of me, and my name was once again dragged through the mud. There's no doubt in my mind that the only reason Mavericks still had that footage was in case I decided to sue them. They would normally destroy CCTV footage after a shorter period of time.

What really angered me, though, was not that this guy had taken the footage and given it to the press, but that the paper had published it. I had just come out of rehab, and this kind of publicity was the last thing I needed. It was not as if it had happened recently – it had happened 18 bladdy months earlier. I've taken a lot on the chin from the press, and most of it was deserved, but this felt like pure opportunism on their part. They were looking for something scandalous so that they could sell newspapers, and they used me. If you're looking for an example of irresponsible journalism, this is it.

Right. I think that's enough *skandaal* for one book. Time to talk a little cricket. Coming up next is a highlights reel that has more to do with bat and ball than having a ball …

7

The big games

These are the games that will always loom large in my personal recollections of a colourful career. Some for good reasons ... some for bad.

When it comes to high-pressure games, I've always done pretty well. My World Cup average is 56.15 from 23 innings, which I reckon proves my ability to handle the unique pressures of a big game. I'm not entirely sure why I am good at handling these types of games – it's probably a combination of factors. I know I like the glamour that accompanies the big occasion. And I like being on the big stage and in the spotlight. Or perhaps I was just born with the ability to handle pressure.

Sure, I do get a little nervous, but even at school I was always amped to play in front of the crowds on the big occasions. I remember a couple of pretty big rugby games when I was in the Bishops First XV. Some guys in the team would be talking about the size of the crowd while biting their nails, whereas I was like, 'Bring it on, boet!'

I remember playing rugby for the SA Schools team against Nampak Schools (basically the SA Schools B-team) as a curtain-raiser before the Springboks took on Australia in 1992. It was a capacity crowd at Newlands and the atmosphere was awesome. I absolutely loved it. Big crowds, all the razzmatazz – I love that sort of thing.

Funnily enough, though, when it comes to semis and finals, I tend to play within myself. Again, I don't know why, but I am not as flashy in those games. I become a little more circumspect and apply a little more *kop*. I also tend to be a little less instinctive. But once I'm 'in' in a final, I genuinely feel I can run the show. I guess some people can handle pressure and others can't. And if you are one of those who *can* handle it, then you have to do what it takes to get the team through.

The question you're probably asking is: If that kind of strategy has worked for me successfully in pressure games, why haven't I applied it to all the other games I've played? Fact is, I'm an instinctive type of player who just goes out and plays. I don't think too much about what I am doing once I'm out there, to be honest. Sometimes I play a shot and I don't know why I'm playing it. No idea. I just play it.

Indian batsman Virender Sehwag is similar in his approach, and he's one of the highest-scoring batsmen in Test and ODI cricket in recent years. He only knows one way to play, and that's his way. His game is either going to come off or it's not, whether it is a Test match or an ODI. He's not going to change his approach from one match to another. I mean, the guy doesn't know how to play himself in – he just blasts away from ball one.

Chris Gayle and Brendon McCullum are the same, as were Adam Gilchrist and Matthew Hayden when they were playing Test cricket. They don't have the finesse of a Sachin Tendulkar, but what they do have are terrific timing and a great eye. They just go out there and murder the ball.

I've got to tell you, it's a *great* feeling when you know that today everything is going to come together and you are going to smash the ball all over the place. In the Proteas 2009 tour to Australia, for example, Mark Boucher came up to me during the third ODI at the Sydney Cricket Ground and said, 'Hersch, entertain us tonight. We're chasing 270, and no one's chased down 270 at Sydney before.' And I was like, 'Yes, Bouchie, I do believe I'll be playing a few shots today.'

So I went out with that mindset. I played myself in for the first over or two, and then, after I mishit a drive to the fielder at point, who promptly dropped it, I said to myself, 'Okay, boet, this is your cue. Now you've got to play shots.' Shaun Tait was running in, and the next minute I'm walking up the pitch and popping the ball back over his head for a one-bouncer. The SCG is a big ground, and Tait wasn't bowling slow either – around 149 km/h – and I was just like, *bang*! So I thought, okay, cool, we're starting to get going here. The next ball, I ran down at him again and again hit the ball straight over his head for another one-bounce four. And I just took off from there. I ended up getting 64 in no time at all.

Looking back over my career, these are the games that stand out the most for me …

My first 100 for South Africa

I got my first 100 against New Zealand, during the second Test in Christchurch, in 1999. And I owe it to Gary Kirsten. It happened in the first innings, and I remember being exceptionally focused that day. I didn't play too many loose shots, left balls very well and just played within my strengths.

By then I'd been playing Test cricket for nearly three years and this was my 24th Test. My highest score up till then had been a 54 against the Aussies in Sydney the year before. That day, for some reason, Gary's advice just clicked with me. I mean, we weren't really talking much at the wicket – we never really did – but Gary just kept me focused, telling me what he thought the bowler was trying to do and what the wicket was doing. We kept it simple. From that perspective, I really enjoyed Gary. He was a great thinker.

I not only got a 100 … I turned it into a double: 211 not out. I guess I've never been one to do things in half-measures, have I? I always did like ordering doubles. Actually, I probably could have made more that day, but rain interrupted play and we declared. Jacques Kallis and I set up a 300-run partnership that day – he got 148 not out, if I remember correctly.

Unfortunately, though, almost 90 overs of that Test were lost to rain. The Black Caps had batted first and we'd skittled them for 168 – we then declared on 442/1 and had them at 127/1 before the match was declared a draw.

My first Test 100 at Newlands

My first Test century at my home ground will always be special to me. Not just because I finally scored a 100 there – in the second Test against Pakistan in 2003, so it came pretty late in my Test career – but I turned it into a double again, scoring 228. It was my highest Test score and, after Kiwi Stephen Fleming's 262 against the Proteas in 2006, the second-highest Test score ever at Newlands.

I don't really know why it took me so long to get a Test 100 at my home ground. I had obviously always felt some pressure playing in front of my home crowd, and the expectation for me to do well is higher there than anywhere else. Still, nothing gives me more pleasure than scoring runs in front of the Newlands crowd. It's not easy, though – especially in Test cricket – as on the first day the Newlands wicket is always quite lively. In all my innings up till then, I'd either nicked off or done something wrong, and just never got going.

But this day, against Pakistan, was different. It was a really good wicket and I was seeing the ball very well. Graeme Smith and I made 360-odd runs for the first wicket. And Pakistan didn't exactly have a weak bowling attack either: Mohammad Sami, Saqlain Mushtaq and a few other seamers. Their legendary quickie, Waqar Younis – though admittedly past his best – was also playing.

But, man, we were blazing hot that day. We almost reached a score of 500 on the first day. We were on about 410 when I finally went out. I think there were only 11 or 13 overs left before the close of play. So, ja, it was special.

The 1999 World Cup

Of all my performances, I'm probably the proudest of my World Cup record. And of all those innings, I reckon my best was in a Super Six game against the Aussies at Leeds during the 1999 World Cup. I played a really well-paced and composed knock – the wicket was good, and I played within myself in that innings. Nothing flashy, just percentage shots, and I went on to get 101 before Glenn McGrath bowled me.

It's funny, but when I'd woken up that morning, the first thing that popped into my mind was that I was going to score a 100. I just knew I was going to get a century. Perhaps the girl lying in bed beside me had inspired me. She worked at the hotel, where I had befriended her. I guess she was my lucky charm – she certainly was when it came to my batting. I just wish her powers had extended to my fielding and the bladdy 'dropped catch' …

For seven or eight months leading up to the tournament, I'd got into the habit of immediately throwing the ball away right after I'd caught it and got someone out. Some people thought my action was a sign of arrogance, but for me it was more about confidence … making the catch look easy. I celebrated in this way. I back myself to take every catch that comes my way, no matter how tough. And, ja, sometimes with the really easy ones I did make a bit of a meal of it, which is what I did that day. I caught the ball and quickly threw it away.

But this time, the umpires thought I hadn't had the ball under control before I tossed it and ruled it a dropped catch. But I have honestly *always* believed that I'd had the ball under control. If you watch the slo-mo replays closely, you can see that I've actually caught the ball. I caught it and chucked it away. That constitutes control in my book. You can even tell that I've caught it by the look on my face. I'm looking over at the Aussie dressing room, wanting to send them the message, 'That's you gone, done and dusted.' From my point of view, I caught the ball … I caught it 100 per cent.

But of course I should not have thrown it away so quickly. And in throwing it away, I dropped it.

I was shocked when the umpires ruled Waugh 'not out'. Seriously shocked. I remember Hansie coming over to me and asking, 'Hersch, did you catch the ball, or what's the story?' I think I was in more shock than anybody else. I remember looking up at the replay on the big screen and seeing that I'd caught the ball, but then had spilt it in my haste to get rid of it.

So, to be on the safe side, I told Hansie, 'No, I dropped it.' It was a major game and there would've been huge drama if I had claimed the catch. It looked like I'd dropped it, but I knew I had had that ball under control. Looking back now, obviously I should have held it for another second before throwing it in the air. Steve Waugh would've walked back to the dressing room, having scored 56 instead of going on to play one of his best one-day innings, scoring 120 not out. At that stage, it was only his second ton (in 266 ODIs).

Then, of course, there's the myth of what Steve Waugh said to me afterwards. Some people claim that he'd said, 'You have just dropped the World Cup,' but, like I've said many times since, I never ever heard him say those words on the field. Perhaps he said it later, at a press conference, but I never heard him say it on the field.

Anyway, Waugh's century helped Australia chase down our total of 271, and they won by five wickets with a couple of balls to spare. And that, of course, meant we had to face them again in the semis. Had we beaten them in the Super Six game, we would have knocked them out of the tournament and we would've had an easier semi. We could have carried that momentum into the final. But, ja, we had to face the Australians again in the semis.

In the semi-final we had to chase a reasonably easy target of 213. Allan and Polly's bowling had been great – Polly took five wickets and Allan four. Gary and I opened our innings, and we were going great guns. Both of us really got hold of Damien Fleming.

Then, with my score on 30, Shane Warne let rip with probably the best ball I've ever faced from a spinner. He was getting a lot of in-drift and turn from the ball, and the length of this delivery was just perfect. I couldn't go 'back to' and I couldn't go 'forward to'. I didn't want to sweep the ball either, because I didn't think it was full enough. The ball was right on the money and caught me playing from the crease. It hit the deck outside leg, spun past my bat and knocked the bail off my off-stump.

I heard their wicketkeeper, Adam Gilchrist, go up, and I remember thinking, 'What the hell's he going on about?' I didn't think there was any way Warne could've bowled me. I mean, I didn't even hear the bails come off! But I turned around and saw that one of the bails *had* come off. The *perfect* ball ... perfect. Warney reckons it's the second-best ball he's ever bowled (the best being the one he bowled to get Mike Gatting in the 1993 Ashes series).

As we all know, this semi-final was one of *the* toughest games South African cricket fans have ever had to watch. After it looked like we were dead and buried, Lance 'Zulu' Klusener brought us back to the brink of victory ... and then that notorious run-out happened. During the game, I couldn't even watch the last 20 overs. I couldn't bear it. I was in the physio room with Nicky Bojé and I looked only at his face for his reactions, while he was watching the telly.

Lance hit two fours in the last over and then almost got run out. And then we did get run out. I mean, our emotions went from rock-bottom to ecstasy and then all the way down again in the space of half a minute!

With the run-out in the last over, the scores were level, which meant that the Australians would go through to the finals, as they had finished higher than us in the earlier Super Six round. I remember the atmosphere in the dressing room afterwards ... you could virtually hear a pin drop for at least ten minutes after coming off the field. No one said a word. We just couldn't believe it.

It was rough. I mean, there's dead silence in our changing room and next door – back then at Edgbaston the changing rooms used to be right next door to each other – they're going bananas. I still haven't asked Zulu or Allan to this day what actually happened out there; it's something I just want to forget.

Our coach Bob Woolmer said a few words, and then Hansie made a speech. He said how proud he was of the way in which we had gone about the match and, you know, I think he was just very, very sad that we had drawn and ended up going out of the tournament. He burst out crying after his speech.

But the 1999 Proteas squad was just a great team – no, a fantastic team. I still think it was the team with which South Africa had the best chance of winning the World Cup. With all those guys in their prime – Donald, Pollock, Kirsten, Klusener, Cullinan, Cronjé – it was a wonderful one-day outfit. The way in which we'd lost that semi-final was just – excuse my language – fucking tragic.

The 2003 World Cup

This game was a totally different story. Eric Simons was now the Proteas coach after taking over from Graham Ford in 2002. Fordie had replaced Bob Woolmer after Bob had resigned in the wake of the dramatic loss discussed above. And then poor Fordie was made the scapegoat for our disastrous tour of Australia in 2001/02, when we were blitzed 0-3 in the Test series.

Anyway, so with Eric now at the helm, things were not looking promising even in the lead-up to the World Cup. We'd lost one or two practice games before the start of the tournament, and there wasn't a hell of a lot of confidence in the camp before our opening game against the West Indies. We tried to make light of our poor performances in those warm-up games, but the fact was that we were a team without proper focus.

The World Cup was being held in South Africa, and, as a result, the team was in constant demand for functions and press calls. There were just too many damn distractions and extra activities throughout the entire tournament, which was one of the reasons the guys would later use as an excuse for our poor performance. Look, I do think they were right, to a certain extent, because there genuinely was a huge demand for our attention, and questions probably did need to be asked of the Proteas management back then. But it didn't really affect me personally. For me, the main problem was that we were just not operating as a team. And it's a problem that has plagued the Proteas ever since. I'll go into more detail in Chapter 10.

I guess some players need to find excuses for poor performances, but I didn't mind how hectic things got. This was a World Cup. Things were supposed to get hectic. I always wanted to play World Cup games, irrespective of how little sleep I got or how busy I was kept between games.

Perhaps some of the team's problems in the 2003 Word Cup stemmed from Shaun Pollock. Polly was one helluva cricketer – one of the best this country has ever had – but he wasn't a natural leader. Certainly not in the way Hansie had been. But to be fair to Shaun, it could not have been easy taking over from Hansie, given the former captain's powerful personality *and* the mess he'd left behind. Polly always led by example on the pitch, but he was a little too distant from his teammates.

Polly was also one for the disciplinarian approach. He was like a teacher in a lot of ways, especially the way he spoke at team meetings. He made me think of school a lot, and I never did very well at school. For Polly, it was all about what happened out in the middle – the actual cricket – and not about getting to know his teammates off the field. I guess he was very professional, but maybe too much so, as he never really came out and partied with us. Polly doesn't drink, but I'd always hoped he would join us socially more often.

Of course it is unfair to lay all the blame at Polly's door, but, fact is, we were not the tight unit we had been under Hansie.

We lost that opening game to the West Indies by three runs – Brian Lara got 116 – which basically set the tone for the rest of our games. One of my personal highlights was smacking 143 off 141 deliveries against New Zealand in a pool game – my third-highest ODI score after making 153 against Bangladesh in 2002, and 175 against the Aussies in 2006's famous 438 game.

Unfortunately, a rain interruption led to a revised target of 226 runs in 39 overs for the Black Caps according to the Duckworth-Lewis method, after we'd posted 306 in our innings. The Kiwi captain, Stephen Fleming, scored 134 after we dropped him when he hadn't got past 20 yet, and we lost the game. We did beat minnows Kenya, Bangladesh and Canada, but so did everyone else, which meant we needed to beat Sri Lanka in our final pool game to go through to the Super Six stage of the tournament. I don't think there's a cricket fan in South Africa who doesn't know what happened next.

What a cock-up.

Batting first at Kingsmead, the Sri Lankans scored 268, after which we seemed to be gunning along nicely. I scored 73, then Mark Boucher came in and was looking strong on 45 ... and then the rain came bucketing down. As we all now know, there was confusion about the revised total set by the Duckworth-Lewis method, and this extended from the dressing room to Mark Boucher out in the middle. With our total on 229, Bouch, thinking we were home safe, blocked the last ball before the umpires called off the game.

But the thing was, we actually needed 230 to win ...

With 229 on the board we only tied the game, and with that we were out of our own World Cup. I'm still not entirely sure how they managed to screw that one up. After all, we knew that the rain was coming. At the start of our innings, we were given a list of revised targets – Eric and Polly had the list – *and* we saw the rain as it started coming down. Nicky Bojé had been dispatched down to the boundary rope to tell Bouch we still needed one more run. For some reason, the umpires didn't allow him onto the field to give Bouch the message, but Nicky was still trying to indicate to him that we needed one more run ... only Bouch thought he meant one more ball to block. Which he promptly did.

Everyone was in complete disbelief in the changing room afterwards. The players pretty much held the coach and the captain responsible for the debacle. But no one could really explain why they hadn't got the right message out to Bouchie.

It was really awful for the team to go out like that – I mean, it was shocking, actually, especially after our previous eliminations from earlier World Cups. The press had an almighty go at us for our decision-making skills, which were not so much poor as they were embarrassing. I was pretty frustrated personally, as I was in good form; I averaged 96 in that tournament. So ja, I was obviously a bit pissed off about it all. It would have been nice to win the World Cup in South Africa.

The 2007 World Cup

No rain excuses here. In the West Indies we just got our arses properly kicked, and this despite a lot of pre-tournament preparation. Mickey Arthur was our coach, and one thing about Mickey: he was always very efficient in his preparation. He not only had a detailed itinerary of when and where we would be practising, but he'd done plenty of research on the conditions we could expect on the islands. All good and proper stuff. We arrived two weeks early for the tournament and spent the time preparing in Trinidad.

Perhaps that was one of the problems for us in that tournament: we spent too much time 'preparing'. The Caribbean is a fantastic place to tour – it's beautiful, with a very chilled-out atmosphere, and you've got plenty of South African supporters around. Understandably, the guys in the team were enjoying themselves. I wouldn't say more drinking than usual was going on, but the guys certainly put back a beverage or two.

That said, the training in those two weeks went really well. The guys were sharp in the warm-up games and all seemed fine. In the group games we thumped everyone, until we got to our nemesis, the Aussies. Clearly looking for some revenge after losing the 438 game, they came out guns blazing and klapped 377, with Matthew Hayden in a particularly vicious mood, hitting 101 off 68 balls. There were some wide-eyed Proteas bowlers that day. We managed 294 in reply.

A couple of the guys had been cramping during the group games, and the press and fans speculated that we were both unfit and overweight. *Sports Illustrated* South Africa published some images of the guys with their kit off playing volleyball and lounging around the pool during some time off, and the shots weren't very flattering. Maybe the photographer had used a wide-angle lens; I don't know. Anyway, the okes in the pictures – Smithy, Kallis, Boucher and Justin Kemp – were really pissed off about the article.

To be honest, I think the fact that they weren't drinking enough fluids to compensate for the heat was the cause of the cramping rather than them being unfit and/or overweight. Some of the guys might not exactly have been lean, but they always passed the fitness bleep tests we were all put through (more about those tests later).

Anyway, so we qualified for the Super Eight phase, where we started blowing a little hot and cold. We beat Sri Lanka – very satisfying after 2003 – Ireland and the West Indies, and we creamed England. But then we lost to New Zealand and suffered a shock defeat against Bangladesh, where I was the only player for South Africa to score any meaningful runs. I got 56 not out in a team total of 184, chasing Bangladesh's 251. Still ... at least we had made the semis. Problem was, we were up against the Aussies again.

The night before the semi-final, we were just trying to be really calm about the whole thing. We had done our analyses and had studied all their strengths and weaknesses. We now had a game plan for how we were going to bowl to each Aussie batsman. We even had separate meetings for the batters and the bowlers. At the batting meeting, as far as I was concerned, the plan was to stick to our assigned tasks calmly and not to try to rush out and score too quickly.

But – and this is the part I find so flipping bizarre – we did *exactly* the opposite. Our top order went bananas, trying to blast the Aussies, and within no time at all we were 27/5. And that was pretty much it. Game over. Graeme Smith, AB de Villiers, Ashwell Prince, Mark Boucher – all gone.

You simply don't recover from that position when you are up against Australia. I remember thinking while I was batting: 'No man, I can't believe the guys actually did that!' I knew the damage had been done, but I just couldn't figure out what had happened to our supposed game plan. I couldn't understand why the batsmen had just changed their minds entirely. I scratched around with Justin Kemp, getting 39, and Kempie was not out on 49 for a miserable total of 149 in 43.5 overs. Predictably, the Aussies took no prisoners, overtaking our total inside of 32 overs.

Whether or not our guys were carrying the scars from previous World Cups, I don't know. But to me it looked like we had just plain panicked. Our performance could only have been the result of not being able to handle the pressure of being in a major semi-final. When it comes to big-match temperament, you can have the most experienced guys in your team, but in these situations, even they can't handle the pressure.

And did we sit down and analyse our (lack of) performance after the game? Nope, no discussion at all. When I got out and returned to the dressing room, Jacques' bag was already packed and he was sitting there reading a magazine, while our innings was grounding to a complete halt. I kept on looking over at Mickey, and he seemed as bewildered by what was happening as I was. The guys looked like they were just relieved that the pressure was finally off, that the whole thing was over and that we could now go home. Weird.

The only thought going through my head was, 'No ... not *again*.' Maybe if there had been more of a team spirit in the squad I might have stood up and said something, or shook Mickey by the shoulders.

When we got back to the hotel, it was a case of, 'Well, everything's good now. At least we're on our way back to South Africa.' I, on the other hand, felt pretty sad and empty as I left the West Indies that year.

Unsurprisingly, the label 'chokers' was pinned on our jerseys by the world media, and I'm finding it increasingly tough to float a counter-argument. If a team cannot handle the pressure, then they are chokers. And a choker is someone who doesn't have the stomach or nerve for the big game. The situation is immensely frustrating for me, because I'm exactly the opposite. I live for the big games – these are the games that motivate me to perform at my best. At the end of the day, experience means nothing if you can't handle big-game pressure.

So, are the Proteas chokers? I'm not saying that it's right that we have been given that label, but I think it's a an accurate assessment of some situations the team has been in.

Hey, but that's way too miserable a note on which to end my World Cup recollections, isn't it? Which is why I've saved this little cameo for the end ...

Six sixes

There was one upside to the 2007 World Cup, and it happened in one particular over I faced against Daan van Bunge of the Netherlands. In previous World Cups I tended to play within myself to start off with, and then I turned it on towards the end. When I scored 143 against New Zealand in 2003, for example,

Eric Simons had said to me, 'I know you're in really good nick at the moment, but I'd like to see you get a scratchy 50 today against New Zealand.' I could easily have been out once or twice, but I did scratch my way to 50 ... and then turned on the taps to get 100 ... and then 143.

But this group game against the Dutch was another story. For one, I had the luxury of knowing that we were going to get a big total anyway – Jacques Kallis was purring along and would end up scoring 128 off 157 balls – and even though they had shocked the English at the start of the tournament, the Dutch didn't have enough firepower to worry us. For another, the straight boundaries on this pitch at Basseterre in St Kitts were pretty short, and right from the start of my innings, therefore, I decided to have a proper go.

It wasn't as if I had taken a particular liking to Daan van Bunge's spin-bowling either. I think I was just going to try to smash every ball irrespective of who the bowler was. I also wasn't thinking I would hit six sixes from the outset; the idea only entered my head after I'd clocked the first two.

For the first six, I charged down the wicket and hit the ball over long-on. For the second six, I moved up the pitch again and this time smacked it over long-off. Because I'd danced down the pitch for the first two deliveries, I decided to stay in the crease for the next delivery and play Van Bunge from there. I was like, 'Let me just hang back to see where he bowls.' Van Bunge obviously thought I was coming down the pitch again, and he dropped the ball a bit shorter, outside off-stump.

Now, along with most batsmen, I would usually cut that shot and go for a four, but usually you find a sweeper on the boundary and you only get one. In that split second I decided to flat-bat the ball straight back over his head. As I said, the boundaries were short. It was risky, but I absolutely nailed it and hit another six.

It was the key shot in that over – that unorthodox six set me up for the rest. The poor Van Bunge didn't know where to bowl from then on. He tried to dart the fourth ball in quicker and flatter, but I was expecting something along those lines, and I posted it over deep mid-wicket. The fifth ball was short outside off-stump, and I was able to rock back and pull over wide-long-off. One more to go …

At that moment, Jacques came up to me and said, 'Well, you've got five now; there's no need for a sixth.' Funny. I was like, 'Bugger that, boet. I'm going for another one.' I mean, how many such chances do you get in international cricket? *'You've got five now, there's no need for a sixth'* … he must have been having a laugh.

It's odd, but I just knew that the sixth delivery was going to go for a six as well. And the prospect of actually getting six sixes in a row wasn't making me nervous at all. In fact, I didn't even realise I was on the brink of a record, to be honest. I thought Sir Garfield Sobers had already done it, but I later learnt that his six sixes had occurred in a first-class county game for Nottinghamshire against Glamorgan and not in an international. So ja, I felt a certain inevitability about that final ball. And I think Van Bunge did too. He bowled it full outside off, and again I lofted it over the mid-wicket boundary for six.

Ba-da-boom. I became the first person to hit six sixes in succession in an international.

I didn't quite know how to celebrate, as I'd already got my half-century halfway through the over, and now I didn't know whether to raise my bat or lift my helmet or what. I also didn't know at the time that the tournament's sponsor, Johnnie Walker, had put up a one-million-dollar prize for anyone who managed this feat. The guys in the dressing room had cottoned on to this, so they were getting really excited at the prospect of sharing in some serious money.

The Proteas squad works as follows in terms of individual prize money: if, for example, you are Man of the Match, you get half the prize money and the team splits the rest. The ous were understandably amped – US$500 000 split among them would be a tidy and unexpected little bonus. Obviously most of the people I'd ever met must have known this too, because when I looked at my cellphone later, I had received tons more messages than I usually do when I've played well. If I get a century or something big, I probably receive about 80 or 90 congratulatory SMSes … that day I got 130. Clearly they all thought I'd hit the jackpot.

Unfortunately not, as it turned out …

The prize money was actually supposed to be allocated to a charity of my choice and would not be given to me personally. I won't lie and say that I wasn't a little disappointed. I mean, in what other international sport do you not get a financial reward for setting a world record? Be that as it may, I am proud of the fact that I was able to donate a million to the Habitat for Humanity foundation, which provides homes for underprivileged people. Some of the money went to people in Trinidad and the rest to people in Johannesburg. All in all, the cash prize meant that over a thousand people benefited from my six sixes.

The same deal applied to Matthew Hayden, who got a 100 off 66 balls – the quickest 100 in World Cup history. We were both also awarded honorary citizenship of St Kitts and Nevis, which I would put to good use, getting married on the island later that year. Apparently this citizenship is worth in the region of US$300 000, so I guess I did get some reward!

The 438 game
As you will have gathered from Chapter 4, with the amount of alcohol I had consumed the previous night, I should not even have been on the field for the start of this momentous game on the morning of 12 March 2006. This was a massive game for the team. After winning the initial two ODIs easily, the Aussies – predictably – had come back at us, winning the next two, so we had everything to play for in the decider.

Remember that this was on the back of a very disappointing tour Down Under, where we'd failed to reach the final of the triangular ODI tournament against the Aussies and Sri Lanka (we had lost three of our four games against Australia). The Australians had also hammered us 2-0 in the Test series – results that only reinforced the 'chokers' tag the media had pinned on our jerseys.

All of which makes getting pissed the night before the big game not a very good idea at all. But that's me, I guess. I do stuff. Often it's only in hindsight that I am able to judge the merits of my decisions. Fortunately I got away with this one. And I have, besides my natural talent, two things to thank for what's probably my most famous innings ... Mypaid and Red Bull.

Before leaving my hotel room that morning I had grabbed two Red Bull energy drinks from the mini-bar and a handful of Mypaid tablets. These little tablets, let me tell you, are the best things ever invented. Especially for hangovers. And I should know – I've had a few. Mypaid is a superb cocktail of painkilling substances with an anti-inflammatory, which just zaps anything resembling a hangover. You can buy them over the counter, too. I'm never without them. (Jeez, this is such a good punt, the pharmaceutical company should be paying me for this.)

Anyway, so I knocked back my little cocktail and, under the highly annoyed gaze of our bowling coach Vinnie Barnes (who knew what I'd been up to the night before), took to the field.

Thank the Lord we were fielding. I really, really wasn't feeling very good at all. Fortunately, though, that wasn't evident to anyone watching. I did drop one catch, but it was a total screamer from Adam Gilchrist. Even getting to that ball had been an unbelievable effort on my part. I doubt that I would've caught it even without a hangover. But my head was gradually clearing and, as luck would have it, not many balls were coming my way on the field.

The Australian innings was a bit of a blur, to be honest – not

Attending a 2003 World Cup welcoming function in Cape Town with my dad, Herman (next to me). With us are two former presidents of WP cricket, Fritz Bing (left) and Ron Delport (back)

© Gallo Images

Chatting to cricket fans, signing autographs for the young ones and having a drink with the older ones has never been a chore for me. I've always loved this part of being a professional cricketer

© Gallo Images

Funny photo, this. These are the three protagonists at the heart of the Duckworth-Lewis debacle at the 2003 World Cup: coach Eric Simons (left), captain Shaun Pollock (middle) and Mark Boucher (right). I felt for Bouch – he received the wrong instructions. Polly was a decent captain, though – just don't cock up in the field when he's bowling. Ja, big-time sense-of-humour failure then!

© AP Photo/Andres Leighton

With Graeme Smith. Smithy and I have had our ups and downs, but you've got to give the guy credit. He took on the job pretty young and has improved a lot as a captain

Leaving the field after scoring 175 off 111 balls to help the Proteas beat the Aussies in what is our most famous ODI win. All in all a surprising turn of events, given my activities the night before

Sitting in the changing room, holding my Man of the Match award and, with the help of Proteas fitness trainer Adrian le Roux (left) and Proteas bowling coach and my very good mate Vinnie Barnes (middle), signalling my innings of 175

AUSTRALIA		18:57		S AFRICA		TOTAL	438
✳ LEE	7.5	68	1	SMITH	90	WICKETS	9
┕ BRACKEN	10	67	5	DIPPENAAR	1		
CLARK	6	54	0	GIBBS	175	OVERS	49
LEWIS	10	113	0	deVILIERS	14	BATSMAN	-
SYMONDS	9	75	2	KALLIS	20	BATSMAN	✗ 50
CLARKE	7	49	1	✳ BOUCHER	50	PARTNERSHIP	5
				KEMP	13	RUNS TO WIN	
Keeper: GILCHRIST				VD WATH	35	OVERS LEFT	
EXTRAS	BALLS LEFT	TO WIN		TELEMACUS	12	RATE ACH'D	8.8
				HALL	7	RATE REQ'D	
20	1			┕ NTINI	1		

Vinnie took this photo of the scoreboard … not that I'll need photos to remind me of this epic game

© Gallo Images

I know some of my national and provincial teammates have been given some stick for appearing to be a little out of shape at times. I've taken plenty of abuse for other stuff, but never for my conditioning

© The Bigger Picture/Reuters

© Gallo Images

Shirt off in a practice session during the 2006 ICC Champions Trophy in Jaipur, India … because you never know when the ladies are watching

Dusting off some of those silky rugby skills at a Proteas fielding and fitness session at Kingsmead, Durban, in 2009

Michael Walker © Sunday Times

The 2007 running of the J&B Met at Kenilworth, Cape Town. That's me with a bunch of models. Apparently they have horse racing at the Met too

Max Berg © Sunday Times

Happier days with my ex-wife, Tenielle. The divorce was messy and she never deserved the press's portrayals of her. I was not exactly a model husband

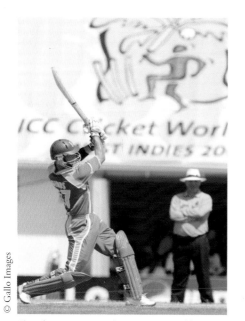

© Gallo Images

© Gallo Images

I've always come to the party at World Cups. Never more so than against the Netherlands during the 2007 World Cup, where I got a 72 that included – for the first time ever in international cricket – hitting six sixes in one over. The pic on the right is me klapping the final six

© The Bigger Picture/Reuters

At first the guys and I thought the $1 million on offer for breaking that record would be shared by me and the team. Turned out it wasn't. At least it went to a worthy cause. Presenting the cheque to me is the first man to hit six sixes in first-class cricket, the legendary Sir Garfield Sobers

© Gallo Images/AFP

Not bad for a 36-year-old: as always, putting in the hard yards during practice. This was in Jaipur ahead of the first ODI game against India in February 2010

© AP Photo/Aman Sharma

Giving the IPL trophy a little bit of a buff after beating the Royal Challengers Bangalore in the 2009 final at the Wanderers

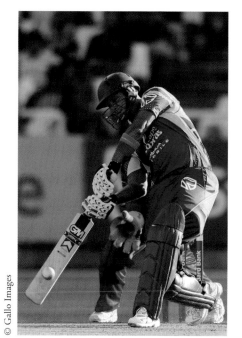

T20 cricket: my game these days is perfect for this new form of cricket – I've done well for both the Cape Cobras (left) and other teams, like Yorkshire (right), in English county cricket. There are quite a few more years of quality cricket left in Herschelle Herman Gibbs

This is my son, Rashard. I'm immensely proud of him and the way his mom has brought him up. He's 14 now and looks like a chip off the old block. In a good way ... obviously!

only because of my state of mind, but also because of their batting performance. Adam Gilchrist, Simon Katich and Michael Hussey all hammered us, but that was nothing compared to captain Ricky Ponting's 164 off 105 balls. I remember Mark Boucher and I sort of looked at each other at about 350 and Bouchie said, 'Jeez, we're going to be chasing 380 here.'

My money was on something closer to 400. As it turns out, we were both wrong. Ponting and Andrew Symonds climbed into Roger Telemachus, hitting him for plenty in the 48th over. Our bowlers also sent down a few no-balls, which didn't help matters. Australia ended on 434/4, breaking the record of 398/5 Sri Lanka had set against lowly Kenya in 1996. We walked off the field in complete embarrassed silence. It was a terrible feeling to be the first team to concede 400 runs, on our own turf, and it wasn't as if we were a Mickey Mouse side like Kenya either. We were among the top cricket teams in the world. It was downright humiliating.

The upside was that I was beginning to feel like my old self again.

At the turnover in the changing room there was complete silence for 10 or 15 minutes. We were all shell-shocked. This was obviously unknown territory for us, and we had no idea what bladdy targets to set along the way, or how we were going to get to 434. Coach Mickey Arthur gave a very short speech, pointing out that the wicket was perfect for batting and that the boundaries were fairly short. If the Aussies could do it, there was every chance we could too … *if* we remained positive.

'Listen,' said Mickey, 'just try to get to 200-odd in 19 overs and we'll take it from there.' Not the most sophisticated game plan ever conceived, but no one had ever thought Australia would get 400+ against us either.

While Mickey was talking, he looked straight at me, which made me wonder whether he'd heard about my exploits of the night before. I held his gaze and smiled as if to say, 'Well, Mick, if that's the going rate, someone has to give it a go. Might as well be me.' But I didn't really think we would end up chasing down the total, to be honest, especially after Boeta Dippenaar got out for one in the second over.

So there I am, walking out to the middle at number three. Memories of my big night had not receded quite as far back as I would've liked … and the Aussies started to chirp me. As I mentioned earlier in the book, the Aussie management had also been in the Sandton Sun Hotel bar, bearing witness to a good part of my drinking spell. Obviously they'd spread the word that I had been as pissed as a fart the night before. I could hear Michael Hussey saying, 'Come on, boy. Are you still happy? You don't look so happy.' The remarks were flying: 'Somebody give Hersch another glass of wine. Come on, Hersch, just one more.' And all that sort of shit.

Sledging never really bothers me, so I wasn't really taking too much notice. And, as my innings progressed, they quickly shut up. To this day I cannot explain it, but suddenly I was seeing the ball as if it were a football. I couldn't miss a shot – 21 fours and seven sixes later, I had swatted 175 runs to put South Africa in sight of the Aussie total. If I look back at the footage of the match I can see my eyes look deep-set in my skull – always a sure sign that I've had a big night. No doubt I was tired, but in a way that helped. I didn't run a hell of a lot that day. I just stood there and teed off. After I was out, Bouchie's gutsy 50 off 43 balls saw us home to a win that's universally acknowledged as the greatest game of cricket ever played.

I subsequently discovered that the Proteas team management had found out about my drunken night and were planning to kak me out after the game. Mickey actually said to me, 'Hersch, I was going to give you the biggest lecture of your life, but now, how can I?' He was laughing as he said it. That evening we had the biggest fines meeting ever. As I mention elsewhere, it was the first time I ever saw Mickey Arthur so drunk that he threw up.

The 2009 Indian Premier League final

To be honest, I still don't know how we, the Deccan Chargers, won the damn thing in 2009. As you know, the series was moved to South Africa for safety reasons, and our opening game in Cape Town was against the Kolkata Knight Riders. I think that game set the tone for us. It was an unbelievable effort. For one thing, I've never seen a fielding display in a similar vein from an IPL team. I've seen it playing for the Proteas at times, but on that particular day … man, everything just stuck. I took a good catch to get Brad Hodge, Rohit Sharma took a brilliant catch to get Moisés Henriques, and he also ran out Ajit Agarkar.

This was our current fielding coach Mike Young's first game as part of the Chargers squad and he was like, 'If this is the standard you've already got going, then what the hell am I doing here?' It was just that good. The intensity, the energy … everything … That game set the standard and we got off to a flyer. We won four games in a row before hitting a bit of a wobble. Then Adam Gilchrist basically won the semi-final against the Delhi Daredevils on his own, with an unbelievable knock of 85. He took Dirk 'Diggler' Nannes for 20 in his first over, and that took the wind out of their sails completely, because obviously the Devils used him to strike early on. Gilly just klapped him, and after that they didn't have an answer.

And then I took care of the final.

Playing for the Deccan Chargers against the Royal Challengers Bangalore in the 2009 IPL final was one game that proved just how unpredictable finals can be. This is where you find out which guys can or can't handle the pressure. And that pressure sometimes makes you do silly things.

The final was played at the Wanderers in front of a capacity crowd. It was loud, and it was just the kind of scenario I love. We batted first; Gilly and I were opening. Once we'd walked out onto the field and got to the middle, we realised that they were going to open the bowling with Indian spinner Anil Kumble. I see him warming up and setting the field, so I walk up to Gilly and say, 'Listen, boet, just give yourself a few balls so that you can have a look.' I probably didn't say 'boet'; probably 'mate'. I dunno.

But Gilly hits the first ball straight to a fielder, blocks the second, and then, with the third bladdy ball, runs down the pitch, misses the ball and gets bowled. Unbelievable. A prime example of how the Aussie confidence can sometimes work to their players' detriment. Sometimes they go out once too often to try to dominate, irrespective of the situation.

So now our main guy is out, and it's the final … We've got a fair number of younger, inexperienced guys in the team, and it's a funny sort of wicket – a little bit slow. You just couldn't get the ball away. I had no choice but to drop anchor and, after 10 overs, I'm on, like, 20. Ridiculous for a 20-over game! Still, somebody had to try to bat through the innings.

Andrew Symonds joined me and smashed a few quick ones before being really unlucky to get out, while trying to pull Kumble. The ball came off Symonds's thigh pad and rolled right onto his stumps. Meanwhile I was telling myself, 'Just hang in there; hang in there, and you'll be able to get the run rate up in the last few overs.' Which, luckily, I was able to do. Unfortunately, I didn't get to face a ball in the last over, or we might have scored in the range of 155.

I walked off knowing we had a total of only 143, but that it was a final, after all. And anything can happen when the pressure is on.

Rahul Dravid's dismissal in that game was a perfect example. I mean, here was a guy who had played in numerous high-pressure games. He was usually as unflappable as one got, but in this final, at a crucial time for the Royal Challengers, he played a ridiculous shot to get out. He tried to play a little paddle against Harmeet Singh and got bowled. In a normal game he would never have tried that shot at that time. There was panic written all over it.

But, as I said, funny things happen in a final.

There were a couple of good stumpings by Gilly, and Mark Boucher hit the ball straight to me at point ... but by then the game was over anyway. There were loud celebrations in the changing room after the game, I can tell you that much. My Indian teammates might be frustratingly quiet on the field, but put a trophy in their hands and the celebrations are about as loud and as noisy as they get. I don't think I've ever seen guys so happy at winning something in my life.

The Indian guys don't drink much – having said that, Rohit Sharma can put a couple away when he puts his mind to it – and our fines master, Andrew Symonds, showed admirable restraint by getting everyone in the mood without bringing anyone's evening to a premature halt.

Afterwards we all went to a nearby hotel for the official IPL after-party. As with any bash thrown by former IPL supremo Lalit Modi, there was champagne on tap and plenty of the fairer sex in attendance. Good times were had by all ...

8

My teammates

**These are the guys who influenced me … and one whom
I could never quite figure out.**

Since I started playing senior cricket – as a 16-year-old for
Western Province in 1990, and then in 1996 for the Proteas –
I've obviously come across some characters in this interesting
and pretty long career of mine. Unfortunately, I've only got to
know a handful of them really well, through no fault of my own,
I assure you. There are not many people easier to get along with
than Herschelle Gibbs.

The reality of international cricket, though, is that you don't
actually socialise much with players from other teams. I know the
rugby guys hang out with each other quite a bit, but they only
see each other for 80 minutes on the field, before they are off to
the next game. Not only are we playing five-day Test matches
against the opposition, but sometimes we're touring their country
for a couple of months. You see the guys nearly every day, so you
don't really want to be socialising with them too.

Having said that, the Indian Premier League has changed this
situation somewhat, and more friendships have been struck
among players of different nationalities. The IPL has certainly
broken down barriers, even with some of the Indian, Sri Lankan
and Pakistani guys, whose English isn't that good.

For example, until the IPL, I'd never really got to know any of
the Aussies. We never spent time with them off the pitch, even if
they stayed in the same hotel as us, but this has changed with the
advent of the IPL. I've become good friends with Adam Gilchrist

(more about him later in this chapter) and I've had the unique pleasure of spending some quality time with that wild man of Australian cricket, Andrew Symonds.

What a character. Andrew Symonds is not at all like I thought he was. When he was still playing for his country's national team, he came across as this hard-arsed, in-your-face kind of guy. However, having played with him at the Deccan Chargers for the past two years, it turns out he's hilarious – one of the funniest guys I know. He's got a great sense of humour. Problem is, when he's had one too many beers, he's not such an easy guy to be around. He is genuinely scary when he's pissed, but man, when he's sober, he's very funny.

Symonds has a really dry sense of humour, which is complemented by his thick Queensland accent. He loves, for example, to tease Goolam Rajah. Goolam is not only the Proteas' long-time team manager, but the Chargers have also, very wisely, employed this great man's services. Goolam has been doing this job for 17 years and knows everybody in the cricket world. When it comes to a logistical issue, Goolam is your man. I mean, *everyone* respects him, including Symonds, or 'Roy' as we all call him. Apparently it's short for 'Leroy', after Australian basketball star Leroy Loggins. One of Roy's early coaches gave him the nickname because he reckoned he looked like the guy. Amazing what you can find on Wikipedia.

Still, Roy can't resist taking the mickey out of Goolam, especially when it comes to one of his little 'faults'. Goolam is very obliging when the press want an interview or fans want their bats signed. He's like, 'We need to have these bats signed, and then we have a function at 6 p.m.' And then Roy will say, 'Goolam,' in that accent of his, 'Goolam, you always have to say "yes", don't you? You *always* have to say yes. Can't you just say *no* every now and again?' And then he'll look at Goolam with this serious expression. We'll all know that he is taking the piss, but it takes Goolam a moment longer to cotton on.

Ja, once you get to know Roy, he's a very funny guy.

Except, as I said, when he gets drunk. Then he gets a little aggressive. After one of the IPL games this past season, Roy wanted to hit our video analyst. I mean, this guy is part of the squad ... one of the boys ... and he is small compared to Roy, like ... *my* size. We had to talk Roy out of that. Then, later the same evening, Roy took a chair and poked people in the backside. He loves to drink, does Roy. I think he'd drink every day of his life if he could. And fish. Drink and go fishing.

Brett Lee is another Australian player whom I've got to know pretty well, and he is the only Aussie I have befriended outside of the IPL. Interestingly, our friendship started when I left my pants at his digs. No. Let me explain ...

During the 2006 tour to Australia, the one just prior to them coming to South Africa, his fiancée, Liz, got on really well with my fiancée, Tenielle, when all the wives and girlfriends sat together at the Perth Test. Anyway, so the two girls are chatting and Tenielle asks Liz about laundry, as the hotel laundry service never seemed to get the grass stains out of one's cricket kit.

All the Aussie guys were staying in hotel suites, with their own washing machines and other facilities, so Liz says, 'Well, bring it over to me. I'll clean Herschelle's pants.' Talk about the irony: my kit being washed by Australia's opening bowler.

Fortunately Brett 'Binga' Lee found it quite funny as well, and when I was batting, every time I got to his end, I'd hear, 'Nice pants, mate. Who is doing your laundry then? It's a fine job.' So I was laughing my damn head off when I should have been concentrating, because moments later he was going to be steaming in, trying to knock my head off.

Since then we've become quite good mates. When I was still with Tenielle, we used to go out quite a lot with Brett and Liz on double dates, but I've never really socialised in the same way with any of the other players. Other than Adam Gilchrist, Binga is probably the friendliest Aussie I've played. Odd ... like Tenielle and me, he and Liz are now also divorced.

Of the English guys, I know Jonathan Trott the best. He's essentially still a South African oke, and we were teammates for a couple of games at Western Province. So, ja, we've had a couple of drinks and quite a few laughs together.

Despite his South African roots, I haven't interacted much with Kevin Pietersen. It's pretty clear, though, that the best thing he ever did – and the best thing he did for his cricket – was to go to the UK. I remember him when he played here – no great shakes whatsoever. He was just this guy playing for Natal B – an ordinary off-spinner and an average batsman. So, when I first heard his name mentioned in connection with the England team, I was somewhat surprised, to put it politely.

The West Indians come across as a fairly arrogant lot, swaggering around in their fancy clothes, with the whole bling vibe going on, but – and this is why I love the IPL – once you get to know the guys, they are not like that at all. The IPL is ultra-competitive; players put their pride and status on the line in the IPL, and of course there is a lot of money involved too. Yet the IPL allows you to become friends with players with whom you wouldn't normally spend time. Fidel Edwards, for example, is a really funny oke, and I've enjoyed getting to know Dwayne Bravo a little better too.

These players, though, have been on the periphery of my cricketing career. I would rather tell you more about the guys who featured significantly in my career. These are the players (and coaches) who, through their actions, whether negative or positive, have made an impression on me. And I thought I'd also give you a list of my favourite cricketers of all time …

Let's start with the good guys.

Vincent Barnes

Vinnie's been my best friend and mate for the past 20 years. Our friendship began when I first started playing for Western Province – he was one of my first roommates. Vinnie is 14 years older than me and was, at the time, nearing the end of his playing days. He would go on to become the Proteas bowling coach, which means that he has probably seen more of me than my family has.

Many a time Vinnie and I have shared a pot of tea together and discussed the intricacies and vagaries of the life we lead. It is something of a ritual – whenever he wants to chat, he'll always say, 'I think it's time for a pot of tea,' and we'll spend hours talking about life in general.

Whenever I've needed any kind of advice, I have turned to Vinnie. And whenever I've needed to open up and speak from my heart, Vinnie's been there for me. He's a really good listener and understands me completely. And he knows how to handle me. Sometimes he'll tell me what I want to hear, but at other times, he'll be completely blunt and say exactly how he feels.

Vinnie and I hardly ever talk about cricket, but he has always urged me to be more outspoken within the Proteas set-up. He feels I don't share enough of my thoughts or give enough input at team meetings and practices. Vinnie reckons if I were more vocal and shared my experience with the younger guys, it would be good for the team. I keep saying that if the team were more together, I would talk a lot more.

To be honest, and as I've touched upon, I've never felt any true sense of team spirit within the current team. But more on that in Chapter 10.

As a counterpoint, my role in and relationship with the Cape Cobras is totally different. I've become a lot more outspoken in the Cobras set-up, for the simple reason that I love playing in a *team*. There are no issues in that team, no egos; everybody gets along well. It's a great team to play in, just like Glamorgan, my county club. There are no damn status and ego issues, man.

That's why I've just never bothered speaking my mind in the South African team. In 1999 I was still fairly new and had only been playing for two years. But that, by the way, was a *real* team; there were no dramas. Everybody got on like a house on fire.

I know there are people in the squad with whom Vinnie hasn't always quite seen eye to eye. I know that one or two players think, 'Well, Vinnie didn't play international cricket, so what has he got to offer?' Proteas fast bowler Makhaya Ntini, however, would be the first to tell you how valuable Vinnie's cricketing input is. Same applies to our off-spinner, Johan Botha.

Vinnie has been a figure far more valuable than a coach to me. He's been more like a best mate, an older brother and a father figure rolled into one. Vinnie is just great to talk to, and I can offload whatever's in my heart and on my mind when I need advice on relationships and other personal stuff.

Hansie Cronjé

If there's one name mine will always be linked with, it is Wessel Johannes Cronjé's. And yes, the match-fixing scandal may have cuffed us together, but Hansie was a man I will always admire. He had his faults, I know. When he accepted money from book-ies, he deserved the censure his actions received. If he were still alive, Hansie would undoubtedly be the first to admit that.

I am often asked whether I ever forgave Hansie for the whole drama. Of course I did. I mean, I was an adult too, and I take responsibility for my decisions. What there was to forgive, I for-gave him for long ago. I don't hold any grudges at all. People make mistakes, and I, of all people, am not going to be the one pointing fingers, that's for sure. Hansie was human; he made a serious blunder, but I dare you to put your hand up if you've never made a serious mistake in your life. Hansie's was a very public mistake, and the consequences were far-reaching, but I don't think any of us on this planet is qualified to make a call on when a misjudgement cannot be forgiven.

Hansie was certainly the best captain for whom I've ever played. Despite the cloud that hangs over his legacy, I can tell you that I've never played with anyone who possessed such a die-hard attitude to winning. Hansie wanted to win at any cost; he was a *great* competitor. We were all in awe of the guy – Hansie was one of those men who had a special presence towards which others gravitate. His other great asset as a captain – actually the *biggest* positive, as far as I am concerned – was that he never got too close to his players. Maintaining a distance allowed him to put players in their place when it was required. From what I've heard, as captains, Steve Waugh was and Ricky Ponting is much the same.

And, man, could Hansie lay down the law! *No one* would contradict him – not even the senior guys like Brian McMillan or Allan Donald – not only because his teammates had respect for him, but also because Hansie basically took no shit.

Hansie was also hard core about players' fitness. For example, in a training session ahead of a tour, Hansie told Pat Symcox that if he didn't run a certain amount on the bleep test, he wouldn't go on tour. 'If you can't run this on the bleep test, you can't go. Simple as that. I don't care whether you're in or out of form – if you can't run the bleep test well, you are not fit enough. And then you're not going.'

Bleep tests are shuttle runs between two lines that are 20 metres apart. You start off almost at a walking pace. There are 10 or 11 shuttles at every level, and every subsequent level gets quicker and quicker. You've got to reach at least level 12 or 13, which means doing 120 or 130 shuttles. Old Patrick liked his beer and his cigarettes, but somehow he managed to run it.

Along with his no-shit attitude, Hansie also had a tremendous sense of humour, and he'd occasionally surprise us with his fun and mischievous side. One night in particular illustrates this side of the man perfectly …

The West Indies were touring South Africa in 1998. The second Test was in Port Elizabeth and, thanks to an 'interesting' pitch, the wickets were tumbling. We'd batted first, getting 245, then skittled the opposition for 121. By the end of the second day, we were already 145/5.

Still, with a lead of 266 and five wickets in hand, it was pretty clear we were going to win the game. We'd also won the first Test, at a canter, by four wickets. I must admit, I had a bit of a 'mare in this game – scoring two in the first innings, which I doubled to four in the second innings. In my defence, though, it was the first time I had ever opened the batting for South Africa.

I guess Hansie knew that the game was probably in the bag and that, having already been dismissed, the top five in the batting order would only be taking their small tog bags to the game the next day. And so he decided we were going to make a night of it. Six of us – me, Hansie, Daryll Cullinan, Jacques Kallis, Gary Kirsten and Pat Symcox, who, even though he still had to bat, was always game for a piss-up – appropriated the team Kombi and headed out to PE's infamous eatery and bar, The Ranch, where, it was rumoured, there were some very tasty off-menu dishes one could order should one feel the need. Symmo liked to claim that he was just 'in the wrong place at the wrong time' that night, but, knowing Symmo like we knew Symmo, no one ever bought his story.

The Ranch has closed down now, and I know I speak for all cricketers – the South African guys as well as any visiting international team who ever played in PE – when I say that it was a very sad day. The quality of the food was only matched by the quality of the waitresses and, as mentioned, rumours abounded that they were on the 'specials list' too.

The girls were indeed unbelievably pretty, and they all wore tight black dresses. There was supposed to be a room above the restaurant where one could allegedly get a little bit extra if you forked out the right sort of cash, but sadly I never got to substantiate that particular rumour. I do know, however, that one or two of my teammates – the single guys, of course – flew the odd Ranch waitress out to join them on tour.

Of course this evening with Hansie and the boys was by no means the first time I had visited this fine establishment. As a teenager, with the Western Province team, I had accepted many an invitation to join the likes of teammates Kenny Jackson, Adrian Kuiper and Meyrick Pringle for an evening of entertainment at The Ranch. As I recall, Meyrick was particularly fond of the place ... and fond of a few beers too.

Back to Hansie, though – he really surprised me that night. And I'm sure a few South African cricket fans are also surprised to hear that their national team was out on the piss midway through a Test, especially with the captain leading the charge!

With Hansie, though, you could never know when he was serious or when he was joking. He'd play a prank on someone out of the blue and everyone would laugh. And then other times you'd think he was being funny, but in the meantime he was being dead serious.

Hansie would sometimes leave messages under your door to inform you that there would be a 6.30 a.m. team meeting and that you had to attend. Except, of course, no one would be there when you rocked up. And then sometimes he would crack a joke and you'd be rolling around laughing, and he would be like, 'What are you laughing at?' You didn't know what was potting half the time – whether you should smile or be upset. Hansie just had an aura about him, you know, a presence. But you could never tell whether he was being serious or not.

So Hansie makes the call that night, and you know me. Especially in those days, I was going to be at anything that resembled half a party. Despite being keen myself, the bottom line was that when Hansie made a call, his teammates bought into it.

We had a great time that night. We weren't misbehaving too badly, but plenty of beers and shooters were involved, and we got back to the hotel pretty late and quite drunk. I'm not entirely sure why Hansie had wanted to party on that specific night. Perhaps, because we had all batted badly, he wanted us to let off a little steam and indicate that we needn't worry too much about it. But I never got over the idea that the person he most wanted to reassure was me. After all, it had been the first time

I had opened the Test batting, and I had failed badly in both innings.

Another reason why I thought this was because I was sharing a room with Hansie during that Test – it was one of the few times we would share a room. In those days, even though all the other players shared rooms, it was the team captain's privilege to have his own space. At that time I used to share with Paul Adams, but in PE, Hansie said, 'No, Hersch, you and I are going to share a room for a few nights.'

Given the match-fixing scandal we'd both become embroiled in two years later, you might think that a more sinister reason lay behind his invitation to share a room, but I can assure you nothing of the kind happened on that occasion. I think Hansie knew the pressure I felt as a 24-year-old opener, and he was offering me his guidance and support.

The following day, the five batsmen who were already out watched their teammates – including a hung-over Pat Symcox – add another 52 runs to the total before we were all out for 195. The following day the Proteas bowled the West Indies out for 141, to win the Test easily by 178 runs. In fact, we won all five Tests against the Windies – to date the only time the Proteas have registered a series whitewash.

After the King Commission had concluded, I saw Hansie once or twice at Fancourt Golf Estate, where he lived. But we didn't really stay in touch. Things were a little awkward between us, given what we had been through. Also, I was once again playing cricket after my six-month ban, but Hansie's cricket career was over. It was difficult.

All of us, his former teammates, were shocked when we learnt of the tragic circumstances of his death. At his funeral, I was sitting in front of Lance Klusener, who cried throughout the entire service. I held back my tears until they carried the coffin from the church ... then I sobbed.

Hansie's life was tragic after the match fixing, but I'll say this much for him: the man was an inspirational cricket captain. The team we had was a proper team, not a bunch of individuals.

Gary Kirsten

Among all the players, I was probably closest to Gary Kirsten. He had a huge impact on my life – especially in my career. I wasn't a natural opening batsman, as my inclination was to be aggressive and hit the ball from the word go. But Gary helped me to curb my instincts somewhat and be more disciplined in my approach. Gary's work ethic is phenomenal and, through his example, I was motivated to put in the extra hours.

The two of us went through a lot out there in the middle. As opening partners we went through the same emotions, especially in Test cricket. It's not like Gary and I discussed a helluva lot of stuff, but when we walked out to the wicket together, we knew that we were having the same thoughts: how we felt when we were preparing for a Test match, as opposed to when we were actually walking out to face the world's fastest bowlers, who were all going to try to knock our bladdy heads off with the new ball.

Gary and I prepared for matches very intensely. We practised with the same intensity we had to face in a match, which meant that we were always ready for anything when we went out to bat. We used to take a new ball and throw it at each other from about 16 yards and bounce the living kak out of one another. Gary hit me on the helmet many times and, you know, I naturally returned the favour.

The practice sessions Gary and I had together were sometimes more draining than actually facing the bowlers in the middle – that's how hard we used to work. It's easily the hardest I have ever worked with a batting partner. Gary practised like he played – with a lot of heart and determination. He always wanted to get things right. He always believed that you needed to practise specifics, like being able to play the short ball as an opening batter, or else you would quickly be found wanting at international level.

I reckon we could do with commitment like this in the South African team at the moment. It's flipping silly, because we're a little spoilt these days. At practice, either a Corrie van Zyl or a Vinnie Barnes throws at us. The guys won't throw to each other. I know that Gary spends hour upon hour practising in the same way he and I used to with the Indian national team he's currently coaching, so you don't have to wonder why they're currently number one in the world. And why the Proteas aren't …

So ja, I think our attitude and hard work contributed a great deal to our success. Gary and I also knew each other's strengths – if one of us was doing something wrong, we would correct the other. This could be one of the reasons why I couldn't play the same standard of cricket in 2006 and 2007, the last two years I played Test cricket. Graeme Smith simply doesn't do throw-downs.

To be fair to Graeme, though, he can't throw, as his arm is crocked. But ja, the other guys don't throw to each other, not because their arms hurt, but because they actually just don't want to. They'd rather ask Vinnie or current coach Corrie van Zyl to throw to them. Hard-core practising not only made Gary and me a successful opening pair, but it also brought us closer together.

That work ethic is just one side of Gary, though. Most people won't know this, but Gary was a helluva lot of fun off the field. Obviously he made the most of his professional cricket career, but he always had time for a laugh. We used to have this private joke going: every time we'd bump into each other while on tour – like in the lift on the way to breakfast, or at lunch – I'd say to him, 'So, what's news on the Rialto?' It's a line from Shakespeare's *Merchant of Venice*. Don't ask me *why* I remember that particular line – especially given my suspect academic record – but every time I said it, Gary would pack up laughing. 'What's done cannot be undone' is the other snippet of Shakespearean prose I remember. From The Scottish Play, I believe. Weird that I should remember it, isn't it?

After a few pots, Gary can also become quite dilly ... funny and, like, mad. In Antigua on the 2001 tour, for example, the night after we'd won the series against the West Indies, Gary decided to go bodysurfing in these tiny two-foot waves. Obviously he'd had a couple, and at about six or seven o'clock that evening he got it into his head that he wanted to go bodysurfing. The next morning he woke up with these abrasions all over his chest ... obviously he'd kept on ploughing straight into the sand without feeling a thing.

I cried the day Gary retired in 2004. I cried like never before. I think I cried even more than *he* did. It was Gary's final game, the third Test against New Zealand in Wellington, and I remember the tears started flowing after he'd got out. We were playing in the third Test after drawing the first and losing the second, and we needed the win to tie up a very even and hard-fought series. Thanks to Graeme Smith's second-innings 125 and a typically gutsy 76 off 227 balls from Gary to stop a middle-order collapse, we beat the Black Caps by six wickets.

It is not often that a great cricketer ends his career with a great innings, but fortunately this servant of South African cricket left the field having given his team one last master class on how talent and application make a formidable combination. Two hours after Gary had walked off, the tears were still there ... The only time I'd every cried like that was at Hansie Cronjé's funeral. But, ja, Gary Kirsten is just a genuine, true and complete human being.

Goolam Rajah

Our revered team manager has been part of the Proteas set-up for 17 years, and when it comes to team logistics, I don't think there is a problem Goolam cannot overcome. I reckon the man works harder than anyone else in the team – he is often up until the early hours of the morning getting the preparations in order for his players. We never have to worry about a thing when we're travelling, because we know that Goolam has all the bases covered.

And we know that even if something crops up, Goolam will find a way around it.

It's just amazing that you have absolutely nothing to worry about when you're travelling, because everything is done for you. Even your bags are checked in for you. There's never an issue with excess baggage, for example, which is a real bonus when you come back from an extended overseas tour. The guys are *always* overweight – we're talking excess baggage now.

But before I digress ... So, ja, our luggage always weighs too much, especially after a trip to the subcontinent. In Pakistan, for example, the guys buy tons of carpets and leather jackets. Don't ask me why. I mean, I can understand the carpets, but not the leather jackets. It must say something about some of the guys' dress sense! Anyway, excess luggage is never ever an issue when Goolam's in the house. After being in the business for so long, he's made so many contacts all over the world that any problems just seem to melt away. Another benefit of being part of an international sports team is that we never have to clear customs either.

Goolam is so good at what he does that I got the Deccan Chargers to sign him up for the IPL. When the tournament was held in South Africa in 2009, the Chargers needed a team manager, and I was like, 'Well, you guys had better get Goolam on board before anyone else snaps him up.'

It's also great to have Goolam in India – he understands Indian culture. He's always telling us, 'Whenever you come to the subcontinent, make sure you pack an extra bag. That's the bag of patience.' He knows that everything takes just that little bit longer to happen in India. The job will get done, but it just takes a while.

Fortunately, the Chargers signed him just in time. I think Graeme Smith had been keen to get him for the Rajasthan Royals, but Goolam opted for the Chargers and his favourite son ...

That's Goolam the team manager. But Goolam is also one of the most humble and kindest people I've ever met. The Proteas regard him as a father figure, and I secretly think Goolam sees us all as his kids. He's very soft-spoken, courteous and quite shy. You often see Goolam blush – even through his complexion – when he has to say a few things that he's not comfortable saying. Goolam also withdraws into his shell when he feels people are talking in a provocative manner. He goes quiet and just sort of sits back, and he never really challenges people. And as I illustrated in the story about Andrew Symonds teasing Goolam, he finds it difficult to say no to people, because he genuinely wants to help and accommodate everyone.

Goolam has tried to retire before, but he came back when the UCB sent out a desperate SOS. When Goolam finally takes a very well-earned rest, it will be a huge loss to South African cricket. While some of the Proteas have taken Goolam for granted over the years, the rest of us treat him with the utmost respect. Most of the guys call him 'Gools', but I'm sticking with the name Gary Kirsten gave him – 'Ledge'.

Because Goolam Rajah *is* a legend.

Allan Donald

I played with Allan from 1996 to 2003, and every time we got together, we had at least five beers! I could never understand how this man could drink so much and then still bowl so well the next day. He'd have a bottle of wine with his supper, and sometimes drink four beers in a team meeting. Ja, Allan Donald ... he loves his beer. Allan's got his own 50-litre keg at home, which was a present from Castle Lager.

On our first full tour of the West Indies in 2001, Allan and I drank *every day*. Put it this way, I decided that every time he drank, I'd have a drink with him ... which, of course, was a mistake. Allan is phenomenal and handles his drink better than anybody else I know. When we had a day off on the tour, or after we'd finished a match, we'd have a couple of pots. You'd be on, like, your sixth or seventh beer and Allan would be on his tenth. He'd still be behaving like nothing was happening. You're getting slaugh-tered and he's going, 'Are you okay? What's going on?'

The one time I did see Allan pissed, though, was on a tour. We were with a mutual friend of ours and drinking whisky. Allan could put the beers away – and stay stick thin, I never knew how he managed that – but he couldn't quite handle spirits with the same aplomb.

I reckon Allan learnt to drink in the years he played county cricket. I mean, he went over to Warwickshire when he was, like, 18 or 19. And anybody who goes to play in England year after year is going to learn how to drink.

I'm only telling you about the drinking because I'm proud to have played with Allan and to have known him. The drinking is just a very small part of Allan. As a cricketer, I've always regarded him as a total professional. And he's just a champion guy, you know … a very, very nice guy. I always felt very close to him and could talk to him about anything.

Allan actually kicked off my wristwatch fetish too. Not that he kicked off my drinking fetish – I reckon I did that on my own – but he used to buy a pair of golf shoes on every Proteas tour. Every time, he had to get at least one pair. So I started buy-ing watches on tour, and I bought my first TAG Heuer with Allan on the 1998 tour to Australia. So, ja, he buys golf shoes and I buy TAGs. Different product, but the same concept!

I didn't always get on with everyone, though …

Daryll Cullinan

Daryll was the one teammate I could never figure out. Obviously, he was one helluva gifted cricketer; as a batsman, the guy was a genius. I have always thought that, out of all the players I've played with and against, Daryll always looked like he had more time to play the ball than anyone else. He looked like he was playing the ball in slow-mo, that's how good he was. He had the ability to make the quickest bowler in the world look like a medium-pacer. That said, he wasn't that great against a certain Aussie leggie, though, was he?

Daryll and I didn't get off to the best start (as discussed in Chapter 6), and for the rest of our time as teammates, the two of us never got on. At all. I always felt that I had to force a conversation with Daryll, as he wouldn't just come and talk to you, you know. You never felt that you could actually have a decent conversation with the man, and I believe most guys in our team shared my feelings.

At first, though, Daryll was mates with Pat Symcox and Brian McMillan, but when they retired, he got quite isolated ... which was a little sad, as I'd always admired him as a player.

Daryll even managed to get up my nose when he finished playing cricket and started to do some TV commentary. When I got three centuries in a row against the West Indies during the 2004 Test series in South Africa – two 142s and a 192 – he didn't congratulate me and say 'well done'. No, he asks me: 'So, when are the 300s coming?' He was being dead serious too. It wasn't just some off-the-cuff remark. He was obviously implying that I was incapable of getting a triple century ... unlike him. But that's Daryll; he always liked to say his little piece. He was never shy of a word.

Daryll met his nemesis in the spin-bowling of Shane Warne, though. There was Daryll, one of the few guys I'd pay good money to go and watch, and Warnie put the brakes on his career a little. I never quite understood why Daryll couldn't play Warnie. Perhaps if he was a more likeable chap I would have asked him. But someone – I think it was Robin Jackman – had an interesting theory about this. According to him, it was the trajectory and bounce of the flipper with which Shane often got Daryll out – the ball that pitched shorter than normal, but skidded through and didn't bounce at all – that was the secret.

Warnie would bowl this ball with the same arm position and at the same arm speed – it would look like his stock ball – but then it would come out of the bottom of his hand instead, and all the speed would be generated through his wrist, which made the ball come out much quicker. Warne used to say that bowling this ball hurt his wrist, but it really was the most unbelievable delivery.

But the real secret to the delivery – and this is the part that used to bamboozle Daryll – was that because the ball was pitched shorter, Daryll thought he could play back to the bowler, and even attack. But because of the ball's flatter trajectory, it would come skidding through pretty low. And so Daryll would keep on either getting bowled or given out lbw. He just couldn't grasp the fact that he had to play forward.

I think Daryll also struggled to pick up the length of that ball. Brian McMillan was the same. Warnie got Mackie with the flipper a few times too; I remember a couple of stone-dead lbws. To be fair, there are not many batsmen on this planet who ever played Warnie with any degree of comfort.

So that was Daryll for me. Not a person I could get on with, but a great cricketer who – apart from Shane Warne – could take any bowler apart. For the last three years of Daryll's Test career, he averaged 51, which is bladdy impressive. As I said, he was the one guy I would pay money to watch.

In the following chapter, I'll give you the names of some other players whose cricketing talents I have admired through the years. Actually, there are a couple of bowlers on that list too.

9

My top 10(ish) players

I say Top 10(ish) because I included an extra guy, but kept him outside the Top 10. He's a bit of a nutter compared to the exulted company in this chapter, but certainly worthy of a mention. So ... my Top 10(ish). A little weird, sure, but think of it as another of the little 'discrepancies' that are sprinkled throughout my life and career.

Adam Gilchrist

The thing I love about Adam Gilchrist is that, with him, it is always all or nothing, which is also the way in which he approaches his batting. Irrespective of what the situation in the game is, whether he is opening in a limited-overs game or coming in at seven in a Test match, he always has the same approach. Although some may think all Gilly wanted to do was slog, for him it was about playing positive cricket. Essentially batting is all about hitting a ball with a bat, which Gilly understood and executed, often with frightening ferocity. He always wanted to make the game move forward.

Even if Gilly was going through a bit of a lean spell – as in the 2005 Ashes series, when Freddie Flintoff seemed to have his number – he'd never doubt his ability or withdraw into his shell. Nope, Gilly would still be out there, trying to klap the ball over the top from the word go.

And when he was on song – which was most of the time – his hitting was sublime. I don't think anyone quite timed the ball like Gilly. His ability to pick up the length of the ball very early is a gift that helped him tremendously. I think that the Aussie wickets contributed to Gilly's approach, as the pitches don't seam much and the ball comes on quite nicely. All of the Aussies tend to hit through the line of the ball really well.

Gilly also has the ability to get under just about anything and launch it into the stands. Any bowler stupid enough to bowl short to Gilly inevitably watches the ball disappear into the stands. Ja, his horizontal bat shots, in particular, are unbelievable.

The 102 not out Gilly got against England in Perth during the 2006 Ashes was one of the greatest innings I've ever seen. It took him 59 balls and was the second-fastest Test century behind Sir Viv Richards's 56-ball explosion in 1985. For me, Gilchrist is just as good as any other batter that I've seen.

The Indian Premier League has given me the opportunity to get to know Adam Gilchrist a lot better. Gilly has been with the Deccan Chargers since the inception of the IPL in 2007, and for the last two years he has been our captain. In this time, Gilly has become almost like an older brother to me. He's played 96 Tests and 287 ODIs, so he obviously has a lot of knowledge and experience and, as we both started our international careers in 1996, we've both been down a similar road.

It's great to see how, as a professional cricketer, he keeps everything nice and simple. And he still leads by example with the amount of work he puts in. He has been a revelation to the younger players in the Deccan Chargers.

As our captain, Gilly runs a tight ship – from making sure we are always dressed in the appropriate kit, both on and off the field, to advising and directing the players on the pitch. For example, this past season we were at a function posing for photographs, and I was resting my elbows on my knees. Gilly was like, 'Hersch, straight up, mate!'

He's meticulous and never misses a detail, especially on the field, always seeming to have everything under control out there in the middle. If a bowler's in trouble, Gilly will go and talk to him, but you will never see him really pissed off. If he gets angry, he certainly never shows it. And you can tell that Gilly is always plotting and strategising. Ja, he's really been great for the Chargers – most of his teammates are just in awe of him. I still enjoy watching him stand tall at the crease and dispensing the ball to all corners after all the years of playing both against and, recently, with him.

Matthew Hayden

Charl Langeveldt finds Matthew Hayden very amusing. He just starts laughing when Hayden comes out to bat, because Matt stands directly in front of his wicket and, as a bowler, you can't see any of the three stumps. Langers is like, 'He always does this! I can't see the damn stumps! Where the hell must I bowl?'

Hayden is a big guy – just unbelievably big and strong – and he's an amazing hitter of the ball. He has all the power in the world, and he doesn't take a step backwards for any bowler. If he wants to stand a metre outside his crease, he'll do it. Shoaib Akhtar can be steaming in, bowling at 160 km/h, and Hayden will walk down the wicket and smack the ball over his head. And he even does that in Test cricket. I mean, the bowlers just shit themselves. Ours certainly did in the 2007 World Cup semi-final against the Aussies. When Hayden was standing there, smacking the ball to all corners, you could see the panic flicker across the bowlers' faces.

And he enforced this fear even though we had a game plan against him. Obviously, in preparation for the match, we went through the Aussie players' strong and weak points. When we had played them in the first group game, they scored 377, and Hayden took Shaun Pollock apart. In the end, Polly had 'the claw', where he was just kakking himself and couldn't release the ball properly. Hayden was smacking him all over the show and Polly had no answer that day. I don't think Polly was the same bowler again in that tournament.

Even in Australia, where the wickets are a lot quicker and

bouncier, Hayden just stands, like, a metre outside his crease and pumps it into the stands. I've chatted to Matt a few times down the years, and he's told me about a particular shot he practises in the nets. He calls it the 'bowler crusher'.

It's a fairly straightforward shot with a fairly obvious purpose where Matt isn't going for a six, but is simply smashing the ball back at the bowler as hard, and preferably as low, as he can. It's pure intimidation, which is part and parcel of the Aussie game plan, whether batting or fielding.

As we all know, sledging is part of the Aussie strategy, and Hayden always had a bit to say when his mates, Justin Langer and Steve Waugh, were with him. He certainly wasn't shy of having a word. Not that I could specifically remember what he had to say, as all that stuff was always just noise to me. Even though it was always there, going on in the background, I never paid it much attention. And most of it didn't come from Shane Warne, either, but from Justin Langer and Steve Waugh – not when Waugh was in the covers, but when he was in the slips with Warne.

Waugh would stand there on the field and, when you walked out to the middle, greet you with a, 'Hey, Hersch, we've been waiting for you.' And I'd think, 'Okay, here we go again.' But when you got to 25 or 30 and it looked like you were going to be in for a bit, they tended to go fairly quiet.

Brian Lara

Brian Lara batted in a way that no one else ever has. He was able to get into positions at the crease that allowed him to hit and score off deliveries that would leave other batsmen floundering.

If you watch footage of Lara batting, you can see that he was always very crouched when he batted. And because he was standing quite low, once the ball got up higher than where he was, he could just pull it.

Whereas most Test batsmen might leave a ball of a certain length, Brian could score off it. As his feet were placed wider apart, it lowered his stance and allowed him to hit the ball really late. Just watch the way he used to cut on the off-side – he'd hit the ball very late, but with a lot of power. As hard as anybody I've ever seen.

Lara also had a very high back-lift, which meant that his bat speed through the hitting zone was immense. That high flourish allowed him to chuck in everything but the kitchen sink whenever a bowler offered any width. Most other batters would have sent this ball flying over slips or got caught at third man, but Brian always got on top of the ball, hit it fairly late and laced it past point, which takes incredible timing and coordination.

Lara didn't deliver his best performances against South Africa – but remember, in his case it means that he didn't score a triple or quadruple century against us! His highest score against the Proteas was 'only' 202 at the Wanderers in 2003 and, apart from that, he scored only three other Test centuries against us. I guess you could say our bowlers had his number … relatively speaking.

Still, the man was a total genius with the bat, scoring 11 953 Test runs (the second-highest total in history after Sachin Tendulkar) and 10 405 ODI runs. And, of course, he holds the highest Test-innings score, with 400 not out against England in 2004.

Ricky Ponting

Ponting represents the modern Aussie approach to cricket, specifically in batting. You hardly ever see the guy block the ball – even in Test cricket. Right from the start you know that he's going after the bowlers, and while that means that he can offer up a chance or two early on, that is something of a rare occurrence, as the Proteas found out too.

I mean, people reckon that I am a fairly attacking Test batsman, but compared to Ponting, I always feel tentative. Ponting believes the ball is there to be hit and that runs are there to be plundered.

It's that Australian mentality, isn't it? As sportsmen and -women, they just ooze confidence, which I believe is instilled in them at an early age. You can see it in their youngsters, and I've even seen it in the fans at the games. These little pikkies are, like, seven or eight years old and they're chirping you from the stands! I remember this one youngster at a game in Adelaide: I was walking onto the field with Mark Boucher and I hear this loud voice shouting, 'Hey, Gibbs ... "Gibbs" me your autograph!' It's this little oke who can't be more than seven. Mark and I just laughed. I think the Australians are just brought up with all that cockiness and self-belief.

And as they get older, their confidence just increases. That may be the reason why young Aussies who break into the national team don't seem to struggle as much as we do. Their self-confidence is already sky-high, so they struggle less when they have to make an adjustment into Test cricket. In fact, the Aussies don't really stand back in any sport, and they never shy away from a challenge. Not only do they always go after the bowling, but they are also bladdy hard to get out.

Back to Ricky Ponting, though – he is as aggressive as he is focused as a batsman. I also think he's very aware of Steve Waugh's legacy and, like Waugh, he's not one for going out and partying too much with the boys. Brett 'Binga' Lee – one of the Aussies I have got to know pretty well – tells me Ponting is very chilled-out and relaxed off the field, but he doesn't often party with the team. According to Binga, when Ponting first took over as captain, he would never go out with his teammates, though it's a little better these days.

I remember bumping into Ponting and some of the team at Caprice in Camps Bay when we played them in the 2009 series. I had a few drinks and kept on ragging him, saying, 'Punter' – everyone calls him that – 'Punter, nice to see you out with your boys.' Every time I saw him, I made a point of saying the same thing. Every time he just smiled.

Glenn McGrath

Glenn McGrath would bowl you a half-volley only once a month. As far as line and length were concerned, he was the most disciplined bowler I have ever faced. You knew you weren't ever going to get a bad ball from him. I mean, the concept of a half-volley outside off-stump was totally alien to him.

McGrath hardly ever bowled bouncers either – he wasn't exactly express pace, especially towards the end of his career, but when he sent a bouncer your way, it always took you by surprise. However, his great strength was definitely his nagging accuracy. McGrath wasn't really interested in bowling you out or going for the leg-before, and he hardly ever went for the stumps. His game was to get you caught behind.

He was able to get the ball to do just that little bit off the seam that would get you to play and nick. There was never any great sideways movement, which you could either leave or would just be unplayable. Nope, McGrath always pitched in the channel outside off-stump, just back of a length, which invariably got you coming forward and, too often, nicking the ball to be caught behind.

Because of his immaculate length and the fact that he hardly ever pitched it up or bowled a yorker, you could actually leave him more on length. Pitching outside off and back of a length meant that getting bowled or out lbw was not much of a threat.

McGrath wasn't shy to have a few words out there either ... and unlike most other Aussies, he could get personal. He really had a go at me about the whole match-fixing saga while I was batting in a Test in Melbourne in 2004. He went on and on, saying, 'Hersch, how much did Hansie give you ... 10 per cent?' For the first and probably only time in an international match, sledging got to me, and I lost my marbles a bit. I said, 'Just fuck off and bowl.'

Ja, McGrath loved to chat. He was always talking, under his breath a lot of the time, and if he could see he was getting to you, he wouldn't stop.

Wasim Akram

In his early days especially, Wasim was unplayable – fortunately I only faced him at the back-end of his career. Wasim was a really unorthodox bowler who'd come in off a short run-up but still whip the ball through, thanks to the incredible arm speed he'd generate. He also never had a big jump in his delivery action, and that jump actually helps a batsman get in sync and time the ball. Wasim just kept running and then, at some point, his left arm would blur and the ball would come skidding through at one helluva pace. He was also the master of late reverse-swing, and that ball of his that swung late and homed in on your toes was bladdy scary, let me tell you.

As I said, I didn't play against him too much, but there was one very memorable game when I played *with* him. In 2008, we were both invited to turn out for the Lashings World XI against Kent. It might have only been a Lashings match and therefore an invitational, semi-social game, but our bowling line-up included Allan Donald, Shoaib Akhtar, Franklyn Rose and Wasim Akram. Not a bad damn line-up at all. Incidentally, this was the first time I played with Sir Viv Richards as well.

Anyway, so we're playing at the Kent ground under lights – and if you know Kent, the lights are more like candles than lights – and Shoaib is charging in, bowling full-on, and our wicketkeeper, Junior Murray, is taking the ball at shoulder height. I mean, the ball is really hitting his gloves hard. I'm laughing myself silly at point, because these Kent guys aren't even close to laying bat on ball. They're just swatting at it, and after four overs they've got nothing – less than 10.

Our captain, Richie Richardson, looks at this lot and reckons, 'No boys, we can't have this. We can't massacre them; we need to give the fans their money's worth.' Sir Viv didn't like this one bit. I mean, he was really pissed off, saying, 'No, we didn't come here to make friends. We're here to beat these guys. Yes, we want to give the fans their money's worth, but we're not going to make it easy for the opposition.' The two of them are having this major argument out there in the middle, and you can basically see the steam coming out of Sir Viv's ears.

Richie is the captain and it is ultimately his decision, so he gives the ball to Jimmy Adams for a little bit. Unfortunately, that backfired, because the game eventually got away from us to such an extent that Kent ended up needing just six off the last over to win. You must understand that Lashings have only lost a couple of games since its inception in 1995. So Richie gives Wasim the ball … and Kent manages just two runs off the last over. Unbelievable bowling. Four balls in the blockhole, and a couple more that went flying past the batsmen. The Kent guys couldn't lay a bat on a ball. Fantastic stuff.

Shane Warne

Warnie always looked like he was enjoying himself, both on and off the pitch – almost as much as me, I suspect. During Warnie's international career, he enjoyed his beer and cigarettes, but he was always still able to go out there and bowl the way he did. He'd chirp batters left, right and centre and get in your face virtually every game you played, but he was also really funny sometimes. It just looked like he was having a great time.

I used to enjoy Warnie's chirps more than anyone else's. He was really clever – he knew just what to say at just the right time. I never felt like he was really having a go at anyone personally, but sometimes he'd say something so bladdy funny that I'd end up laughing out loud. Warnie's got a mouth on him and he can talk lots of shit, but he also comes out with a few gems now and again. I used to try hard to remember what Warnie said to me so I could tell people, but I dunno, his words just never stuck.

Warnie is probably the best spinner the world has ever seen – the fact that he has taken wickets all over the world and that his home-and-away record is almost equally good backs that up.

As a batsman, I was never that confident against him. He was just a different bowler. Unlike, say, a left-arm off-spinner, Warnie used to get the ball to drift in to you. Using his wrist and fingers, he could put so many revs on the ball that it would not only dip down very late, but move towards you like an in-swinger. So, if the ball started on off- or middle-stump, the in-drift would cause it to eventually pitch outside leg. That made it really difficult to use your feet, as you couldn't really predict where the ball would land.

Basically you had to play him like an in-swinger – I'd keep my head still for as long as possible and, if the delivery was full enough and pitching outside leg stump, I'd either sweep him or just defend. I'd wait for anything short and then cut him. But I never felt comfortable using my feet against Warnie. Even with the 100 I got against the Aussies during the 1999 World Cup at Headingly, I hardly ever used my feet. Mostly I just used to sweep him. Without that drift, he would still have been a good bowler, but I don't think he would've been quite so special.

After that game at Headingly, Warnie was the first guy to come and have a drink with me – he's a brilliant bowler on the field and a great bloke off it. When I saw him again at the start of the 2010 IPL season in Mumbai, I said, 'Shane, good to see you again.' And his reply was, 'Hersch, it's always good to be seen.' Never short of a sharp comeback is Warnie.

As tough as it was to have him as an opponent, it was also a privilege to face him – I'm proud to have played against the best spinner ever. I feel sorry for the next generation. They won't have the privilege of playing against a spinner of Warnie's ilk ... there is only ever going to be one Shane Keith Warne.

Muttiah Muralitharan

Murali ... I still can't read him after 14 years of playing against the guy. I got two 90s playing against Murali, and I can honestly say I never read one goddamn ball. Look, he wasn't effective at all in South Africa, as the ball never turns much here, so it was fine. Here, you could play him quite easily. But face him on the subcontinent, in Sri Lanka, where they prepare wickets specifically for him, and it's a completely different proposition. That's why his home-and-away record is so different.

It kind of annoys me that I've never scored a century in Sri Lanka, but I've only got myself to blame, really. I know Jacques Kallis shares a similar frustration. He's scored 35 Test centuries and still hasn't got one against Sri Lanka either, though he does have one ODI 100 scored in Colombo in 2004. But he can read Murali … or so he says.

My strategy was basically just to sweep the living kak out of him. That way, playing the ball on length, even if he spins it away from a right-hand batsman, you can still cover the spin. And if he spins it into you, then you sweep with the spin. Either way, you're smothering his spin. So, if you are going to do that with every second ball he bowls to you, and execute it very well, he's going to start dropping it a little bit shorter, and then you can play him off the back foot. Your default is to play the ball that's spinning into you and, if you see it coming fairly straight, then you know it's going to be the one that turns the other way.

To execute the sweep effectively, you've got to get your front pad in line with the ball so that, if you miss it, at least you don't get bowled. A lot of players don't execute the sweep correctly – the arc of their sweep is horizontal to the ground, which means that they don't cover the spin. The chances of getting a top edge then are high. And, remember, Murali also bowls fairly quickly for a spinner. What you have to do is sweep in an arc from high to low. In other words, you sweep down, and in that way you smother the spin. I play the sweep shot pretty well, so, ja, that's how I play against him. I can't say I've hit too many boundaries against that boy, though. Ja, one of the trickiest bowlers I've come up against.

Peter Kirsten

There's no one player whom I've specifically modelled my own game on, but as a youngster I always liked Peter Kirsten – specifically his basic cover drive. He never moved his feet all that much for the shot, but he had great hands. The way he got his hands through the ball was just amazing. The fact is that when you are playing against genuine quicks, it's not possible to get a good stride in. That 'get your foot to the ball' stuff just doesn't apply when the ball is hurtling towards you at 155km/h. What matters is how quickly you get your hands to, and through, the ball. That's what makes an opening batsman good.

This is also evident in the way Peter played the wide half-volley. His feet would never quite get there, but thanks to his hands, he'd lean back and hit through the ball. Peter was very strong with his wrists, and a lot of people say I'm quite wristy too when I play.

Obviously Peter was a hero to a youngster growing up in the Cape, but unfortunately by the time I made my senior debut, he'd already gone to Border, so I never played with him. He did coach us for a bit at Province, but by then I had already established myself as an international cricketer and he didn't have too much influence on my batting approach.

Peter is also a very nice guy – a great guy, actually; really funny too, with a dry sense of humour. He was always cracking us up. When he was coaching us he used to walk around the changing room in his underpants and long socks, with his comb tucked into his socks. I mean, how the hell can you take a coach seriously when he walks around like that?

So, Peter will always be one of my all-time favourites, simply because of his nature – he's just a phenomenal guy – and his talent as a cricketer. I've always been completely in awe when I'm in his company.

Sir Vivian Richards

I never saw Sir Viv in his prime, but I've watched his exploits on TV countless times. This guy was just a complete murderer of bowlers. He butchered them. Completely annihilated them. He could hit an away-swinger a foot outside off-stump and flick it over square leg. I'm very fortunate to have had the opportunity to play with him in the Lashings team. Sir Viv might be 58 now, but he is still as strong as a bull and oozes confidence. And he's still charging the bowlers. He's always got that swagger, and man, the women love him too.

One benefit he had playing for the West Indies in the 1970s and early 1980s was that he was never going to get bounced too often by opposition bowlers, because he had quickies like Andy Roberts, Michael Holding, Colin Croft, Joel Garner and Malcolm Marshall to back him up. The West Indies had one helluva bowling line-up, and team, back then.

Interestingly, their bowlers also helped their batsmen in a roundabout way. Viv told me how, during net practice, their bowlers used to run in and let their teammates have it. Apparently the bowlers never gave their own guys any rest, even in the nets. They would bomb them just as they would bomb the opposition out in the middle. Obviously this meant that when the West Indies batsmen went out to face the likes of England or Australia, it was a bit of a walk in the park.

And finally ... no. 11, Shoaib Akhtar

Ja ... a bit of a nutter, this guy. I've never ever felt safe facing him – even wearing a helmet – simply because his action makes it so difficult to pick up the ball. He doesn't show you the ball, so you can't read the seam, and he's got this long throwing action ... well, I shouldn't say 'throwing action' ... I'm sure Shoaib's never chucked a ball in his life ... But anyways, let's just say it's a very difficult action with which to pick up the ball. And if that's not tough enough, add inconsistent bounce in the wicket and it becomes even trickier. We're talking a life or death situation here.

Fortunately, I haven't played against Shoaib in South Africa, with our bouncier wickets, often. He's had a lot of injuries, and controversies have also kept him out of the Pakistan team – but I have faced him a lot on the subcontinent. Even on those slower wickets, he's very effective swinging the new ball and reverse-swinging the old one. He has easily bowled the quickest balls I've ever faced. Through the air and off the wicket, he's even quicker than Brett Lee at his quickest. Add that awkward bowling action to the mix, and he's a tough guy to face.

Of course the word 'chucker' often appears in the same sentence as the name 'Shoaib Akhtar', but while he has been called a couple of times, nothing has really come of it. In my opinion, the authorities have been quite lenient with him. His very quick ball, and sometimes his bouncer, stretch the boundaries of legality. And I remember former Aussie opener Justin Langer's comments after a game against Pakistan. 'We,' he said, with a very obvious smirk, 'handled everything he could *throw* at us.'

But, ag you know, players like Shoaib are good for the game and people want to see him bowl. I have always liked making it interesting for the spectators. And he really is an entertaining bowler.

Shoaib even seemed to fake injury in order to confuse batsmen. At times, particularly on the subcontinent, it was really hot and humid, and he'd come running in with his bladdy spikes hitting his arse – I mean, really charging in off that long run-up of his, which gave you, the batsman, plenty of time to think, 'This boy is coming, and he's coming for *you*.'

He'd bowl four really quick overs with that slinging action of his and you'd really be kakking off … and then he'd suddenly pull up like he's tweaked his hamstring. Now you're thinking, 'Great, he's pulled a hammy, or he's cramping. I can relax a little.' Maybe he'd send down a couple of slower ones and by now you're thinking, 'Brilliant, he's going to be heading for the changing room soon …'

And then the next ball is a lightning bolt aimed either at your head or, worse, your toes.

I remember one of the first times I played against Shoaib was in 2000, at the Sharjah tournament in the United Arab Emirates. It was a day/night ODI game against Pakistan, and there he was, charging at Gary Kirsten, my fellow opener, and me. In that first over that Shoaib bowled, not one delivery was slower than 153km/h. I mean, he was blitzing in. So … after two overs he grabbed his hammy and we thought, 'Okay, cool, it'll be nice to relax.' And then he comes back and bowls just as fast. We suddenly lost three or four quick wickets. Actually, I remember that particular game as one of the few times when I carried my bat through an ODI. I opened the batting and was still there at our innings' close.

As I mentioned, I always found Shoaib trickier to face on the subcontinent wickets because the bounce isn't always consistent. Some balls stay low, others bounce, and then it becomes like a lottery, you know. It's almost like you've got to decide what you're going to do beforehand.

Let's say Shoaib throws the ball in short; you're going to pull it and rely on your reactions to execute the shot. At that speed, you can't play each ball on its merit – they just come too fast. You have less than a second to make up your mind. That's not a lot of time to weigh up your options, which are normally 'should I stand up and hit, or should I duck?' So, from that point of view, it was quite frightening to face him.

And it was no less pleasant getting hit by him. Shoaib hit me in the chest once during our tour to Pakistan in 2003. It was the first ball during one of the ODI games – he tried to bounce me, but the ball didn't get up. I just sort of dropped my hands, and the ball klapped me on the chest and ran down to third man. It hit me really, really hard, and that was only a glancing blow, because I was standing fairly side-on.

As I mentioned earlier, those huge in-swingers that zero in on your toes are equally intimidating. I'll never forget that 2003 Test in Lahore, when Shoaib nailed Gary on the cheek. Shoaib was bowling around the wicket, and he pitched one in short and Gary tried to hook him … but he got smacked right in the face. Ten stitches, and a broken eye socket and nose later … Check it on YouTube. Frightening.

Gary showed huge courage to return in the second innings and score a gutsy 46 to help us try to save the Test. It wasn't enough, unfortunately. Back to the story, though – Gary leaves the field, blood pouring from his face, and in comes Neil McKenzie. It might have been the very next ball, but Neil gets a huge reverse-swinger straight on the toe. I mean, the ball bent like a bladdy banana. The direct hit didn't break Neil's toe, but he was out lbw, and he could hardly walk for the rest of the day. Proteas bowling coach Vincent Barnes still reckons it was the best spell of fast bowling he's ever seen.

I've got to know Shoaib a little better, having played quite a few games with him for the Lashings World XI, and let me tell you, he is just as wild off the field as he is on it.

10

The Proteas and me

Some people aren't going to like this chapter, but I've always believed you have to call it like you see it.

I think if we're honest with ourselves – and I'm talking about the players and the fans – we've got to admit that the Proteas have underachieved in international cricket over the past decade. Given the talent we have had at our disposal, we should have won at least one ODI World Cup and been consistently challenging the Aussies as the top Test team in the world.

Yes, we have hit the number-one spot in both ODI and Test cricket, but only briefly. One great highlight – and, ironically, one that I played no part in – was the historic 2009 Test series win in Australia. It's a pity we haven't been able to build on that victory, though. The stone-cold fact is that, when it comes to the crunch – especially in limited-overs cricket – we fail, time and time again. Painful World Cup after painful World Cup. And believe me when I say that no one has felt the pain more acutely than me.

I have thought long and hard about including this chapter in the book. Should I tell you why I think the Proteas have underachieved? I certainly get asked often enough by both cricket supporters and the press to know that it's an issue. Or should I rather keep my mouth shut? I know where *your* vote lies – you wouldn't be reading this book if you thought I should keep my mouth shut – but I do run the risk of sounding like a big fat hypocrite mouthing off when I was part of almost all those teams that failed at the final hurdle.

But I have decided to talk and be damned.

These are my honest views on where I think our national cricket team falls short. This is not press speculation, but a first-hand account of someone who has been inside the team for 14 years. Of course, these are *my* opinions and they are therefore subjective, but they certainly represent a viewpoint shared by quite a few of my teammates over the years. And I say this while acknowledging all my own failings and shortcomings as a player, when the team could've done with more consistent performances from yours truly. Here we go, then ...

I believe that the main factor that has contributed to the Proteas' underachievement is an overly conservative approach to the game.

Putting the 'conservative' back into cricket

I touched on the Proteas' lack of big-match temperament in Chapter 3, but it's a subject that definitely deserves a bit more attention. The press and our opponents love to call us chokers, but I think that's far too simplistic an analysis. Yes, I agree that we don't always have the *kop* for the big occasion, but it's important to understand why that is the case. I believe it comes down to an ingrained fear of failure, reinforced by a fundamentally conservative strategy – particularly in 20- and 50-over cricket.

The fear of failure is our Achilles heel. This fear has overcome us time and time again in big tournaments. Perhaps it stems from that awful semi-final loss against the Aussies in the 1999 World Cup. Maybe those scars run so deep that their memory still hampers any chances we may have of winning when the chips are down. Whatever the reason, we always seem to get paralysed by the occasion. We're so petrified of losing that we tighten up. You never see that happen with teams such as India, Sri Lanka and, obviously, Australia. But we do it, as do England, and the West Indies too – basically the teams that don't consistently perform in limited-overs cricket are always too tentative. I mean, it's not like we don't have enough talented players. Shit … we had enough players to help England win the 2010 T20 World Cup.

Having mentioned it, the recent T20 World Cup in the West Indies illustrates my point perfectly. Prior to the tournament's kick-off, we had a big team meeting aboard a cruise ship in the Caribbean. The aim was to clear the air and for everyone to give their 10 cents' worth. Everyone was supposed to be really honest about what it would take for us to be successful in the tournament.

I made the point that the big tournaments are the ultimate opportunity for us to show the world how good we are at limited-overs cricket, both as individuals and as a team. Mark Boucher backed me up, and he also tried to get the point across that we can't afford to have a fear of failure – we have to go out there and express ourselves. As it turned out, the only South Africans who expressed themselves were Kevin Pietersen and Craig Kieswetter …

In our match against England, for example, Pietersen and Kieswetter came at our bowlers and really took the game to them, and our boys didn't know what to do. There was no Plan B – or if there was a Plan B, they were too shell-shocked to implement it. And I'm standing on the field watching, thinking to myself, 'Okay … here we go *again*!'

As soon as they took the attack to our bowlers, we were found wanting. We also took a couple of wickets off no-balls and dropped some catches, which didn't help. I know the guys don't mean to do it, but standing there on the field, I just think, 'It's a World Cup. This kind of stuff costs you big-time.'

And then in our do-or-die game against Pakistan, even our top batsmen played some pretty weird shots – look at the way a guy like AB de Villiers lost his wicket. Here's proof that even one of the game's best batsmen can play a silly shot – something that I have done plenty of times … that's just what pressure does. He'd been hitting back past the bowler superbly, but then went for a paddle-scoop over the keeper's head and ended up hitting straight into the air, to be caught by Pakistan keeper Kamran Akmal.

Lest you think I'm laying the blame at my teammates' door here, let me say that my own form was far from impressive as well. Against England, I was on eight when Ryan Sidebottom took a great catch at short fine leg to dismiss me; and then against Pakistan I hit a solid pull shot off Abdul Razzaq, but Misbah-ul-Haq managed to pluck the ball out of the air at mid-wicket. On another day it would've been a four. Unlucky? Maybe, but that's cricket. I guess on another day AB's paddle could've gone for four as well.

In that Pakistan game, chasing 148, we left the charge way too late and ended up 11 runs short. We were just too tentative, and despite our little team talk on the boat, again it basically came down to being scared. Look at the Aussies – they chased down 191 in their semi-final against the same Pakistani bowling attack with the ballsiest final two-over run chase I've seen in a long time.

As I said, this fear of failure is really reinforced by an essentially conservative strategic approach to the game. The Proteas' brain trust, for example, has decided that for the first six overs of a 20-over game, we should rather go for consistency than hitting balls over the top. Do you think Aussie opening pair David Warner and Shane Watson have been given that instruction? If they have, they've clearly been doing their level best to ignore it.

Not with us, though, and it's why we never got runs in the games against New Zealand and England. Graeme and Jacques hardly came off, and then it was like, 'Okay, Hersch, now you go out there and play your natural game.' There are too many of the same ideas, no flexibility and no ability to quickly switch to another game plan if the current one isn't working.

At the toss before the final group game against Pakistan, which we had to win to stay in the tournament, commentator and former Pakistani batsman Rameez Raja asked Graeme what it was like to prepare against a team as unpredictable as Pakistan.

Graeme's response was, well, it wasn't too difficult, because we were pretty unpredictable ourselves. I wondered about this. I'm not sure 'unpredictable' is the word I would've used. Inconsistent? Yes. Unpredictable? Not exactly. All this talk of being more instinctive and expressive ... ja ... I've yet to see it.

As I said, Warner and Watson are going hell for leather from ball one – just like Adam Gilchrist and Matthew Hayden did for them in the 50-over game. If they failed, they failed quickly, but if they came off, they got 60 or 70 runs in no time. That's the basis of success in one-day cricket since Sanath Jayasuriya and Romesh Kaluwitharana paved the way in the 1996 World Cup.

The game is becoming more and more attacking each season – particularly on the subcontinent. If you don't have guys who fire upfront there, you leave yourself with far too much to do – especially with our less-than-stellar history against spin-bowling. I reckon the Proteas would really benefit by opening the innings with a Warner or Watson-like batsman who possesses the kind of explosive power and improvisational skills to win you a game upfront.

I think the selectors have tried this route, picking Loots Bosman as a 20-over opener in the 2010 T20 World Cup and the T20 series against the West Indies that followed. Unfortunately for Loots, he wasn't very successful. You've got to feel for the guy in this situation. No doubt, Loots has all those explosive shots in his armoury – his domestic record certainly proves that – but his ability to express himself was clearly hampered by injury. He'd just had a knee op and couldn't field for more than a couple of overs before coming off the pitch.

I'm not exactly sure why they preferred Loots to me in some of those T20 World Cup games. I know I was supposed to play in the game against Afghanistan – coach Corrie van Zyl and Graeme Smith had told me that I was taking the field – then on the morning of the game I heard Loots would play instead of me. The reason for this change was never shared with me. It was whispered by some of the press that it was because Loots had a darker skin than me, but that was ridiculous I'm sure. I am classified as a 'previously disadvantaged' player too and, though my skin tone can look a little fair at times, I thought I was pretty brown in the Caribbean. I'd been working hard on my tan.

I would love to have a go at opening again, but not under the circumstances in which I currently find myself. I feel I have to perform in order to stay in the team, when what I need to hear is, 'Hersch, you're opening the innings. Play as freely as you want and don't worry about your place. If you come off, you come off; if you don't, you won't get dropped. We know a batsman can't always score big runs, but we're confident you'll have more successes than failures.'

If I play 10 games and get the team off to six flyers but fail four times, then I think that's a good return.

The 'clique'

This issue of a clique within the Proteas team has long been a topic of discussion among the press and South African cricket fans. The team has been criticised for being run by a group of senior players – Graeme Smith, Jacques Kallis, Mark Boucher and, more recently, AB de Villiers – and this inner circle splits the team in two and makes any chance of developing true team spirit among the Proteas impossible.

Yes, these guys are very tight mates and do everything together – from hanging out during tours to going on holidays together when we aren't playing. You only have to see AB's photo on his BlackBerry Messenger – it's him, Graeme, Mark and Jacques. They always keep close tabs on what the others are doing – while Graeme was batting in one of his two 2010 IPL innings, AB sent this message around, saying, '*Die buffel bat kwaai*,' so you know they're not only out partying together, but they also watch each other's games. Unfortunately, AB's message was something of a jinx – Smithy went out the very next ball.

Does this make for a clique? Look, it's inevitable that members of an international team will form close bonds. It's what happens when a bunch of guys go to war together. And, make no mistake, international cricket is a war. I guess people have a problem with this when one of the guys in this circle of tight friends is the team captain. There's a perception that it splits the team into 'us' and 'them'.

Other international players have quizzed me on this. One of the benefits of socialising with other international players in the IPL is that you get to hear what they think of the Proteas. One consistent observation has been their surprise at seeing Smith, Bouch and Kallis, in particular, always going out together. I understand where they are coming from but, as I said, war forges close bonds and it's only human nature that Graeme is going to form close ties with his lieutenants.

This is a weird situation for me, because I've always kept myself in the middle, and I'm equally comfortable both in- and outside this group. I can hang out with both Bouch and Makhaya – that's just the sort of person I am. Bouch, for example, has been a really good friend to me over the years and offered me support and valuable advice. He's been a great servant to South African cricket, and his opinion and experience are respected within the team.

With regard to being able to fit in easily, I think JP Duminy is a lot like me ... but I know some players have found it a complicated situation. Perhaps it's a cultural issue, but I can't know for sure. Whatever the reason is, I do think we still have some work ahead of us to build a stronger overall bond within the Proteas.

Obviously there's only one person ultimately responsible for building a unified team, and that's the captain. Graeme is a powerful presence, and his personality is one that almost insists on being a leader. There's also no questioning the guy's courage on the field and his willingness to stand up and take the flak for us when we're under public scrutiny. Given all this, is it a justifiable criticism to say he has got too close to certain players?

Perhaps you might think so, but I have played under enough guys to know what a tough job Graeme has. Plus, I am confident in the knowledge that I'm not a captain's arse. As I've said, I had known from my school days – when there's always pressure on the best player to be captain – that I was not cut out for the captaincy. It takes managerial skills I admit I don't have. Still, I suppose that doesn't disqualify me from having a firm opinion on what makes a good captain. I have played under enough of them to observe different approaches.

As I said earlier, despite his shortcomings, Hansie Cronjé was the best captain I ever played under. He could tread that fine line between bonding with the team while still maintaining sufficient distance so that he could treat everyone equally. It also allowed him to be hard on an individual when the situation demanded it. Every single one of his players had huge respect for the guy.

Things were never the same after Hansie was banned. I sympathised with Shaun Pollock – he had a tough time filling Hansie's shoes and gluing the team back together at the same time. But the Proteas never had that same togetherness under Polly. He never socialised with the boys too much but, that said, like Hansie, Polly also never got too close to any one player, for which I respected him.

If you ask me, I think the issue really became a problem when Mickey Arthur took over. Mickey wasn't the most forceful personality, and I guess he found it tough to coach guys who had played close to 100 Tests. Too often he bowed to senior players' opinions.

I think he made an effort to take them on once or twice, but he wasn't being taken seriously. Simply put, without Graeme's backing, Mickey didn't have much influence over the guys. In the end, Graeme was simply too powerful. If it was indeed the case that he had wanted Mickey out, as many fans and the press speculated, Mickey would have been asked to leave. Of course, as I was not a member of the inner circle, I wasn't privy to why Graeme might have wanted Mickey out.

New coach Corrie van Zyl has talked about how he wants to mould the Proteas into a proper team, and the new convener of selectors, Andrew Hudson, has also made noises about wielding the big broom. Whether that means dropping some of the senior players and bringing in new blood (and I do realise that Mr Hudson's broom could sweep me out too), or using a very firm hand to set up a new player–coach dynamic, I don't know.

My future in the team

I have simply been honest in my preceding comments. I sincerely hope my colleagues and the Proteas team management see it that way. My intention is only to see the Proteas do better, and of course I would also like to be playing better, but, as we speak, I haven't had the best of seasons with the bat.

As always in sport, confidence is a massive factor, and at the moment I feel I still need to convince the Proteas selectors that I can make a positive contribution to the team. Over the past year I've really begun to realise how crucial their backing is for your confidence. As I've said, I'm comfortable with the fact that my Test career is all but over, but I still believe I have what it takes to be a game-winning batsman for South Africa in limited-overs cricket. I just wish I knew where I stand – I mean, you get left out once or twice for no reason, okay, it shakes you up a bit, but the way that I've been in and out of the side over the past year has not exactly been great for my confidence. Let me put you in the picture ...

After coming out of rehab and going straight to Australia at the beginning of 2009, I started off very tentatively, going out for a duck in the first T20 game, then getting only six runs in the second. The Aussies – looking to get back at us after our Test team had just famously beaten them – comfortably took the series 2-0.

After that, though, I started to get back into the swing of international cricket, and during the five-match ODI series I scored a low of seven and a high of 64 to average 30 on the nose and help the Proteas to a convincing 4-1 series win. It got better in the return series here in South Africa a few months later, when I averaged 50, including 110 off 116 balls in the series-clinching fourth ODI in PE, and then 82 in the final dead rubber at the Wanderers.

After that series we headed over to the UK for the 2009 T20 World Cup, where I put on a fairly good show, averaging 19 – the fifth-highest in the team behind Jacques Kallis, who had a great tournament, averaging a shade less than 60. I was in good form going into the semi-final, having scored 30 against the Poms and 55 against the West Indies. Unfortunately, my game went a little pear-shaped thereafter, with a five against India and another five against Pakistan in the finals.

Shahid Afridi got me with a beaut in that game – a slider on off-stump that had me playing for the leg-break … goodbye off-stump.

Our next series was, of course, the ICC Champions Trophy in South Africa in September/October 2009. Once again we bombed on home turf, failing to get past the group stage. I only played one game – the final group game against England, where our bowlers got smashed. We eventually fell 22 runs short of chasing down England's 323. So that's where I was with my batting. All in all, 2009 was a bit of a roller coaster. It started out slowly, then got a whole lot better before tapering off as my opportunities started to dry up. They would dry up completely when, during the Champions Trophy, I got a missed call from the then convener of selectors, Mike Procter.

I had a feeling something was up, so I phoned him back, which is when I found out that I was to be dropped from the squad for the upcoming home series against the Poms.

'Hersch, did you get my message?' Procter asked.

'No, why?' I replied.

'Well, we haven't included you in the ODI squad against England.'

The reason was that I wasn't 'consistent' enough. And Mickey Arthur was questioning my preparation. According to him, I hadn't prepared sufficiently for the Champions Trophy – a statement I found bizarre. I had prepared exactly the same way I have for my whole career, but this time it wasn't good enough? I played one game in that tournament and I mistimed a pull shot off James Anderson's bowling.

'Inconsistent and ill-prepared.'

Whatever. Man, was I pissed off. I had been one of the Proteas' most consistent batsmen in the preceding year – it was only when they started yo-yoing me in and out of the starting XI that I started struggling a little. My confidence was shot. I remember the conversation with Procter was rather curt and ended with me saying, 'Okay, well, if that's your story, bye,' and terminating the call.

As you know, the ODI series against England in November/ December 2009 was a disaster. We lost the five-match series 1-2, with both the first and fifth ODIs being abandoned without a ball being bowled. For that final game in Port Elizabeth, I was actually called back into the squad after Jacques Kallis was out injured. Except I was to be twelfth man ... which didn't make me a happy chappy at all.

I was thinking a lot about my future with the Proteas at that point. I mean, not since the earliest days of my international career had I been twelfth man. I was always in the starting XI for Tests and ODIs – especially in the ODIs. And especially in PE, where I have a great record. But no ... here I was, the bladdy waterboy. Obviously there was some ego involved here, but I seriously began to wonder whether or not I should give up on the Proteas and focus on ending my career as a specialist T20 player for teams like the Cape Cobras, the Deccan Chargers and in county cricket. When I was spending time alone in one of my many hotel rooms in India during the 2010 IPL tournament – I spent a lot of time in my room, given that we weren't allowed outside the grounds for security reasons – I came very close to calling it a day.

But then the UCB offered me another contract in April 2010, when all our contracts came up for renewal. Donné and I had a long chat about my future, as I really did not want to be messed around any more. It wasn't good for my head and it wasn't good for my cricket.

As contracts always seem to do, they just appear in your email inbox one day. It's weird, I know. Nobody discusses anything with you beforehand, nor is there any kind of negotiation. The contract simply arrives in your inbox with an instruction to print it, sign it and return it. I know, for example, of one senior Proteas player who recently read his contract to find he'd been dropped two categories ... it was the first he knew about it. This guy has been a mainstay in the batting line-up for the past three years and he suddenly finds he no longer has an A- or B-category contract. As you may well imagine, he's one unhappy Protea.

But this is the way it's always been. I mean, it's not like the coach sits you down and says, 'We'd like to offer you a new contract – do you want one?' There's no opportunity to say (if you wanted to), 'Look, coach, I think I've done my time and I'm thinking of retiring.' Nope, the contract just arrives. All the players know when the contracts are due, and I guess if yours doesn't arrive, you know you're out of the mix. So, ja, like I said. Strange.

Anyway, so now I have a new contract until April 2011, which will include the World Cup in India, Sri Lanka and Bangladesh, starting in February. Which is great – I've made no bones about the fact that winning a World Cup would mean everything to me; it's the one medal I've wanted the most in my career. So all's good. Or not.

When the selectors then dropped me for the May/June 2010 West Indies ODI series, I thought: Go figure. How can I be in their plans for the next World Cup when I'm left out of the team for a major series eight months before the start of the biggest tournament in world cricket?

So that's where I am with the South African team at the moment. I just have to keep on smiling and not let myself get too down about it. I guess everyone's time has to come, but I still believe that Graeme and I remain the best two openers for the Proteas in limited-overs cricket.

As far as the 2011 World Cup is concerned, I think there's still time to experiment with the squad of 16 players that have been selected. I reckon they should give some of the younger guys a chance to put their hands up in the run-up to the World Cup. I think, for example, that David Miller deserved his call-up to the 2010 West Indies tour – he had a really good domestic season for the Dolphins.

Dropping Mark Boucher was a contentious issue. Look, I understand the selectors' dilemma – if someone hasn't been scoring runs for a while, they need to be dropped. The same has applied to me. Stats don't lie, and it's been a while since Bouch has been able to consistently finish a game the way he used to. On the other hand, can we really do without the kind of bulldog, never-say-die attitude Bouch brings to the team? Not to mention the guy's massive experience. Remember too that by sticking the gloves on AB, the team is now deprived of our best fielder. I mean, point – where AB normally held station – is such a valuable position in one-day cricket.

There have also been a few calls for Graeme's head. Although he does have some faults as a captain, as I'm sure he would admit, you have to consider who his potential replacements would be. Jacques Kallis is the current vice-captain, but he is not captain material, seriously. The main contender has to be our new T20 captain Johan Botha, who did a great job leading us against Australia in January 2009. Without Graeme and Jacques, we beat the Aussies 4-1 in their own backyard.

I still find it hard to understand why Botha wasn't made vice-captain after that series instead of Jacques. As captain he was genuinely impressive – very confident and outspoken on the field. I think he lost a little confidence in the subsequent ODI series in India in February 2010 when we lost 1-2, but I think now he's got his confidence back. And I thought he bowled really well at the recent T20 World Cup. Botha's a complete cricketer. He's fit, he's hungry and he knows what he wants to do on the field. Most importantly, like Hansie, Johan never gets too close to the other players. The selectors have clearly shown confidence in him by awarding him the T20 job after Graeme stood down, and I think he would make a great 50-over captain as well.

The World Cup is being held in India, which means that you need at least two spinners. There's no one pushing Johan Botha or Roelof van der Merwe at the moment ... but the guys seem to have worked Roelof out a little. He's basically got one delivery and only varies his pace. I think Wayne Parnell is going to be a key bowler. Wayne has the ability to do the same job that Lasith Malinga does for Sri Lanka.

Malinga's economy rate is helluva impressive – 7.02 runs per over at the 2010 IPL and 7.92 at the T20 World Cup – the way he mixes up three deliveries is the key to his success. Firstly, he's got a great yorker – and his lack of height and that slinger delivery action of his are tailor-made to bowl this kind of ball. There's a lot less margin for error on a yorker if the ball is coming in low than when it is bowled by someone as tall as Morné Morkel, for example.

Secondly, Malinga's got a good slower ball. And, thirdly, he has a bouncer. Malinga mixes up those three deliveries right from the start of his bowling spell – it doesn't matter whether he's bowling during the opening Power Play or the last few overs. That's all you get from him. Those last two deliveries, combined with the accuracy of his yorker, make him really tough to score against. I mean, the guy does not bowl a length ball. Maybe if he's getting some swing, he might send down the odd length ball to induce a nick, but that's about it. Bowl a length ball in 20-over cricket and whether you are Morné Morkel or Dale Steyn, the guys are going to send it over the boundary.

Proteas bowling coach Vinnie Barnes keeps telling me how tough it is to bowl a yorker from nine feet up (or however tall Morné is with his hand up), but that's the way the game is going. Morné's a helluva talented bowler and I've no doubt he will be able to adjust his sights. Look at Pakistan's Umar Gul – he's pretty tall and he has a great yorker, so it's not like it can't be done.

When our guys were under the cosh from England in that T20 World Cup game, they didn't know what to do. They kept trying to bowl bouncers, and those were travelling as far as the nice, juicy length balls they were bowling. The bouncer seems to be our bowler's stock dot ball. In South African conditions, if our bowlers need a dot ball or two, they go for the short-pitched delivery. And that does work *here*.

On Indian pitches, where we'll be playing the next 50-over World Cup, that strategy is going to be much less effective than it was in the West Indies. As you know, the ball just doesn't get up there at all. It'll get messy, unless we utilise bowlers who have a good yorker in their arsenal. As good as these guys think they are, without a consistent yorker they're going to get hit, and hit far. You have to have a banker ball in limited-overs cricket. It's weird – I mean, our guys practise yorkers for all they're worth in the nets, but they can't execute them well enough in a game.

Along with Rusty Theron, who I think has all the variations needed for the subcontinent, I think Wayne is the guy who can really do the business for us. Apart from the fact that he is a lefty, he has the potential to bowl a good variety of balls, including an in-swinging yorker-length ball. All the signs are there for Wayne to play a big part in Proteas cricket in the coming years – in all forms of the game.

11

The future
and what it holds

The future of cricket … and of Herschelle Gibbs.

Let's start with the game and end with me, personally. It's my
book, after all, and having it end with me just seems right. And
I do so at the risk of unleashing the traditionalists, who are just
waiting to intone: 'You're not bigger than the game, boy! *No one*
is bigger than the game!'

Ja, I know that, but, like, it's my book.

CRICKET

Is it the end of Test cricket?

So what is happening to the game, then? Cricket has certainly
changed a great deal with the introduction of 20-over cricket,
which has gained massive popularity in a very short space of time.
For many fans, 20-over cricket is a better version of the game than
Test cricket. It's like the game itself – and not me – has got bigger
than the game. Yet I know that some of those above-mentioned
traditionalists do not love the new development at all.

There are a lot of concerns that the new, shorter form of the
game could spell the end of Test cricket – or at least see the five-
day game take a back seat to the new pyrotechnics. But I don't
think that will be the case. I reckon there will be a much clearer
division between Test and limited-overs cricket, from the players
who play each respective format of the game to the fans who
watch the games.

In my opinion, if there is going to be a casualty down the line, it's going to be the 50-over form of the game. In the future I think we're going to see two types of players and two types of fans embracing their favourite format of the game. We are going to reach a point where there will be enough commercial leagues for a player to have a successful career in ODIs and 20/20 without having to play Tests.

I have mixed feelings about it all, to be honest. On the one hand, the shorter format has opened the door for guys like me, Adam Gilchrist, Matthew Hayden and Andrew Symonds – all big hitters from the previous generation who have now been given a bit of a second wind. As 20-over 'mercenaries', it's been a really lucrative innovation for us too. It's funny how the wheel has turned. As youngsters the only route to fame and fortune was to work your butt off to get into the Test team – and even then the South African guys were a little bitter because they were getting paid peanuts compared to their colleagues in the English Test squad. Convert into rands what those guys earned in pounds and it was like chalk and cheese.

On the other hand, I do feel a little sad to see the new-generation youngsters disregard Test cricket. It's a form of the game that tests strength of character and resolve like no other. Only in Test cricket do you get enough twists and turns to keep you on the edge of your seat for days. The downside of 20/20 cricket is that the game can pretty much be decided in the first five overs of the first innings if the team opening the innings has a 'mare. So, ja, I think gone are the days when a young cricketer starts out with a hunger for Test cricket and sets as his goals those golden milestones of 100 Tests or 10 000 Test runs.

Neither will these young pups get the opportunity to play epic games against the likes of the great Aussie teams under Steve Waugh and Ricky Ponting. Even though they klapped us most of the time, it's a genuine highlight of my career to have played against one of the best teams in Test cricket (along with that legendary West Indian team of the late 1970s and 1980s). I get a real sense of accomplishment knowing that I was able to score Test runs against bowlers such as Shane Warne and Glenn McGrath. Gary Kirsten and I were chatting about this recently – Eric Simons was with us too – and we're proud to say that we held our own in Test cricket and were able to make our mark in the limited-overs game as well. Not like these youngsters nowadays who have become so specialised.

Young Australian David Warner is the perfect example of the new breed of international cricketer. He's an explosive batsman the likes of which we haven't really seen before – he's like me, times two. When he comes off, he comes off big, but he doesn't always come off. Thank goodness. The chances of Warner ever being picked for a Test team – or even wanting to play Test cricket – are slim. Why would he? The guy is travelling the world playing really exciting cricket, having the time of his life and earning a ton of money – more than he would have earned in Test cricket, certainly. The same applies to guys like Kieron Pollard of the West Indies and India's Yusuf Pathan – you don't hear their names mentioned in Test cricket.

I do understand it, though – why would you want to play Test cricket when you've got money coming at you left, right and centre for just 20/20 cricket? Pollard (along with Kiwi Shane Bond) was sold for the player-cap maximum of US$750 000 at the last Indian Premier League player auction in January 2009. And young South African fast bowler Wayne Parnell went for US$610 000.

Those sums make these youngsters instant millionaires. And remember, that's not the total fee for their three-year contract – it's what they get *per year* for three years. Who needs to play Test cricket if you are earning that kind of cash for six weeks' work per year? Now add a county contract, plus your own domestic-franchise contract, and you are smiling, boet.

You have to remember, though, that the only reason 20-over

cricket has so much cash at its disposal is because fans want to go and watch the games. Take the IPL, for example – easily the most successful tournament currently out there. In fact, it's one of the most successful tournaments in world sport as far as spectator attendance is concerned – reports state that IPL 3 attracted more eyeballs than any other sports tournament in history.

The popularity of the game is reflected in the amounts that the two new franchises – Pune and Kochi – were sold for in March 2010. At US$370 million for Pune and US$333.33 million for Kochi, that is three times more than the original franchises were sold for just three years earlier. I mean, that is phenomenal growth! Even within the increasing popularity of 20-over cricket, nothing compares to the IPL as far as the vibe of the tournament goes. The T20 World Cup doesn't even come close to the razzmatazz and heightened feeling of excitement that spectators, players and the organisers experience with the IPL.

Not only has 20-over cricket changed the format of the game; it's also having an impact on the design of the equipment. Matthew Hayden's revolutionary Mongoose bat got a lot of attention at IPL 3. With a handle that is 43 per cent longer and a blade 33 per cent shorter but thicker than a 'normal' bat, it is supposed to give you 20 per cent more hitting power. And the new bat still falls within the ICC's regulations, so it's legal. In the hands of a smasher like Hayden – not a guy who really needs any extra help when it comes to launching balls over the ropes – the Mongoose was devastating.

I haven't tried the Mongoose yet, but my Deccan Chargers teammate Dwayne Smith had a couple in his possession and I picked one up in the changing room during one of our games. But it just felt too weird to me. I wanted to assume the stance of a baseball player, not a cricketer. I think with the smaller blade, you're at a disadvantage against quick, short-pitched bowling. But the bat clearly works for Hayden. Besides the fact that the ball doesn't get up much on the Indian wickets, any bowler with half a brain knows that, no matter what wicket you're playing on, pitching anything short to Hayden is a *bad* idea. You *are* going to get pumped. It's as certain as death and taxes.

I have absolutely loved playing in the IPL. With Adam Gilchrist as captain, Darren Lehmann as coach and South African legend Goolam Rajah as team manager, the Chargers are among the most professional outfits I have ever played for, especially in team preparation.

But, there's a relaxed side to it too. The sponsors arrange a lot of social functions to which at least 40 models are invited at a time. Seriously. At least 40 models at every party. Everything has to be ultra-glamorous. This sort of thing doesn't happen anywhere else in the cricket world, believe me. I think it's particularly great for the older guys, like me, who have played international cricket for such a long time. While we are still able to be professional in a tournament, we also make the most of the ample opportunities to relax and enjoy ourselves, which is probably the part I enjoy the most.

Even though we're the defending champions, the Chargers aren't one of the glam teams in the IPL. Our owners aren't Bollywood stars like the Royals' Shilpa Shetty or the Knight Riders' Shahrukh Khan. The Chargers feels more like a family. They're just a great bunch of lads, from legends like Gilchrist and characters like Andrew Symonds, to the younger Indian players like Rohit Sharma and RP Singh.

And the buzz at the ground is just incredible to witness in person. You get some idea of the noise the Indian cricket fans generate if you watch it on TV, but actually experiencing it in person is something else. It's so bladdy loud that even if you yell at a teammate 25 metres away, he won't hear you.

The crowd go ape-shit even if you just walk out onto the field prior to the game for a bit of a warm-up. I mean, you have never seen people who love cricket as much as these Indian chaps. And obviously they get revved up by all the music blaring out from the PA system and watching the gorgeous cheerleaders – who, in 2010, were all South African girls. What a bonus. We were in India with a squad of lovely South African lasses following us around. I got to know a couple quite well.

I always used to love coming to India as it is – especially after the match-fixing issue was settled and I knew I wasn't going to get arrested the minute I set foot in the country. But ja, India is a special place. There are challenges, as I've mentioned, but it's a gentle country. You can see it in the way the locals drive. There are no road signs and the traffic looks chaotic, but everyone drives slowly and they even stop for a dog crossing the road.

India is always full of surprises. A totally unexpected surprise came my way recently when I was offered a role in a Bollywood movie that will start filming at the end of May 2011. I'm not sure what the part is or what I'm supposed to do, but my agent has told me it's very good money for only a day's work. I should probably find out a little more about it, though. Playing a bad-boy cricketer who gets involved in match fixing probably won't be the smartest career move.

Umpires
The debate on the use of technology has been raging for some time now. Should technology be used to help umpires make the correct decisions? Lord knows, I've seen some umpires in my career who needed all the help they could get. In modern professional sport there is a lot of money involved, and making the correct call can have a monumental financial impact on both players and their teams. One argument is based on the premise that there should never be any doubt about whether a football has crossed the goal line, a tennis ball has touched the tramline, or a cricket ball has nicked a bat. Now that we have the technology to make the correct calls, we should use it, even if it slows the game down.

I'm not so sure, though.

Although I'm not what you'd call a traditionalist by any stretch of the imagination, I have been on the receiving end of some shocking decisions in my career. However, I, for one, would be very sad to see the human element disappear from cricket. And I'm not a fan of the referral system that's been used over the past couple of years either. The human element is part and parcel of cricket, and you've got to take the good with the bad, I reckon. I think all this referring nonsense undermines the guys on the field. The umpires have been standing there for hours and then, when they're asked to make a decision, the players want someone else to give a second opinion? I mean, what's that all about?

You've got to feel for the umps. They must be wondering why they even bother going out there on the pitch other than to hold the players' jerseys, hats and sunglasses. They may as well just plant a hat stand out at point and another behind the bowler's stumps. I don't know about you, but I'd rather have someone like Billy Bowden and his legendary antics out there in the middle than a hat stand. I love all his crazy signals – especially his ultra-quirky 20/20 versions. And the guy very rarely makes a mistake. Simon Taufel, who was the ICC's Umpire of the Year between 2004 and 2008, and Aleem Dar, the current holder of the crown, are also excellent umpires.

To be honest, I've never had one guy umpiring a game I've played in who's made me think, 'Okay, here comes trouble.' Sure, I've been given some kak decisions, but I've also had a few go my way. I recall Dave Orchard giving me a shocker in a domestic game – this must've been, like, 10 years ago – but afterwards he came up to me and apologised. I remember him saying, 'I got that one wrong. Next time, I owe you.'

Obviously, when it's a big nick, it's easy to call. Everyone hears the nick and there's no point in hanging around – you just look like an idiot if you stay there. But there are times when the touch is so faint that you're not even sure whether you touched it or not; I mean, I don't know how the hell an *umpire* is supposed to know. In such a case, I'll definitely stick around and wait for the finger.

The funny thing about batsmen is that their desire to walk (or not) is often determined by their form. If they're going through a bad trot, they very rarely walk when they nick the ball. If they've had a good run of form, though, and they are scoring runs consistently, they will often walk when they nick one. In other words, it's a lot easier to show your more honourable qualities when you have some runs in the bank.

But World Cups are a different story. Well, for me, anyway. I *never* want to go out in a World Cup match. And I have nicked a ball in a World Cup game – I knew it, the fielding team knew it – but I stood my ground, as I am entitled to do … and the ump turned down the appeal. Bladdy miracle!

It was in a semi-final too – in 2007 against the Aussies. We were already deep in the shit, with five wickets down for 27, and Shaun Tait was the bowler. I got a big inside edge to a Tait in-swinger that Adam Gilchrist, diving to his left, took cleanly. It was a clear nick, no doubt, but I was like, 'No. Why walk now? The match is already down the toilet. You might as well try to get a 100 while you're at the crease.'

For some reason umpire Steve Bucknor didn't give me out and, as you can expect from a pumped-up and competitive bunch like Ricky Ponting's men, they were not at all happy about it. All sorts of comments came flying my way. They were pissed off, obviously, but at least they weren't swearing. Probably only because they had us by the balls anyway … I was thinking, 'This is a World Cup, and if you stand your ground, you might get away with it.' Which I did. Not that it helped. As I already said, we got our butts kicked.

I don't know if you've noticed, but my long-term colleague, Jacques Kallis, is a genius at standing. He's a total expert at never looking back – a really tough skill to master, because 99 per cent of us automatically look behind us when we've nicked

THE FUTURE AND WHAT IT HOLDS

the ball. Jacques never changes his expression either. Old Jacques just loves batting so much that he's learnt to cover his mistakes very well.

Actually, I did too. It's a funny story. The exact dates are a little hazy, but I was playing for Western Province against Griquas in a final at Newlands. I remember Peter Kirsten was our coach. Griquas batted first and didn't get too much. The total looked very gettable – the only problem was that it had been raining on and off. Before going out to bat, I remember Kirzie saying, 'Hersch, it rained on the way here … We are not going to lose this game because of the damn rain.' I said, 'Cool,' and went out and played some shots. Some serious shots, as I recall.

Lloyd Ferreira and I were going great guns when, on 49, I got the biggest nick. It was a *huge* deflection. I think the keeper caught the ball in front of first slip. I just stood there thinking, 'The rain is on the way. I've got to finish this game!'

Fortunately umpire Rudi Koertzen was of the same opinion, and he just shook his head and said in that firm, square-jawed voice of his, 'Not out! *Nee man, ons moet nou die game klaarkry!*' It was really funny. I don't think the Griquas okes were even too upset about it.

With that lifeline, I managed to hit the winning runs just before the rains came. I spoke to Rudi about the incident years later and he just laughed, claiming – as I'm sure he would to this day – that he'd never heard a nick. I don't see how that's possible, though. It was as loud a nick as it gets … and as far as I know, Rudi's hearing is pretty top-notch. With his retirement earlier this year, international cricket lost a great umpire.

So ja, to get back to where I started about umpiring … I think the game would be more boring and less quirky without the human element the umpires bring to it. Perhaps we need to keep the technology but make it available to the umpire only. And if he's not sure, then he can go upstairs if he so chooses.

ME
Regrets, I have a few

Looking back on my cricketing career, I have very few regrets about not achieving on-field goals. If I had to pick one, though, it would be that I would have liked to have been a bit more expressive … a bit more attacking, especially in Test cricket. Remember how Brian Lara climbed into Robbie Peterson during the first Test of the West Indies 2003/04 tour to South Africa? He smacked 28 runs off that one over. I should've been more of an out-and-out attacking Test batsman like Lara and India's current opener, Virender Sehwag.

But, as I've touched on, the Proteas' approach to the game is not exactly conducive to playing this kind of attacking cricket. Our approach has always been conservative, no matter what might've been said in the press. If you hit a couple of fours in an over, you're expected to block out the rest of it. Jacques Kallis's comments during my 'six sixes' over against the Netherlands in the 2007 World Cup prove my point. I'm not having a go at Jacques, but his words reflect how we've been taught to play.

Then Proteas coach Mickey Arthur, for example, always told us that the first 20 balls in an ODI should be used to play ourselves in. I'd think, '*Twenty* balls? If you said that to Hayden or Gilchrist, they'd tell you to piss right off.' Do you think those Aussie batsmen ever thought, 'Yeah mate, tell you what, let's just block out the first 20 and then take it from there, shall we?' No. Exactly. Unfortunately, though, that's the sort of mindset we've had, and frankly, I've always thought it to be utter bullshit.

To my detriment, I spent too many innings walking out onto the pitch trying to execute a conservative game plan. I just should have said, 'To hell with what the coach says; I am just going to go out there and play my natural game.' I always appreciated Duncan Fletcher for letting me be myself on the field. Whenever he was involved with a team I played for, his advice to me would be: 'If you want to hit the first ball of the game over extra cover, well, go for it.'

Not the Proteas, though. Once or twice I tried to suggest that we do things a bit differently, but my input would just get pushed aside. I wouldn't say laughed off, but they weren't really interested. Everything is so structured, you know, nothing instinctive or spontaneous is allowed.

The point I'm trying to make is that I really should've been more carefree in my cricket back then, because these days, despite wanting to play an all-out aggressive innings, I find myself batting really responsibly. I find there's a bit of inner conflict in my game at the moment, which is the result of my stay at Harmony Clinic. It's made me regret that I didn't go for it more when I was younger, when I would have revelled in the freedom.

What I'm going through now is necessary for my development as a cricketer and as a person, but it's not easy. My time at Harmony Clinic was a life-changing experience. Ever since, I've been thinking very deeply about my life, which obviously includes my cricket. This notion of 'responsibility' has been bouncing around my head ever since I left the clinic, and the role I feel I need to play in all my teams as a senior player has subdued my out-and-out aggressiveness. The more I think about stuff, the more the word 'responsibility' comes up ... and they say that you take your personality onto the field with you.

A reporter recently asked me what was happening with my batting. Why wasn't I going after the ball quite like I used to – even in 20/20 cricket? I couldn't answer the guy, because I know that no matter whether it is the Proteas, the Deccan Chargers or the Cobras, I *have* to bat through most of the overs. I've sort of got into that way of thinking. At the Chargers, if Adam Gilchrist, Andrew Symonds, Rohit Sharma or I didn't fire, it put too much pressure on the rest of the guys, which they can't handle because a lot of them are still so young. The same principle applies at the Cobras.

The situation has created a real conflict inside me. I really don't want to lose my aggressiveness – especially in the 20/20 game – but at the same time I have to consider what's best for the team. Man, since I've come out of that clinic, I haven't been the same. I think it was evident on the tour to Australia in 2009. I mean, I couldn't wait to get to Australia, because I knew it was probably going to be my last tour there with the Proteas. We're not scheduled to play in Australia again until September/October 2011, and it's unlikely I'll be part of the Proteas set-up after the 2011 World Cup in February and March.

As I was no longer in the Test team, I should've just gone out there and had a blast, but instead I was thinking about the team's welfare and ended up playing way too tentatively in the first two 20/20 games. And in the first ODI, I scored 22 off 28 balls. In the second ODI we weren't chasing a hell of a total, but I put the team first again. I thought, 'Well, if you just bat for 40 overs, it should be fine.' And then I tried a pull shot and got caught. It was a half-arsed, overly tentative shot. I was out for 19 off 37 balls. Not great.

For the third game, I was like, 'This is bullshit, I'm just going to go out there and blast away.' The result: 65 off 52 balls. Although I admit I wasn't thinking about the team at all, I did score the runs.

On the other hand, my newfound calm has also worked in my favour – particularly at the Cobras, where we won the Standard Bank Pro20 competition and played in the inaugural Champions League Twenty20 in 2009. The more I settle into the number three batting position, the more I'm figuring out that I am responsible for seeing an innings through. It's not exactly my personality to play like this, but ja, I can see a calmer sort of Herschelle at the wicket these days.

So that's my dilemma. Being too tentative does not work for me ... but I also feel the need to assume more responsibility and bat through an innings. It might eventually boil down to just making sure that I play the kind of innings appropriate to the game. Some days I'm going to have to bat through, and other days I'm going to be charging.

Even in 20-over cricket, the basic principles still apply. You still need both big partnerships and someone who will take on the bowling during the game, like I have always tried to do. If I walk out and I feel it's going to be my day – I'm seeing the ball like a football and everything is nice and loose – then yes, I am going to hit the ball and play my shots.

If we're in trouble, though, I'm prepared to accept the responsibility to scratch around and bat through. In World Cups I have always played within myself at the start of an innings and then opened up. I'll work it out, though. I know I had a bit of a dip in form in the latter half of the 2010 IPL, and none of us scored any meaningful runs at the T20 World Cup in the West Indies, but overall I think my new maturity should still see me play plenty of big innings.

My form in the recent Friends Provident T20 competition – county cricket's 20/20 tournament – was, for example, very promising. For Yorkshire, I averaged 36.91 and scored my first 20/20 100 as well.

I got a 90 not out against the West Indies at the Wanderers in 2007, a 98 against Northants for Glamorgan in 2008, and 92 for the Cape Cobras against the Dolphins in 2009, but that's the closest I had got.

My new sense of responsibility has also contributed to my willingness to be more outspoken at team meetings. Not when I'm playing for the Proteas, obviously, for reasons I have already outlined, but certainly with the Cape Cobras and the Deccan Chargers. Provided the team is unified, then I have the confidence to say my piece at meetings.

At the Cobras, for example, I've been helping out the younger guys with technical aspects of their game, and I've also given them advice on what to do in certain situations in a match. Senior players gave me some crucial advice when I first started out – I mentioned Brian McMillan telling me to line up my head with off-stump in Chapter 2 – and I've been passing some of that information on. I don't try to be too prescriptive. I just give the guys food for thought, really.

I think I can play a role in helping some of the youngsters raise their goals so that they can realise their true potential. I had a long chat with a few of my younger Cobras teammates in 2009. I told them that they were in a comfort zone and were not working hard enough to improve their game beyond being domestic stars. I think I have a lot to offer these youngsters, as many of them coming through now probably have a similar mindset to the one I had back then, both regarding their cricket and how they live their lives. Especially in the new world of 20-over cricket, these guys are earning money, playing aggressive cricket and leading quite fast lifestyles. I have been through it all, and I've come out the other end.

I look at these okes and see how, season after season, they're just not improving to higher levels, as they should be. There might be a slight improvement from one year to the next, but it's not enough. In your early twenties, you've got, like, five or six years to use domestic cricket as a platform to gain experience – to help improve your physical and mental abilities – and really make your mark, and then to take your game to the next level. Instead, some of the young guys appear totally satisfied to be local franchise players for their entire careers.

A few of them come from tough backgrounds, where they did not have a lot of money, and they are more than happy to be earning whatever they are getting paid at Western Province. They've got some money and a little local fame, with which they're happy. Some of the guys are even getting a little thick around the middle, and that's just inexcusable in my book, and plain lazy. Look, I have my faults, but I've always worked damned hard to stay in top shape. My fitness is a big part of who I am. I've grown to love being fit, and when I can't train, I'm probably the most frustrated guy around.

I'm trying to make these guys realise that with hard work and application, they can take their natural talent and *really* make it work for them. The occasional national team call-up should not be enough. They should be working their flabby butts off to secure a place in the national team, or at least help the Cobras get into the Standard Bank Pro20 final. They then have a chance to shine at the Champions League tournament, from where they could get an IPL contract. And that's where the *real* money is.

I've also started to have a little say in my IPL team too. This past season I worked hard to up the Deccan Chargers' energy levels while we were fielding. At one post-match debriefing, after we had lost a game, coach Darren Lehmann asked us if anyone wanted to say anything. I put up my hand and said how important a little encouragement was on the field, and what a huge difference it could make: it not only lifted your teammates when they were defending a low total, but also let the batsmen know that we were the bladdy defending champs and that we were not going down without a fight.

The Indian players are generally quiet by nature. They are not very outspoken, and they tend to talk in a quiet, mellow tone of voice. But I got them to understand the value of making a noise so that your teammates could benefit. Why keep quiet when you can be offering words of encouragement … when you can keep a buzz going on the field? I say something every second ball, not only because it is a part of me, but also because I feel it's my duty to my teammates. It doesn't take much effort to say 'Come on, boys' every second or third ball. I mean, let's face it, fielding isn't the most exciting activity in the world – especially if you've been at it the whole day. At least keeping the vibe going adds a little to the experience.

Not that this is a Chargers issue only. A couple of my national teammates are also a little too quiet on the field for my liking.

My old friend Jacques Kallis doesn't say much when he's fielding – he's probably the quietest one on the field. That's just his nature, I guess. I asked him once why he doesn't say anything on the pitch. And he didn't say anything.

I often get asked if I regret not achieving the 100 Test-cap mark. Well, even though I haven't officially retired from Test cricket and I'm still contracted to the UCB, I do know that my Test cricket career is pretty much over. Maybe some part of me is disappointed. I got close – I have 90 Tests to my name – but to be honest, I'm not really too bothered. After all, I had a little over 11 great years from November 1996 to January 2008.

If I have to be frank, I didn't really justify my place in the Test team in 2008. The selectors did the right thing to drop me. I probably had my best years in Test cricket as an opener between 2001 and 2005 – at one stage, my average was up to 51. Unfortunately the rot set in when I moved down the order. I became really inconsistent. After I went back to opening, I didn't make any runs. The last Test century I scored was back in 2005, when I hit 161 off England at the Wanderers. So, ja, I have no complaints about being dropped, really. I had a good-enough run.

Funny, I'd always thought I would be the first black or coloured player to reach the 100-Test milestone, but it was not to be. In those 11 or so years I reckon I probably missed about six or seven Tests through injuries, so I could've got even closer. Still, compared to most other players, I had a lot of injury-free time, so it's not a big deal. A hundred Tests would have been nice, but it's not the end of the world not making it – after all, 90 Tests is still 90 Tests. In my Test career, I scored 6 167 runs at an average of 41.95, with 14 centuries and 26 fifties. That's still an achievement of which to be proud.

The one milestone I am genuinely disappointed not to have achieved was scoring 250 runs in a Test. That score was on the cards for me in the second Test against Pakistan in 2003. We were playing at Newlands, and all was going well for me until I was given out, caught at silly point by Younis Khan off Saqlain Mushtaq's bowling. My bat had been nowhere near the ball. Man, I was pissed off. I know 'ifs' and 'buts' mean nothing, 'but' I got a shocker of a decision from umpire Srinivas Venkataraghavan. To be given out like that in front of my home supporters while I was in such great form was particularly galling.

'If' I had batted out that whole day, I am confident I would have got to 250. It was a tough call for me, especially as I was having one of those 'in the zone' days, where I felt invincible – Graeme Smith and I put on 368 for the opening partnership. Ja, Venkat was never my favourite man behind the stumps, but thems the breaks, I guess. Still, I did score 228 – not too bad – and it remains my highest Test score.

I was also disappointed not to get a century against the Aussies in Australia and also on the subcontinent. I came so flipping close too. During the second Test at the MCG in Melbourne in 2005 I was on 94 when Andrew Symonds – of all people – got me with a medium-pacer. He was bowling with the new ball, and he got one delivery to bounce a little, which came off my elbow and went onto the stumps. I got a few 90s on the subcontinent – 98 against Pakistan at Faisalabad in 2003, and 92 against Sri Lanka at Colombo in 2006, but I never got that elusive 100.

In terms of my Test career, then, I'm more than happy to have got as many as 90 Test caps, but there are those three disappointments: not getting to 250 in an innings, and not scoring centuries in Australia or on the subcontinent. They do linger with me.

I've still got a couple of goals, though ...

Presuming I remain injury free and in good enough nick, I would like to continue my cricket career for another four to five years. I see no reason why I can't carry on until I'm 40. Look at old Sanath Jayasuriya – the Sri Lankan legend is 41 and played for Sri Lanka in the 2010 T20 World Cup in the West Indies. And what about Adam Gilchrist and Matthew Hayden? Both are approaching 40, and they're still very influential in the IPL. I think, particularly in 20-over cricket, you can easily play until that age if you're in shape.

Actually, the biggest issue in the longevity of one's career is mental and not physical. A 20-over game is only three hours long, so that's not a problem. The problem starts when you're playing in 20-over tournaments like the IPL, *and* you're still involved in international Test and ODI cricket. That's a pretty hectic schedule, and competing at such a high level of intensity week in and week out can be mentally exhausting.

International cricketers often take a lot of stick from the press and public if they complain that they're tired and need a break. The common perception is that we're a bunch of overpaid prima donnas who don't appreciate how lucky we are to be making a living out of playing sport. But people don't appreciate that when we say we are tired, we are referring not to physical fatigue, but being knackered mentally. International cricket is played at a high intensity, the stakes are high, and the pressures and expectations are huge. You can really take strain with that. I don't care who you are or how big you reckon your balls are – do this for a living and you'll appreciate what I mean.

But, back to my initial point: because older guys like Hayden and Gilchrist have now retired from the international scene, and they're both in top shape, they come into tournaments like the IPL nice and fresh. And the pressure they feel is a world apart from what they experienced when playing for their country. They just go out there and have a blast, klapping the ball all over the show.

I'm looking forward to being in their position, but before I bow out of international cricket completely, I still want one more bash at the World Cup. Ja, a World Cup medal is the one thing I want very badly. And I'm talking proper 50-over ODI cricket here, not T20. As mentioned in the previous chapter, I have re-signed my UCB contract until April 2011, and Corrie van Zyl has made it clear to me that I am in their plans for the 2011 World Cup. The teams I have played for in the past have come so close – particularly in 1999 – and I'd love to be able to erase the painful memories with a shiny gold medal and the title of world champions.

I'm still fit and trim, and my reflexes are spot-on. Look, I might be a yard slower than I was at 20, but I still put myself about. I have never *not* put my body on the line in practices, and I still flipping dive around like an idiot on the square. It's a part of me; it's just who I am.

Ja, so touch wood, I haven't had any major injuries since I did my knee all those years ago. A lot of it has got to do with maintaining myself in the gym. I'm also lucky that I have a good metabolism – I eat a lot of rubbish, and the booze doesn't help, but if I put in the hard yards on the treadmill, I work it all off.

I know that, at 36, you are supposed to be getting a little long in the tooth for professional sports, but, honestly, I don't feel it physically. There's nothing in my physical attributes to say that I am 36, and no one can tell me that I'm any slower than anybody else on the field. Basically I'm going to keep on playing for as long as I can. As I've said, hopefully that will be for another four to six years. I'm still amped to hit big scores, and I'm particularly motivated by the 20-over format of the game, of which I'm going to be playing a lot.

Cricket has been my life; it's the only life I've known, so obviously I want to carry on playing for as long as I can. When my international career is over – and it looks like it won't go on past the World Cup in 2011 – I reckon I'll focus primarily on 20-over cricket. Hopefully I can divide my time between the Cape Cobras, an IPL franchise and a county cricket T20 team. And, of course, Lashings Cricket Club.

A few more Lashings would be great too

Lashings CC is a wonderful institution. I've been involved with the club for the past few years. Lashings began in 1984 as the brainchild of English businessman David Folb, who started a pub team in Maidstone, Kent, playing in the local village league. David then expanded his business interests to Antigua in 1995, where he met West Indies captain Richie Richardson, who was just about to retire. Lashings really took off from their collaboration.

Richie still wanted to play cricket, but he was looking for something chilled-out and fun. I think David asked him, jokingly, to come and play for his pub side back in the UK ... and Richie said yes. Or probably, 'Yeah, mon.' From there on Lashings grew and started attracting big-name players – both active and retired. The club basically plays exhibition matches against schoolboy, club and county teams, and it is obviously a helluva thrill for these club or schoolboy cricketers to play against the biggest names in the business.

These days Lashings CC also has quite a few sponsors on board. One of them is an auction company for sports memorabilia, and before every game a big auction takes place for which corporates buy tables, which is how Lashings makes money for the sponsors and the club. David is obviously quite wealthy, and the club makes enough money to pay the players pretty well. These games take place in a relaxed atmosphere, and at lunch the team is split up so that the players can socialise with the guests. And if the players feel like a beer or two at lunch time – which they often do – then they go ahead and have a beer or two. It's really chilled.

The whole squad attends each game, so that if anyone doesn't feel like playing in the afternoon, there's always someone to fill in for him. In one game, Kiwi cricketer Hamish Marshall and Aussie Greg Blewett got absolutely wasted at the lunch and couldn't go in to bat in the afternoon.

Lashings has also afforded me the privilege of playing with

some great legends of the game, and my own cricketing heroes – Richie Richardson, who is the club captain, Sir Viv Richards, and that great gentleman of the gentlemen's game, Alvin Kallicharran. It has been wonderful for me to talk to these guys about cricket and hear about all their great experiences. Sir Viv, for one, has some great stories to tell. I remember one particular tale about Aussie fast bowler Craig McDermott.

Apparently McDermott used to chirp quite a lot when he bowled. During one Test in Australia, he was getting so mouthy that the West Indians decided to teach him a lesson. They waited for McDermott to come in to bat at the tail-end of the Aussie innings, and then proceeded to absolutely pepper him with short stuff. Apparently he was getting pinned left, right and centre. I mean, can you imagine what it must be like out there when you're on the receiving end of balls bowled by the likes of Malcolm Marshall, Joel Garner and Michael Holding when they've got it in for you? I'd crap myself. And I'm an opening batsman, not a tail-ender.

Malcolm Marshall, in particular, was as scary as hell. I remember Desmond Haynes – another great West Indian batsman of that golden era – telling me of an incident that occurred in England's 1984 tour to the West Indies, when Marshall bowled to English captain Mike Gatting. The ball went straight through Gatting's grill and smacked him so hard, they found pieces of bone from Gatting's broken nose embedded in the ball.

But to get back to poor Craig McDermott: according to Sir Viv, they were so determined to rough him up that, when McDermott offered a simple catch to one of the West Indians fielding at gully – no doubt just wanting to get the hell out of there – the guy deliberately dropped the ball so that they could continue physically abusing him. That's Test cricket for you. It's a big man's game and there's no place to hide. I believe that for the remainder of his Test career, whenever Craig McDermott played against the West Indies, he was unusually subdued.

Apart from the social side of things, Lashings also gives you some decent time in the middle during the winter months, depending on how seriously you want to take the game. You'll often come up against a team that has a couple of decent pace bowlers. Obviously they are taking the game dead seriously, so you can't just mess around. But sometimes the opposition isn't too strong and, if the mood takes you, you can haul out the long handle and have a good old tonk. In one game, big-hitting New Zealander Chris Cairns let loose and helped himself to a 100 off about 30 balls.

Look, there's still a lot of pride at stake in these matches, and the Lashings CC very seldom lose a game. To give everyone a fair chance, we always bat first – it's best to get some runs on the board, as it's no fun when someone's paid money to watch the game if the opposition bat first and we proceed to get them out for next to nothing.

I've had great times with the team, and David Folb has always said he would love me to come back any year. Apparently my willingness to sign autographs and be part of all the social events adds value to the team … which is all good with me, because I want to continue playing for this great institution.

Life after cricket

I have no idea what I'm going to do when I finish cricket. Seriously. No plan whatsoever. I probably know more about what I *don't* want to do than what I want to do. I don't, for example, want to get into coaching. Yes, the post-rehab Herschelle has enjoyed passing on his experience to the younger guys, but I also know from having played under so many coaches that it's a very complex job. It takes a lot of organisational skill and a practical mind, and that just isn't me. Ja, me a coach. It's amusing even to think about it.

I've also always been an instinctive player relying on his natural abilities, and so have never been very analytical about my game – or anyone else's game. But I think being able to pick apart your opponents' defences is a vital skill for a coach. I basically had to work out for myself what was required to perform well at international level. I was never technically good, like a Tendulkar or a Kallis, and have always relied on my hand-eye coordination.

What I had to learn was how to be disciplined at the crease – particularly as an opener in Test cricket. I had to learn where my off-stump is all the time, which meant I could leave balls with much greater confidence – and on a really good wicket, you can even leave on length.

So, no coaching for me. I can't see myself in any kind of corporate environment either. And I'm sure I don't even have to explain why. I have thought of getting into property develop-ment. I love property; I like everything about it, and I've done fairly well buying and selling my own houses.

I made good friends with some of the big property developers when I got married in St Kitts, and they are turning the whole island inside out. They are doing phenomenal things. St Kitts is competing for foreign investment and tourism with the other islands, Barbados, Antigua and Jamaica, and they want to attract and accommodate the big cruise liners. These developers are busy upgrading all the hotels on the island, as well as building new ones. There's a lot of commercial development too, and they have told me that I'm welcome to come and join them.

So that could be an option, but I haven't made up my mind yet on what I really want to do. And it's not like I'm the only one in this dilemma either. It's tough for professional sportspeople to find something that they can tackle with the same degree of passion that they put into their sport. Cricket was such a massive part of my life for so long that it's going to be difficult finding something to replace it.

Even someone like Shaun Pollock has found it tough adapt-ing to life after sport. I mean, Polly is one of the most together people I have ever met, and he had no idea what he wanted to do when he retired. All he said when I asked him was, 'I don't know. I'll just take a bit of time off and decide.' As far as I can tell, he's doing a bit of commentating, some public speaking – he's a really good speaker – and some charity work. I haven't heard of him being involved in any business ventures, for example.

I don't think I'll miss being in the public eye too much. I certainly have enjoyed my time on centre stage but, in these closing stages of my career, I have got used to the spotlight falling on the younger guys. This is something I have accepted. I've had my time. I've been in the business for 20 years now. I have signed all the autographs, posed for all the photographs, done all the newspaper articles, magazine covers and features, and been on all the TV shows. Often enough I've been in the press for reasons I'd rather not have been, and I'll be happy to see that quieten down. Although, having said that, one has to take responsibility for one's actions and, for me, part of that was to accept that the press were going to have a field day with some of my indiscretions.

If I look ahead to the next 20 years, I'd like to see myself living in Cape Town in the home in Camps Bay I have just bought. I love this city and the people who live in it. Throughout this long career of mine I've been out of the country for long periods of time, and I can never wait to get back to the Mother City. It's such a beautiful place. I've never once flown into Cape Town where people on the aeroplane haven't started looking out the windows 10 minutes before landing, wanting to catch a glimpse of the place. I've lived here all my life, and I *always* look out the window. It's just an amazing place, and I can't see myself ever leaving it.

I doubt whether I'll be married in 20 years' time – who knows: if it happens, it happens. I'll be in my mid-fifties, and my son Rashard will be in his early thirties. Perhaps I would have had the pleasure of watching him play some form of representative sport for South Africa – and, hey, who knows, I might have a couple of grandchildren by then too. Whatever happens to me, and whatever I end up doing, as long as I am still able to be the same Herschelle Gibbs, I'll be happy. Whatever comes my way from now on, I'll be ready for it. I'll embrace it and give it the same amount of passion with which I've always lived my life.

Finally, at least remember me for this ...

Brian Lara's words, on his retirement from international cricket in 2007, have always stuck with me. After his last game for the West Indies at the 2007 World Cup, he was asked in an interview how he'd like to be remembered. He didn't say anything about being remembered for scoring 11 953 Test runs at an average of 52.88, and 10 405 ODI runs at an average of 40.48. Nor did he mention his record Test score of 400 not out. None of that.

His reply was to ask the crowd, 'Did I entertain?' and he's right on the money. Professional sportspeople exist only because of the fans who watch them at the games or on TV. Ultimately, they are the source of all the money. To generate TV rights or ticket sales, you have to put on a good show. If we don't entertain the fans, then they don't watch, and the whole professional sports model collapses.

So, I can only echo Brian's question: Have I entertained? I hope so, because it's what I have always set out to do. If I walk off the field after scoring a 100 – be it off 50 balls or 200 balls – I'm probably the most satisfied person in the ground, because I got to entertain the crowd on that particular day.

Stats honestly mean very little to me, in the sense that I don't play for them at all. I've never batted in an attempt to maintain or improve my average. Yes, the stats don't lie, and my Test and ODI averages (41.95 and 36.13 as I write) are not bad, but everybody's got periods when they're more consistent than at other times. Those stats don't tell of the times – particularly between 2002 and 2005 – when I was averaging as much as the best in the business.

No, what I have wanted to do more than anything else is give people their money's worth. I was born to entertain, and that was always going to be the way I was going to approach my game. If you ask Sir Viv Richards if he would have liked to have scored more runs, he will probably say yes. But whether he got 20 or 40 centuries was not really going to make all that much difference. What really mattered was the way in which he played the game, for which cricket fans still revere him. I mean, no one says that maybe Sir Viv's average could've been a bit higher or he could've scored a few more 100s!

Instead, it was all about how batsmen like him played the game. Whether it is four-day domestic stuff, Test matches or limited-overs internationals, it's all about entertaining the people who have come to watch. I'll give you an example of what I mean: take Sachin Tendulkar's 200 against us in the second ODI in Gwalior, India, early in 2010. He played a brilliant innings – 200 off 147 balls, and the first-ever double ton in an ODI. I was watching his innings on the field that day, and he slowed down in the final four or five overs to make sure he got the record.

Now, I take nothing away from Sachin – the guy is a total genius, probably the best ever – but I would've approached those final overs totally differently. Maybe I would've gone out within touching distance of the record – like I did in the 438 game, when I had plenty of time to get a double ton – but if I was in Sachin's position, I would've really gone balls-to-the-wall to try to see if I could get my team close to 480 or 500 runs, rather than focus on my own double century.

Of course it crossed my mind that I might get 200 in the 438 game, but I just said to myself, 'If I get it, I get it; if I don't, so be it.' On that particular day, if I could've hit every ball for six, I would have done so. It's pretty much exactly what I tried to do! I went out after hitting two sixes and then going for a third. I dragged the ball and got caught. I wasn't going to die wondering.

I have always wanted to entertain with both my batting and

my fielding. I think in this day and age of professional sport there's so much control over everything that it's increasingly difficult for individuals to stand out. I'm all for professionalism, but everyone is petrified of stepping out of line in any way, lest they insult, I dunno, the sponsors or the administrators or the fans in some way.

Actually, it's more accurate to say: what the sponsors or administrators *think* will insult the fans. And so everyone toes the line, which results in predictable, by-the-numbers behaviour. But I reckon sports fans love nothing more than seeing a little individuality in their sport. As a tennis fan, for example, I'd love to hear what Roger Federer *really* feels like when he loses, rather than the usual safe media soundbyte he delivers.

Naturally, there have been times in my own career where I have held my tongue concerning an issue of team selection, or strategy, or even how good or bad the umpiring was. We players all have our opinions, and sometimes they clash with those of the administrators. I reckon it will always be so. The more prudent route is to keep your mouth shut, unless you like getting into a whole lot of trouble with the UCB and/or the ICC.

However, the one way in which I have been able to express myself is on the cricket pitch, a) with a bat, and b) in the field. In my fielding, which I'm proud to say has been among the best in the sport, I could express myself in the way I celebrated taking a catch.

Obviously a sport like cricket has a different ethos to football. The way footballers celebrate a goal would be a little over the top for the more conventional cricket, but I admit to taking a couple of cues from former Manchester United player Eric Cantona. I've supported United since I was a *laaitie*, and I loved the way that Cantona would just stand there with his trademark collar sticking up after scoring, gazing at the crowd for about 10 seconds. He would display some miraculous piece of footballing skill, like chipping the keeper from way outside the box ... and then he would just stand there as the crowd went totally bananas. His was the ultimate expression of self-confidence.

I've celebrated in a number of ways over the years – from sticking out my tongue to tossing the ball away as soon as I'd caught it. Though I did put an end to that little habit after the 1999 World Cup semi-final. After that incident, I started putting the ball in my pocket right after I caught it.

I've also set up some routines with my teammates. In the 2006 series against New Zealand, played in South Africa, Ashwell Prince and I planned a little celebration for when one of us took a catch. When one of us caught the ball, the other one would run over and pretend to start taking photos. I happened to take a catch against the Black Caps at SuperSport Park in Centurion, and Ashwell duly came running over with his imaginary camera.

And in the West Indies during the ODI series in 2005, I was standing inside the circle – at short extra cover – when Chris Gayle hit one in the screws off Makhaya Ntini's bowling. Somehow I managed to dive and pluck the ball out of the air with only one hand. It was one of those catches that you take but you don't quite know how the hell you did it. That was probably one of the best I've ever taken. All I did though, once I had got up off the ground, was to turn towards the crowd and put my finger to my lips in a gesture of silence.

I did it on the spur of the moment. I could have run around the ground celebrating like a nutcase – I was certainly entitled to, given the nature of the catch I had just pulled off – but instead I just jogged back towards the middle. Most of the guys were running after Makhaya anyway. Whenever he took a wicket, he would peel off and run across the field, even if one of us had taken the catch to help him get his wicket. That was just Makhaya's way of celebrating – I think he picked it up from Curtly Ambrose, who did something similar in the latter part of his career.

Actually, I think Makhaya saw himself as a West Indian a lot of the time – especially when he was in the West Indies. He'd suddenly develop this West Indian accent. Makhaya is a funny guy, and he always looked like he was enjoying his cricket. He always had a smile on his face.

Wayne Parnell and I also had a little something worked out if either of us pulled something off in the third ODI against the Poms in Cape Town in November 2009. Although I was twelfth man for that game, it so happened that I was on the field when our plan came off. Both Wayne and I are WWF wrestling fans, so we decided to emulate a wrestler by the name of Batista. This oke is huge – he's probably the biggest chap in the business – and he's got these big tattoos over his shoulders and on his back, with massive muscles bulging everywhere. Actually, it's hard to believe that the oke is actually human and not a computer-generated cartoon.

Anyway, so whenever Batista walks out to the ring, he pretends he's mowing everyone down with a massive machine gun. Wayne and I decided that it would be cool for us to copy his act.

So Wayne takes a wicket – I forget whose it was; he got five that day. He looks at me standing at short fine leg, and he starts to do his Batista impression. Naturally, I followed suit. As we were running towards each other to celebrate as a group, I heard one of the senior players say to Wayne, 'Don't be like Gibbs. Just be yourself.'

Personally, I've never understood that kind of thinking. Here Wayne and I had planned a little fun celebration, and it was frowned on. Ag, I just told Wayne to celebrate in whatever way he wanted. I'm tired of seeing guys on a cricket field who look like they're not really enjoying themselves.

So, ja, for me the game has always been about entertainment. Have I given cricket fans their hard-earned money's worth? In an MTN40 match – these are 40-over games – against the Dolphins in early 2010, I scored a free-flowing 121 off 98 balls to help us post a game-winning 300/3 (young prospect Stiaan van Zyl also hit a 100 for us). After the game, one of the youngsters in the Dolphins team came up to me and said, 'Great innings, Hersch. Hey, you're still my favourite player.' That made me feel really good and that's exactly what I'm talking about regarding what I have set out to do. This comment came from a fellow player and not a fan, but it illustrates what I mean when I say I want to entertain. I want people to remember me for the kind of innings I play – not for what my damn average is.

For me, it's always about putting on a decent show. I mean, I'm a showman. I'm the first to admit it. I love the stage and I love entertaining people. I was born to do it. If I had tried to be selfish and batted just to make my numbers look good, I would never have played the kind of cricket that people have come to enjoy from me. I'm about to start quoting Frank Sinatra. Somebody stop me …

Index

Do you have any comments, suggestions or
feedback about this book or any other Zebra Press titles?
Contact us at **talkback@zebrapress.co.za**